# Building Political Culture In Nepal

# BUILDING POLITICAL CULTURE IN NEPAL

Meena Vaidya Malla

Adroit Publishers
New Delhi

*Published by*

ADROIT PUBLISHERS

4675/21, Ganpati Bhawan, Ansari Road,
Daryaganj, New Delhi-110 002

Phone : 011-23266030

email: adroitpublishers@gmail.com

*Distributors*

AKHIL BOOK DISTRIBUTORS

email: akhilbooks@yahoo.com
akhilbks@gmail.com



ISBN : 978-81-87393-02-3

*Printed in India on behalf of M/s Adroit Publishers by*
Akhil Sharma, E-mail: adroitpublishers@gmail.com

# Dedication

*I would like to dedicate this book to my beloved father Late Lt. Col. Dr. Krishna Gopal Vaidya for inspiring me to be a responsible citizen of the nation. As the first qualified Dental Surgeon of Nepal, he established Dental Department in Tri-Chandra Military Hospital where he rendered his valuable service for more than three decades.*

# *Contents*

# Preface

A number of problems and questions get involved in politics. How nations accomplish change? Why do some nations survive, grow and expand while others suffer or succumb? What are the roles and obligations of ordinary citizens? How is democracy established, and what makes it survive and prosper? The approach used to address these issues and problems stresses the element of political culture that has laid an increasing focus on the behaviour of individuals. It draws the unity of political science with psychology. Of late, as political science discipline has sought to absorb relevant developments in all social science disciplines, it has laid an increasing focus on the behaviour of individuals. Political culture in this sense is an effort to study the total political system without losing the benefits of individual psychology.

The concept of political culture was developed in response to the need to bridge a growing gap in the behavioural approach between the level of micro-analysis based on the psychological interpretations of the individual's political behaviour and the level of macro-analysis based on the variables common to political sociology. Combining the findings of modern depth psychology and recent advances in sociological techniques, the concept attempts to integrate them for measuring individual attitudes in mass societies. Political culture reveals that although political phenomena may be read from a variety of different perspectives, the cultural approach is a discernible subfield of political inquiry which chooses to investigate phenomena such as political stability, social integration, and economic development using culture as an independent variable. The approach values people's beliefs, attitudes, norms, behaviours and cognitions towards their system rather than the formal political institutions for solving political problems. Political culture can be defined as a set of beliefs, which people in a given society develop over a period of time towards various issues within a political system. Political culture embraces not only what people are taught about politics but is concerned with what they come to feel about politics in which they live.

Against this background, the book is an attempt to uncover deep-seated, long-held value characteristics of Nepali society towards their political system rather than ephemeral attitudes that might be gathered through public-opinion surveys. The book is presented in six chapters. The first chapter explains the basic conceptual terminology of political culture with a purpose to make readers familiar with the related area. This chapter gives the picture of the political culture of the developing and transitional societies in general and Nepal in particular. Chapter two examines the political culture of Nepal in the light of Nepal's geography, economy, ethnic groups, and religion. The chapter investigates the access, barrier, quality, trend dimensions of social hierarchy, ethnic groups, economic condition, gender and the religion. I have explained political socialization process as the basic component of Nepal's political culture in chapter three. Since the work is on the Building Political Culture of Nepal, I have attempted to review political culture during different historical periods of Nepal in chapter four. The chapter gives the historical perception on the (pre-Rana period– the Kirat, Licchavi and Malla period (1769-1846 AD), the Rana period (1846-1951 AD), Democratic Politics (1951-1961 AD), Panchayat period (1961-1990 AD). Chapter five explores and evaluates the restoration of democracy, Jan Andolan I (1990-2000 AD), and the success of Jan Andolan II (2006)) that signaled the end of monarchy and the beginning of a 'Republican Era' in

Nepal. Chapter six brings all together by analyzing a number of recent trends of political culture especially after 1990, which is basically a study of attitude and orientation of people towards political parties, leaders, opposition, union demonstration, bureaucracy, foreign interference and overall satisfaction and dissatisfaction of people in general.

Prior to the dawn of democracy in Nepal in 1951, the feudalistic character of Rana regime did not give way to the emergence of any subject and participant political culture. The spirit of 1950 movement, however, paved its way to open party politics, fundamental rights constitutional order and 1959 general election in the country. The oppositional parties and the groups opposed the ruling party and the then king banned the parliamentary system on December 15, 1960. Party less Panchayat system was introduced by king Mahendra. The feudal and authoritarian system collapsed following a massive popular uprising on April 16, 1990. After the success of Jan Andolan I, democracy was restored and the new constitution promulgated with the sovereignty vested in the people. Jan Andolan brought a myriad of hopes in people but it could not go as expected. The UCPN- (Maoist) launched an armed movement against the constitutional order and aimed at establishing its own system modeled on the Maoist ideology since February, 1996. King Gyanendra– who ascended to the throne after the Royal Massacre in June 2001 in which King Birendra with his family members were killed started ruling the country with monarchic absolutism paving the way for launching Jan Andolan II (people's movement) to establish democracy and purse the peace process.

The success of the historic Jan Andolan II in April 2006 set the pace for the new transition signaled the end of monarchy and the beginning of a republican era in Nepal. Following the peace accord, the Interim Constitution (IC) was adopted, which opened the door for the Maoists to join the transitional political process. They were brought into the interim parliament and government as a force to be reckoned with. The monarchy was denied any right to rule and president to head the republic as head of the state. During the movement, people had explicitly expressed to achieve- the end of monarchy and the dawn of republican democratic era, the end of Maoist people's war and return to peace and redefining the people-state relationship by restructuring the state. The transfer to a republic from that of the 240 years old Shah monarchy, despite many speculations, was accomplished peacefully. However, the peace and the constitution making process have yet to be accomplished. When the people welcomed the 12-point understanding between the Maoists and SPA in November 2005, they were energized by the possibilities of epochal change at the societal level that would be realized with the new constitution drafted by a popularly elected Constituent Assembly (CA) and the restructuring of the state. Through the 12-point understanding, the Maoists agreed to transform themselves into a political party in competitive multi-party politics. Amid the violence of the insurgency, they also contributed much towards raising the awareness of the socially deprived and voiceless section of the population about their right to autonomy, dignity and livelihood. This made people hopeful about positive side of the people's war. They believed it would induce a change in the SPA towards a people-oriented political culture with justice and equitable economic and social programmes. But People's euphoria and enthusiasm awakened by the successful mass movements have turned into the culture of indifference, frustration and disillusionment towards the political parties, leaders and government. The political parties have failed to deliver on the most important of the key promises: framing a new constitution keeping in view the aspirations of the people. The CA elected for a term of two years, has had its term extended as many as four times. The political leaders have turned out to be incompetent, bypassed the democratic decision making process and the CA. Now the government's decision to hold election of the CA in April 2013 disappoints the people yet again.

Nepal is passing through transition. The key transitional problems in many countries with regard to the development of democratic political institutions and democratic political culture are: transition problems that stem directly from the phenomenon of regime change from authoritarianism to democracy. Contextual problems stem from the nature of the society, its economy, culture, and history, and are in some degree endemic to the country, whatever its form of government. Finally as the new democracies become consolidated and achieved certain stability, they would confront systemic problems stemming from the working of a democratic system. Authoritarian political systems suffer from problems that derive from their particular nature, such as overly concentrated decision making, deficient feedback, dependence on performance legitimacy, stalemate, and the inability to reach decisions. As a general phenomenon, democracy in those countries would not be immune to transition, contextual and systemic problems. But it does not mean that those countries cannot consolidate their newly democratic political system or they cannot come out from the grip of transition. Democratic consolidation takes place if people try to cultivate culture that reduces feudal culture, abolish drastically authoritarian agencies, inequality, and establish functional constitution, rule of law and electoral system. Moreover, people should change working pattern, behavior, norms, values and perception that help nurture the civic culture. This civic culture helps build tolerance, compromise, consensus, cooperation, trust in the political atmosphere. This engenders the environment of acceptability ease and coexistence -the synergies of which help in building political culture.

As in all third wave democratic countries, these problems have afflicted democracy in Nepal too and political culture for the consolidation of democracy presumably would not be immune to them. It is natural that the clash of old and new values are embedded in every new democratic system. The problems arise when the feudal, authoritarian culture and practices go strength to strength and dominant than the universally acknowledged values of democratic culture. Some significant variables such as the leadership role, parties' performance, and elite behaviours have been identified for making possible as well as showing caveats for democratic culture. Some crucial variables that work against democratic culture in present day Nepal can broadly be identified as lack of ideological clarity, split political culture, the weak leadership role, the rise of ethnic-nationalism and regionalism, crisis of governance, apolitical mass and disoriented new generation. Culture of dependency on external sources and lack of confidence to insulate politics from external penetrations make democracy more unstable.

Nepali people have whole-heartedly supported the movements. The successive governments failed to lead the country in a healthy direction and provide the citizens with freedom, security and a quality of life. Given the positive attitude of the people towards the system, the governments after 1990 have not shown the kind of image the public expected. Lack of suitable political culture, successive governments more than a dozen formed within two decades failed to address the commitments and aspirations of the popular movements 1990 and 2006. The book also examines what have been the obstacles in the way of promoting democratic culture and institutions. It analyzes the reasons for the dominance of undemocratic forces and how they have succeeded in crippling the vital institutions of the state, the judiciary, parliament and the political parties. Why it has not been successful in bringing about the desired political situation in the country as people have expected? How do people in general assess the country's present situation? The discourse here is about, whether the political culture has changed accordingly following the restoration of multiparty system and recently with the onset of federal democratic system of Nepali politics. The study is intended to response to the queries as to how do the Nepalis believe that their state has become democratic? Do they recognize the changes around them and feel that they can make a difference in politics? The book is also an attempt to assess why even after so many years of democratic revolution, (Jan Andolan I and Jan Andolan II), suitable political culture and behaviour to dovetail the changes have remained elusive.

In Nepal, de-culturation of politics and unethical attitudes of leaders have made culture an oppressed conceptual variable to politics. The dissociation of politics from the moorings of culture has imparted to Nepali politics a typical aculture and anomic character within which culture oriented politics has given way to politics oriented culture. In this framework, the book attempts to explore people's orientation towards their political system and perceive their roles in it relating to the support for the system along with the overall satisfaction and dissatisfaction from the systems.

The development of a stable and effective democratic government depends upon the orientations that people have to the political process-upon the political culture more than the structures of government and politics. Unless a political culture is able to support a democratic system, the chances for the success of that system are slim. It is observed that the quest to study political reality is incomplete without the knowledge of political culture. In the current political context of Nepal where the actual domain of politics has manifestly sided down to ignoble depths of inter and intra party conflicts, non commitment, and disruption instead of the culture of consensus, compromise and commitment, a study of Nepal's political culture is expected to foster a cultural mode of political behavior. A substantial scholarly literature, for instance, suggests that political culture is more important than the model of governance for democrats. Since it encompasses both the political ideals and operating norms of a country, having standard political culture can easily face grave dangers. It is in this connection the importance and validity of this work ought to be judged. It is believed to be a worthy enterprise for every ruling elite and intellectual both for the development of discipline and contribution to civic culture.

The study is based on content analysis. It is descriptive, analytic and explorative. The methodology applied is the collections of literature. Its analysis is based on published books, published and unpublished documents, survey based research, public opinion poll findings, seminar papers, academic and professional journals, news magazines, news papers and human development reports including author's direct observation.

*Meena Vaidya Malla*

# List of Tables



# List of Chart

# Abbreviations

| | | |
|---|---|---|
| BS | - | Bikram Sambat |
| CA | - | Constituent Assembly |
| CBS | - | Central Bureau of Statistics |
| CCASS | - | Centre for Civil Awareness and Social Studies |
| CIAA | - | The Commission for the Investigation of Abuse of Authority |
| CPA | - | Comprehensive Peace Accord |
| CPI | - | Corruption Perception Index |
| CPN-Maoist | - | Communist Party of Nepal-Maoist |
| CPN-UML | - | Communist party of Nepal (United Marxist Lenin) |
| DFHRI | - | Democratic Freedom and Human Rights Institute |
| DFID | - | Department of International Development |
| EC | - | Election Commission |
| EPA | - | Eight Party Alliance |
| EU | - | European Union |
| FPTP | - | First-past-the-Post |
| FSU | - | Free Students' Union |
| GCB | - | Global Corruption Barometer |
| GDP | - | Gross Domestic Product |
| GNI | - | Gross National Income |
| GON | - | Government of Nepal |
| HDI | - | Human Development Index |
| HDRs | - | Human Development Reports |

| | | |
|---|---|---|
| IC | - | Interim Constitution |
| ICC | - | *International Criminal* Court |
| IFAD | - | International Fund for Agricultural Development |
| INSEC | - | Informal Sector Service Centre/Nepal |
| INGO | - | International Non-governmental Organization |
| ISI | - | Inter Service Intelligence |
| MJF | - | Madhese Janadhikar Forum |
| MOGA | - | Ministry of General Administration |
| MP | - | Member of Parliament |
| MoPR | - | Ministry of Peace and Reconstruction/Nepal |
| NA | - | Nepal Army |
| NC | - | Nepali Congress |
| NESAC | - | Nepal South Asia Centre |
| NHRC | - | Nepal Human Right Commission |
| NEFIN | - | Nepal Federation of Indigenous Nationalities |
| NGO | - | Non-governmental Organization |
| NLSS | - | Nepal Living Standards Survey |
| NPC | - | National Planning Commission/Nepal |
| NSP | - | Nepal Sadbhawana Party |
| OPEC | - | Organization of Petroleum Exporting Countries |
| PDI | - | Power Distance Index |
| PLA | - | People's Liberation Army |
| PR | - | Proportional Representation |
| PRSP | - | Poverty Reduction Strategy Papers |
| RPP | - | Rastriya Prajatantra Party |
| SPA | - | Seven Party Alliance |
| TI | - | Transparency International |
| T-MLP | - | Terai-Madhesh Loktantrik Party |
| TRC | - | Truth and Reconciliation Committee |
| UNDP | - | United Nations Development Programme |
| UNMIN | - | United Nations Mission in Nepal |
| UNs | - | United Nations |
| USAID | - | United States Agency for International Development |
| WFP | - | World Food Programme |
| YCL | - | Young Communist League |

# 1.

# Political Culture: A Conceptual Framework

Political culture is a fundamental belief and assumption of people about how government and political process operate and what are its intended and unintended effects on the lives and hopes of citizens. People's overall orientations, emotion, commitments, values, norms and cognitions toward system constitute the core of political culture. Political culture is distinct from the general culture of society in that it is more narrowly concerned to the people's understanding of how power and authority operate in principle and in actuality. It has been recognized that political culture is an integral aspect of more general culture. Culture is the shared pattern of behaviors and interactions, cognitive constructs, and affective understanding. A culture is the manner of doing things individually, or in an organized manner as a group, which the majority of populace in a particular group adheres with and accepts. So, culture can be characterized as individual as well as organized one. Yet often, the individual culture becomes insignificant against the organized culture of the group or society. Socio-political culture of a society represents the methodical organized activities of a society, people as a group, which pertains with the development of socio-political scenario of that society in a particular time period.

Cultures are not given to people by nature; rather they are constructed through collective action and reinforced through the manipulation of collectiveness. Here culture is seen as a resource enabling collective action. It is defined as equilibrium in a well-set of circumstances in which members of a group sharing in common descent, symbolic practices or high levels of interaction-and thereby becoming a cultural group-are able to condition their behavior on common knowledge beliefs about the behaviour of all members of the group.[1] Political culture provides structures and meaning to the political sphere in the same manner as culture in general gives coherence and integration to social life. Political culture sets the ground rules for the play of politics and establishes the shared assumptions and beliefs that are the foundation of a country's political life. Since it relates to emotions, function style and ethical values, it has become an important tool for the understanding of political system in contemporary political analysis. Now, it has come to stand as an important touch stone for a morphological study of the political system.

## Political Culture: Behavioural Analysis of Political Inquiry

The concept of political culture subsumes a natural evolution in the growth of behavioural approach in political science analysis. The entry of the concept of political culture into the lexicon of political studies is most associated with the rise of the behavioural movement[2] after the Second World War. Now, within the discipline of political science, political culture attempts to apply behavioural form of analysis to the study of traditional problems as political ideology, legitimacy, sovereignty, nationhood, and the rule of law. It is related to the study of political defection, political stratification, political socialization and political behaviours.

Political culture, the study of attitudes and beliefs about politics amongst citizens was testimony to the behaviouralists' emphasis on non-institutional form of politics. Of late, as political science discipline sought to absorb relevant developments in all the related social science disciplines, it laid an increasing focus on the behaviour of individuals. Political culture in this sense is an effort to study the total political system without ignoring the benefits of individual. It is a behavioural mode of political inquiry where the main focus of the attention is individual political behaviour that draws the unity of political science with psychology. Political culture can be defined as the political psychology of a country or nation (or community, thereof). The study of political community as a dynamic collective entity or of the total political system makes political science a complete social science through its insistence on a combined micro-macro approach. It has accelerated a process of widening the horizons of political science by laying emphasis on non-political dimension of life, the social and economic parameters having significant bearings on politics. The concept of political culture was developed in response to the need to bridge a growing gap in the behavioural approach between the level of micro-analysis based on the psychological interpretations of the individual's political behaviour and the level of macro-analysis based on the variables common to political sociology. The concept attempts to integrate psychology and sociology to dynamic political analysis combining the findings of modern depth psychology and recent advances in sociological techniques for measuring individual attitudes in mass societies.

Political culture approach encourages political scientists to take up the study of the social and cultural factors which are responsible for giving a broad shape to the political culture of a country. It also helps one to probe into the rational factors which mould the action of individuals and the more latent the irrational determinants of behaviour. Political culture equally bears an important role in the shaping of political development in a country that explains the phenomenon why some societies more easily adapt to democratic institution and other find it more convenient to authoritarian ways. Political scientists conclude that the attitudes, sentiments, and cognitions that inform and govern political behaviour in any society represent coherent patterns, which fit together and are mutually reinforcing. In any particular community, there is a limited and distinct political culture which gives meaning, predictability and forms to the political process that each individual must in his own historical contest learns and incorporates into his own personality the knowledge and feeling about the politics of his people and his community.[3]

## The Intellectual History of Political Culture

The classic study of political culture, a work that established the concept in political science, is Gabriel A. Almond and Sidney Verba's civic culture.[4] The book identifies the essential cultural and attitudinal bases for a stable democracy. The notion of political culture is in existence since men and women have spoken and written about politics. Long before the term political culture was coined, political theorists were exploring the political norms of societies to determine which attitudes are essential precondition for a stable democracy. The Greeks had a cyclic theory of political change and explained the rises and fall of political constitution in social psychological term.[5] We find a stronger affirmation of the importance of political culture in Plato's *Republic*. In the words of Plato… "Governments vary as the dispositions of men vary and that there must be as many of the one as there of the other. For we cannot suppose that states are made of "oak and rock" and not out of the human nature which are in them".[6]

Aristotle, a scientific political culturist, in his *politics* tried to work out the most suitable form of government. To achieve this end he did not focus simply on institutions but also on social structure and their attendant value systems. What emerges is a celebration of the virtues of civility, consensus and partnership in *politic* associated democracy with the values and outlook of a middle class. He argues that the best attainable form of government is the mixed form in a society in which the middle classes predominate. This is in turn associated with a mixture of oligarchic (rule by the few) and democratic characteristics and control by the 'middle classes' (in Aristotle's terms, those who are neither rich nor poor). He remarks:

> … a society in which the middle class is small produces a state consisting of slaves and master, not of free men, and of one class envious and another contemptuous of their fellows. This condition of affairs is very far removed from friendliness, and from political partnership."[7]

The conception of mixed government with a predominant middle class is to some extent related to the civic culture in the modern sense. Because there is a substantial consensus on the legitimacy of political institutions, the direction and content of public policy, there is a widespread tolerance of a plurality of interest and belief in their reconcilability and a widely distributed sense of political competence and mutual trust in the citizenry. Jean –Jacques Rousseau, in the eighteenth century, wrote much about the importance of morality and custom as the basis of political stability from a different perspective. The most famous critic of the French Revolution, Edmund Burke, placed considerable emphasis on the vital importance of tradition and the destructive consequences of uprooting well-established political norms. Progress, argued Burke, is best achieved in the context of continuity and with reference to past precedent and tradition. Machiavelli was aware of the importance of political cultural variable of moral values, of feeling of identity and commitment for political strength and weakness. He further writes:

> … whoever runs through the vast number of exploits performed by the people of Rome as a whole, or by many of the Roman individually, will see that its citizens were more afraid of breaking an oath than of breaking the law since they held in higher esteem the power of god than the power of man.[8]

Montesquieu identified integrity and trustworthiness as the critical values for a democracy. He had recourse to sociological, anthropological and social psychological variables in explaining national history, political institution and process. In the same way the terms Rousseau used to identify political culture are morality, custom and public opinion. He treated them as a kind of law more important than law that is "engraved on the hearts of citizen." He comments: "political system and systems of legislation vary with the "local situation and the temper of the inhabitants."[9] Tocqueville probably went furthest of the classical social theorist in spelling out the essentials of a democratic political culture. He noted that the precondition for democracy is the ability of free citizen to form associations, working together to advance their own interests while respecting the larger need of the political system as a whole. He says:

> … the manner of the people may be considered as one of the great causes to which the maintenance of a democratic republic in the United States is attributable. I here use the word customs with the meaning which the ancients attached to the word mores; for I apply it not only to manners properly so called- that is to what might be termed the habits of the heart-but to the various notions and opinions current among men and to the mass of those ideas which constitute their character of mind. I comprise under this term, therefore, the whole moral and intellectual condition of a people.[10]

The next stream entering into political culture, conceptualization and research is that of anthropology stemming from the work of Freud and later became known as the psycho-cultural approach. The merger of psychoanalysis with the social science began in the 1920s and 1930s with the work of Bronislaw Malinowski, Ruth Benedict and Harold Lasswell. The psycho-cultural literature sought to explain political culture propensities by childhood socialization patterns, unconscious motivation and psychological mechanisms. During and after World War II, efforts were made to characterize and explain the psychological propensities of the major nations at war- Germany, Russia, America, France, and Japan. At about the same time, anthropologists were refining their concepts of culture by incorporating the insights of Freudian psychology to explain the socialization process by which individuals are taught how to be effective members of their culture. Personality and culture came to be seen as opposite sides of the same coin. In the immediate postwar environment there was also great interest in national character studies. Benedict has made a remarkably insightful and solid analysis of Japanese Character.[11] It was soon followed by studies of German and Russian national character. Some of these works were highly speculative, for example, Geoffrey Gorer and

John Richman suggested in 1945 that primary features of Russian behaviour could be traced to the practice of swaddling babies. In 1954 work on national character was thrown into ovation by Alex Inkels and Daniel Levinson, who in their article "National Character" called for extremely indeed high scientific standards in the field.[12]

Studies of political culture took an added vitality in the 1960s as it focused on the less industrialized nations and the problem of political development. The approach offered a solid basis for analyzing the prospects for nation building among the emerging states of the former colonial world. These countries were forced to combine their traditional cultural arrangements with colonial influences. The introduction of the concept of political culture opened the way for renewed research into the psychological and cultural basis of political behaviour. The leading example of the behavioural study of political culture remains *The Civic Culture* by the American political scientists Gabriel Almond and Sidney Verba, first published in 1963.[13] *The Civic Culture* was a report on an extensive survey carried out in five countries-the United States, the United Kingdom, Italy, the Federal Republic of Germany and Mexico in 1959. Almond and Verba's comparative study delineated the cultural basis of stable democracy by identifying the essential compounds of what they called the civic culture. Through sample surveys they tested the concept in the five countries' and thereby advanced a solid empirical theory about the political culture of democracy from the West. Modernization process challenged many countries' tradition and inspired to create transitional political cultures. In the late 1960s and early 1970s, the study of political culture lost favour among political scientists. In part, this shift was a reaction to the Vietnam War and the popularization of radical views in some of the social sciences. Political culture was characterized as a conservative, if not a reactionary concept by those who believed that evolutionary leaders such as Mao-Zedong in China and Fidel Castro in Cuba were successfully transforming their societies virtually overnight. Any suggestion about the enduring power of culture was, therefore, seen as hostile propaganda by opponents of revolutionary change.

## Revival of Political Culture

It became obvious by the late 1970s especially with the opening of China in the Post-Mao era that much of Chinese culture had survived the Marxist attacks on it. During the 1980s the abandonment of communism in many countries aroused interest in questions about the relationship of political culture and democracy. Samuel P. Huntington was a leader to revive the interest in political culture. In the 1980s and 1990s he produced important work focusing on American politics and on democratization in the world.[14] The revival of political culture studies briefly conflicted with the new interest in rational choice theory, a field in which the methods of economics were applied to the study of politics. Aaron Wildavsky demonstrated that the two approaches are important compatible aspects since culture determines the political preferences of individuals. Therefore, rational choice theorists must look to culture to understand the goals of rational choice.

Inglehart advanced the revival of political culture theory by demonstrating that with the rise in affluence in the western democracies, cultural matter-such as ethnic identity, socialization, women's right trade unions, etc. have come to command greater political attention while the economic class and more materialistic issues have receded.[15] Therefore, politics in post-industrial societies increasingly revolved around cultural issues and values not just economic interests. Following Almond and Verba (1963), Inglehart identifies the following seven specific indications of mass political culture:

- Levels of overall life satisfaction
- Levels of interpersonal trust
- Support for moderate change
- Support for the current social order
- Levels of political discussion

- Level of post-materialist values.
- Proportion of the population protestant.[16]

Inglehart's measures of civic culture are based on survey data and on mass civic orientations. He finds out that civic virtue should be more widespread within the wealthier democracies as they are less sensitive to short-term economic condition to temporal fluctuation.

The next rigorous study about political culture and its relation to democracy is provided by Robert Putnam's analysis of civic traditions of Italy.[17] Putnam's statistical analysis of the effect of political culture on democratic government is based on the three variables. They are:

- Institutional performances,
- Civic community, and
- Civic tradition.

Putnam and his associates have discovered that the most critical variable for explaining democratic success is the level of development of what they called a civic community. The key to making democracy work was the political culture and more particularly the existence of attitudes not too different from those of Almond and Verba. Similarly, Putnam argues that cultural norms as reflected in a sense of civic community are responsible for economic, political and institutional performance. In short, the political culture identifies distinctive clusters of attitudes that are widely held across individuals. Cultural factors thus condition how individuals adapt to changes in incentive structures embodied in institutions. Thus, Putnam's and Inglehart's studies are easily the most extensive empirical statements on political culture in recent years. The original studies of political culture drew heavily on anthropological analysis of culture of the 1950$_s$ and 1960$_s$. Almond and Verba (1963) sought to identify the features of political culture that foster democratic performance. They paid special attention to the cultures arguing that democratic outcomes are more likely where participatory norms are widespread. The traditional emphasis on military security and material economic welfare would be displaced by the new politics of ideology, community and popular participation.

## Understanding Political Culture

The exact definition of political culture is vague and broad. It is difficult to provide a precise and acceptable definition. Still, a few definitions by outstanding authorities may be cited to help appreciate the Nepali political culture in its true perspective. Political culture, according to Pye is:

> the set of attitudes, beliefs and sentiments which provides the underlying assumptions and rules that govern behaviour in the political and operating norms of polity. Political culture is the manifestation in aggregate form of the psychological and subjective dimensions of politics.[18]

Verba defines political culture to be:

> the system of beliefs about the patterns of political interaction and political institution. It refers not only to what is happening in the world of politics, but also to what people believe about these happenings. These beliefs may be of several kinds. For example they may be empirical beliefs about what the actual state of political life is; they may be beliefs of goals or values that ought to be pursued in political life and these beliefs may find important expression or have emotional dimensions.[19]

Pye and Verba have offered more comprehensive elaborations of the concept. Pye, focusing on political development themes discussed the variety of ways that: "the concept of political culture can help explain developmental problems and process."[20] Verba defined the important dimension of political culture as including the sense of national identity, attitudes toward oneself as participant, attitudes towards one's fellow citizens, attitudes and expectations regarding governmental output and performance and knowledge about and attitudes towards the political process of decision making.[21] As Verba puts, "the political culture of a society consists of the system of empirical beliefs, expressive symbols and values, which defines the situation in which political action takes place."[22] Encyclopedia of Government and Politics defines political culture as patterns of orientation to political action or objectives. There does seem to be a common theme throughout these diverse writings.

Taking into account all these definitions, I adopt here an operational definition and importance of political culture that equates as the psychological orientation of people towards their political system. It includes knowledge and skills about the operation of the political system, positive and negative emotional feelings towards it and evaluative judgments about the system. It is the study of attitudes, beliefs, and values which underpin the operation of a particular political system. Political culture is of vital importance for understanding the large issue of political development. It is to the political system what culture is to social system. It is composed of impulses, feelings and ways of doing and looking at things. It generates a set of trends, values and is sustained by them. It is a rag-bag stuffed with finely-spun political theories, ideologies, and functional style of leaders. In short, it is an elaborate and comprehensive philosophy indispensable to the political system. Since political culture defines the relationship of citizens to government, it refers to what people believe and feel about government, and how they think people should act towards it. To understand the relationship of a government to its people, and how those people are going to act toward that government and others, it is necessary to study what those people believe about themselves and government. So political culture is the political atmosphere or climate of a nation's government. Political culture is also a distinctive and patterned form of political philosophy that consists of beliefs on how governmental, political and economic life should be carried out. Political cultures create a framework for political change and are unique to nation, state and other groups.

A political culture differs from political ideology in that people can disagree on an ideology (what government should do) but still share a common political culture. Some ideologies, however, are so critical of the status quo that they require a fundamental change in the way government is operated, and therefore embody a different political culture. In the same way, particular regional, ethnic, or other groups within a political system with their own distinctive sets of values, attitudes, and beliefs are referred to as subcultures. The purpose of investigating what we now know as political culture has predominantly been to establish the nature of the relationship between region stability and the structure of beliefs, values and traditions. The claim being made is that political culture filters our perceptions, influences our attitudes and has a major say in the extent and manner of our political participation. Moreover, the makeup of a political culture influences patterns of orientations within a political system. These orientation patterns, in turn, have a major influence on the stability of a regime.

## Patterns of Individual Orientation

Almond argues that: "...every political system is embedded in a particular pattern of orientation of political actions."[23] These patterns of individual orientation according to Almond and Powell involve three components. That is individual orientations towards any political object may be viewed in terms of these three dimensions:

### *Cognitive Orientation*

The cognitive dimension of orientation toward the system implies knowledge and beliefs accurate or otherwise of the political system. An individual may have a relatively high degree of accurate knowledge about how his/her whole political system works, who the leading figures are and what the current problems of polity are.

### *Affective Orientations*

It implies feelings of attachments, involvements, rejection and the like world about the political world. It might, however, have feelings of alienation or rejection towards the system; perhaps the family and friends have long harbored such attitudes. It would be unlikely to respond favourably to demands upon him by the system.

***Evaluative Orientations***

It implies judgments and opinions about the political objects which usually involve applying value standards to political events and objects. One may have some more evaluation of the system perhaps his/her democratic norms lead him to evaluate the system as not sufficiently responsive to political demands or his ethical norms lead him to condemn the level of corruption and nepotism.

These orientations can significantly influence the way a political system works. In fact, the demands made upon a system, the responses to laws and to appeals for support, and the conduct of individuals in their political role, are shaped and conditioned by an orientation pattern. Cognitive, affective and evaluative orientations form the latent political tendencies and propensities for political behavior.

## Classification of Political Culture

Political culture can be classified according to whether the members of a society take an active, moderate or a passive part in the political process. That is, whether they play a part with ardent expectations of tangible benefits from the governmental activity or whether they have very little or almost no knowledge of the decision-making process and have no hopes for a share in the power. So, on the basis of the awareness of the people towards the political objects, Almond and Verba termed the existing political culture of the people at that time as parochial political culture, subject political culture and the participant political culture[24] that is briefly discussed below.

***Parochial Political Culture***

Parochial political culture exists in simple traditional societies in which there is a very little specialization, where actors fulfill a combination of political, economic and religious roles simultaneously.[25] On account of development, some of the individuals may become aware of the existence of central political authority but their feelings for an evaluation of the system as a whole "have not crystallized norms and standards to regulate his relation with the system."[26] It means they are unaware of input/ output process of the system. So parochial political culture is basically characterized by general ignorance about political objects and a consequent lack of involvement in political activity.

### *Subject Political Culture*

Subject political cultures are characterized by widespread knowledge about political process. But there is a disinclination to participate in political activity, often because of feelings of powerlessness. It exists where there is a high frequency of orientations to the system as a whole and to it's specifically output aspects. It occurs in dependent colonies where the people either feel pride or have hostility towards their political system. They either accept the decisions of their rulers as legitimate or struggle against them in the name of their right for self-determination. In subject political culture, people are aware of their political system and the impact of its output. But they hardly know the input mechanism.

### *Participant Political Culture*

Participant political cultures combine knowledge about politics with a willingness to participate in the political process. In such situations, people feel able to affect change; that their political activity will make a difference. It exists in highly developed societies where people take active part in the political sphere by considering themselves as active members of the party. The people are well conscious of their rights and duties. "Evaluation and criticism of the system exists at all levels and it is generally accepted discernible that political activity should be the close scrutiny of individuals and groups within society."[27] The participant political culture is the fully developed political culture in which people participate equally in all the process of the system. Thus, the degree of intensity with which each individual holds each of several sets or clusters of values, beliefs, and symbols makes one primarily a parochial, subject or participant.

**Political Culture in Developing and Transitional Societies**

The three types of political culture discussed above are not possibly present in a pure form. They are intermixed, co-related and inseparable in many situations. Almond and Verba's idea was that democracy is likely to be most stable in societies where a participant political culture is balanced by the survival of subject and parochial attitudes.[28] So the inquiry is to know to which culture the developed and transitional societies belong. If the political culture of the developed countries has a strong participant element, can the developing or Third World be seen in terms of parochial political culture? Is the parochial culture a cause of the weak and developing state? The answer is yes, to some extent. A parochial culture implies that many people are only dimly aware of the national government. However, it does not mean that citizens of developing countries are politically naïve. They are often well aware of the intricacies of local and ethnic politics through which resources are, in reality, distributed. Many developing countries are best considered as poly cultural and poly structural societies rather than as countries with weak national and distinct sub–culture. From this perspective, it is better to describe political culture in the developing countries as local than parochial. When three types of political culture interact, the result is the mixed political culture as developed by Almond and Verba. They are:

- The parochial– subject political culture
- The subject-participant political culture
- The parochial– participant political culture.

It is difficult to put developing countries in any single category of the above-defined political culture in the country. Thus, the degree to which the public is cognitively aware of politics and is active in it, it is key to whether a political culture is parochial, subject or participant. In parochial political culture, the public is only dimly aware of the system and is largely detached from it. In subject political culture, the public awareness at the participation in the political process is limited to the system's output as meted out through the bureaucracy, the executive and judiciary. This is the political culture, the type most commonly found in the developing countries. The largest concentrations of individuals with parochial or subject orientations to politics are found in less developed region like South Asia in general and Nepal in particular. Although these different political cultures are not mutually exclusive and do not exist in complete isolation from one another, parochial tendencies often co-exist side by side with subject or participant political culture in the developing nations.

Developing countries are marked by a number of considerable variations from one country to another and from one region to another where tribal nuances tear nations apart, segregating and separating their people along the lines of racial, tribal and linguistic differences. Regardless of social, cultural, economic and political characteristics that are unique to individual countries throughout the Third World, there are many similarities in people's orientation towards their political system. So, an attempt is made here to find out some of the similar characteristics inherent in developing and transitional societies' political culture, so that, one can get detailed information with regard to the political culture of Nepal, a developing and transitional state in South Asia.

The political culture of the most developing and transitional states is marked by discontinuities and lack of coherence. Fragmented political cultures are, in fact, one of the marked attributes of Third World political system. Fragmented political cultures result from a number of social and cultural characteristics, such as multiplicity of races, languages, ethnic and social groups and religions. Rapid and intense industrialization, wars, revolutions, major fundamental shifts in governmental policies are also likely to disturb the coherence of cultural norms and upset the uniformity of political culture. In such circumstances people are suddenly thrown into a political whirlwind and the political orientations to which they have become accustomed and disrupted by sudden and fundamental shifts in politics.[29] It gives rise to fractured political culture where neither the government is responsible to the people nor it concentrates on the development in the words of Baral.[30] In such a situation there is thus no movement towards achievement of national goals and objectives. Because of fractured and fragmented political culture, most of the Third World countries are more prone to political instability and disruptions than an integrated one. The result is a weak civil society that has undermined the development of pluralist politics.

Political culture in stable political system is different as compared to transitional societies. In the former, it is relatively homogenous, where there is a general agreement about the proper limits and functions of politics. Whereas in the later, it is often fragmented and people do not share common orientations towards political action or there is congruence between public issues and private interests. In the developing or transitional societies, wedded to representative institutions, it should steadily reinforce the agents of political socialization and spell out the meaning, the means and the ends of political actions. It moves in this direction, it is viable enough to establish stability in the political system, but if the process is reversed, it results imbalance, stagnation and decay. Once dysfunctional becomes acute and chronic, it poses a serious threat to the political system.[31]

Culture anomie is only one of the features of political culture in the Third World. Within each Third World country, it is not uncommon to find a plurality of political culture. These political cultures are marked by a sharp dichotomy into the political culture of the elites and that, of the masses, each differentiated from the other by its unique features and characteristics. Elite political culture consists of the beliefs, attitudes and ideal about politics held by those who are closest to the centers of political power. The elite political culture involves not only those in authoritative structures but also the leadership element of the non-authoritative structures and processes. In countries with a parochial or subject political culture, elite political culture dominates the policy process. In such circumstances, political culture arises out of incomplete and misdirected political socialization. The result is resistance of old orientations towards new political norms, values, limited public awareness and participation in the political processes. Developing countries are now hoping to discredit old political orientation and instill new one in their place.

## Civic Culture: Stable Democracy

Almond and Verba regard three types of political cultures as the properties of both individuals and political systems as a whole. The assumption, therefore, is that it is possible to link the 'micro' and the 'macro' aspects of politics. Second, the three categories are ideal types. This means that they represent an attempt to impose a classification upon the disordered and messy reality of human world. Real world political cultures invariably appear as some sort of mixture of these ideal types and this is very much what Almond and Verba's research shows. Their study concludes that all three ideal types would be unsatisfactory as cultural underpinnings for a stable democratic polity. Parochialism is a characteristic of 'traditional societies' and not of mature democracies, where developed institutions require a qualitatively different sort of value system. Subject political cultures are also deemed unsuitable. While citizens in such situations possess the requisite political knowledge, they do not possess the sense that they can be effective democratic actors. On the other hand, a participant political culture carries with it the danger of a kind of democratic overload. Too many citizens trying to influence change through mass participation would be a source of instability that could seriously undermine the normative ideal of democratic stability. Thus, in terms of their conclusions, Almond and Verba argue that the best sort of political culture for a stable democratic system would involve a mix of subject and participant elements. They label this mixture the civic culture. In a civic culture, citizens possess high levels of knowledge about the political process and feel empowered as political actors. Crucially, however they would recognize the legitimacy of the elites to make decisions on their behalf. At the same time, elites will be sensitive to the preferences of the mass population. The resultant system is a balance.

It is in this context the political culture of the United States and in particular, the United Kingdom comes near to civic culture ideal. Civic culture is the type of political culture that provides the best environment for stable democratic politics to occur. It combines the optimum mix of subject and participant political attitudes. In the concluding pages of The Civic Culture, Almond and Verba argue:

> The development of a stable and effective democratic government depends upon more than the structures of government and politics; it depends upon the orientations that people have to the political process-upon the political culture. Unless a political culture is able to support a democratic system, the chances for the success of that system are slim….The civic culture appears to be particularly appropriate for a democratic political culture, but it seems to be the one most congruent with a stable democratic system.[32]

Almond and Verba assume that political structures could be explained with reference to political culture. The authors of the civic culture understood degrees of democratic stability as being determined or caused by political culture. So we can explain the level of civic culture in a society with reference to the level of democratic stability. Democratic stability creates and sustains what is understood as the civic culture. It shows that cultures and structures are interdependent and mutually reinforcing.

## Nepal's Political Culture: Half Way Developed towards a Full-Fledged Democracy

Every particular community has a limited and distinct political culture which gives meaning, predictability and form to the political process. Based on it, Nepal's political culture includes the study of people's faith, attitude, values and beliefs towards their political system, whether; it is traditional or modern, rural or agricultural, urban–industrial, homogeneous or heterogeneous, mass or elite. The degree of tradition and modernity can be found on the basis of economic status, educational background, social hierarchy, religion, regionalism, and age factor and socialization process. These variables are almost universal but their applications in Nepal are more acute because of the less developed social, political and economic environment.

The democratic traditions have become the significant components of political culture of many developing nations, but the democratic traditions and behaviour have not been unified. Contemporary political culture of developing nations is based upon creating the new post-totalitarian tradition in politics. The study of Nepal's political culture imbibes the aspects of both tradition and modernity that is the existence of bi-culturism. The Nepali society can be described as a marginal case between the two– traditional and modern. The former signifies people's attachment with the casteism, linguism, authoritarianism, while the principle of mass education, mass communication, mass political participation with republicanism and federalism are instances of change and modernity. Modernity rejects the traditional values, beliefs and emotional sentiments of the social life and stands for adult franchise, periodic elections, social equality, fundamental rights, rule of law, and independence of judiciary, so has helped greatly to root out the evils such as illiteracy, exploitations, land lordship, exclusion, marginalization and localism.

The present political system is a compromise between the two sets of basically incompatible demands. Now, the hard question is how the political system can accommodate both sets of culture? The political culture is a dynamic phenomenon; so it responds to the needs and pressures coming from its social structure. The slow process of social transformation in Nepali political culture has slowly reconciled both the trends of traditionalism and modernism. The social tradition and political culture have slowly assimilated the impact of modernity as Nepal is transforming its old structures to the new one. It is a transitional society moving away from traditional and feudal structures to more advanced, differentiated and pluralistic society. Political culture in such a stage is more authoritarian than democratic, where assertive culture and considerations dominate politics. The social stratification among caste, class and gender lines restrict social mobility of majority of people shaping a value system in the society which conflicts with material aspirations and democratic culture based on freedom, social justice and culture of inclusion. In such a situation, both traditional and modern values mix and modern political institutions are found. This sort of political bi-cultarism of Nepal has marked many changes due to the process of the people's movements and democratic restoration. If the people have adopted new values of life, the sentiments of castes, authoritarism, communalism and regionalism may have been weakened. But on the other hand, these sentiments have also divided the masses or the voters as these forces have gradually been polarized in the new political culture, i.e. in the politics of struggle for power. The trend has virtually created a gap between values and institutions of Nepali political culture.

It is observed that the present political system in Nepal is a compromise between the two sets of basically incompatible demands. Though the conservative people still may desist any radical and sudden social change, Nepali political culture still allows the assimilation of the new trends. In a transitional stage, the assimilation is in a slow and gradual process. Culture is a dynamic flux. The aspirations of the individuals of the society and the values of the community clash with each other. So it provides a middle path of change satisfying both the aspirations and value premises of the members of the society.

The noticeable fact of this flux is aspirations of the youth or new members often wins over the value premises of old that brings about a change in outlook of the society and its values. There is no dichotomy between the two sets of cultures, although the elite culture overshadows the mass culture in the sphere of decision making and participation of the people. Nevertheless, the political bi-culturism has the abundant capacity to absorb the impact of the two cultures- traditional and modern, rural and urban and elite and mass ignorant.

## Social Transformation: Historical Break

Social change is a gradual process. Literature review in this field suggests that social transformation is a process of wide-ranging change in the thinking, nature, structure, institution, rules, technology and cultural patterns of society through human actions. It aims to replace the crisis-prone and dysfunctional system by new values, processes and division of labour in search of a new but more humanized social equilibrium. It clinches a considerable amount of overlap between old and new forces. It does not seek any structural alterations in the way the state is organized to help the society's productive life but rationalizes the society and legitimizes the state's guardianship. The idea of social transformation, in contrast, seeks historical break. It also transcends the prevailing linear assumptions of theories and practices of development and accepts the tolerance of social, cultural and political diversity. In this sense, social transformation is a systemic process.

It inexorably leads to a dynamic equilibrium of society where the power of society to self-organize is brought to the level of political power. Due to the existence of dynamic tension, the level of Nepal's social transformation is, however, unclear whether the historically dominant class will prevail, or it will accommodate the new class or bring back to the forefront of history the hitherto subordinated class to impose its interest in the state and society. Obviously, newly gained political consciousness is moderately expanding the social base of political power in Nepal and forcing the old political class to play by new rules of the game. But, in no way has it restructured the social stratification arrangements. There is, however, also a huge cost in expanding the size of political class. No one knows how long and how far poor people of Nepal would be able to subsidize the swelling political class which is interested more over the domination of political process by any sort of political combination than democratic alteration in office for gender, social and inter-generational justice. Devoid of these virtues, this class is rife on all sides by a widespread social revolt.

The huge disproportion between social force of diverse people and the supremacy of incumbent political class has made possible to bring continuous political disequilibrium. Growing bodies of historical analysis affirm that Nepal's major obstacle to progress is the patrimonial political culture of ruling elites which is incompatible with genuine pluralistic politics, entrepreneurship and social justice. Such practices have weakened the vital agendas of socio-economic and political transformation as expected by the people. Change in political culture of excessive passion for the concentration of power and authority on individual leaders is a precondition of modernization. Transformation in Nepal is premised on the inclusion of marginalized forces of society to reshape governing institutions, undertaking the process of democratization, decentralization and devolution of power, abolition of feudalism, transformation of a centralized and unitary state into a decentralized and federal one and providing proportional representation of women, Dalits, Madhesis, Janajatis, Aadibasis and marginalized in the state power. The purpose of restructuring, according to the preamble of the Interim Constitution is to resolve the existing class, caste, regional and gender problems of the country and set the path of the nation towards participatory democracy and shared rule.

The Interim Constitution thus purports to transform the concept of citizenship based exclusively on civil and political rights to the possession of full social rights. The high level political participation of these social classes in the face of puny socialization on citizenship and weak political institutionalization, however, might provoke a hatred and conflict between citizens and the social classes. It may cause the instability of the political system in the future. The new constitution should glue the reconciliation process. The test of new constitution would be measured as a capacity of removal of these social anomalies. It can be forecasted that the political bi-cultarism in Nepal is bound to remain operative in near future as an essential part of our political change.

The contradiction and conflict between the two political cultures are likely to prevail until old and traditional politics is thoroughly replaced by the new mass political culture. It needs a harmonious synthesis of the two cultures in this transitional stage. So at this juncture, the political change in Nepali political culture warrants the establishment of an egalitarian social order and eradication of social and economic injustice which can be achieved by mass movements and political consciousness among the masses and political leaders.

Nepal is moving from a hierarchical culture in which one's place was dictated by gender, caste and ethnicity, religion, region to one that aspires to making human dignity and equality as its fundamental culture. In such a transitional stage, the creation of new roles, institutions, values, and social relationships during meaningful state transformation may produce instability that may lead to anomie. Adjustments and compromises made by the leadership in the interest of social order and survival may delay or distort programmes of social change beyond the delays and distortions caused by the expected difficulties in attitudinal changes and institutionalization. So, Nepal in this transition is placed with the problems of adapting and adjusting her ancient political cultural heritage to a set of new rapidly altering conditions brought about by the immense science and technological changes in recent decades. Therefore, Nepal's political culture can be named as the transient political culture, pursuing democratic norms and values with traditional and modern attitudes, so to be less than half way developed toward a full-fledged democracy. One of the major problems of Nepal's democratic republic is that the transition which is expected to be smooth, goal –oriented, and more or less consensual, has become not only uncertain and turbulent but is also likely to erase the political achievements made over the years. Many are also of the view that the foregoing trends in Nepal are inherent characteristics of a transitional stage of development; so there is no cause of alarm. But any transition has definite ideology, direction and leadership role. Given the present Nepali situation, if such transition becomes too long to accomplish its set goals, its chance of becoming unsuccessful is also pretty high. Political heterogeneity and spurious ideological and normative commitment may in all probability not make the transition a success.

A long period of confusion, uncertainty and mixed purposes may further contribute to a state of chronic frustration and a pervasive cynicism in collective orientations. In the same way, weak supportive orientation towards authority may prolong the period of transition. This feature of Nepali political culture in present day is mainly responsible for slow and sluggish development in all the sectors. It should be understood that no cultural system has more than two alternatives in a transitional situation- either it adapts itself to the new conditions or doggedly resist them rather than being dragged by them. The latter alternative has no chance of success in the contemporary world.

## NOTES

1. David, D. Laitin, *Nations States and Violence,* (Oxford: Oxford University Press, 2007), p. 64.
2. Behaviouralism is a movement in postwar political science, notably in the USA, concerned with establishing law- like generalizations about the political world with shifting the emphasis of political studies away from its traditional, legal and institutional manifestation. With a focus on individual behaviour, the behavioural approach is linked with quantitative research technique designed to generate testable hypothesis about measurable attitudes and observable behaviour, rendering the study of politics more scientific.
3. Lucian W. Pye, "Introduction: Political Culture and Political Development," *Political Culture and Political Development*, Pye and Sydney Verba (eds.), (New Jersey: Princton, 1965), p. 7.
4. Gabriel A. Almond and Sidney Verba, *The Civic Culture: Political Attitudes and Democracy in Five Nations,* (New Jersey: Princeton University Press, 1963), p. 15.

5. Plato, *The Works of Plato,* Trans. Jowett (ed.), Vol. 1, (New York: Dial Press, 1932), p. 307.
6. *Ibid*, p. 445.
7. Gabriel A. Almond and Sidney Verba (eds.), *The Civic Culture Revisited,* (New Delhi: Sage Publication, 1989), p. 4.
8. Niccolo Machiavelli, *The Discourses,* Trans Leslie Walker (Trans.), (New Haven: Yale University Press, 1950), p. 240.
9. Jean Jacque Rousseau, *The Social Contract*, (New York: Carlton House, 1968), pp. 41-43.
10. Alexis de Tocqueville, *Democracy in America*, (New York: Alfred A. Knoph. 1945), p. 299.
11. Ruth Benedict, *The Chrysanthemum and the Sword: Patterns of Japanese Culture*, (Boston: Houghton Mifflin, 1946), p. 60.
12. Geoffrey Gorer, *National Character: Theory and Practice,* (New York: Norton, 1953), pp. 57-82.
13. Almond and Verba, *op cit.*, f.n. No. 4, p. 18.
14. Samuel P. Huntington, *The Third Wave: Democratization in the Late Twentieth Century,* (Norman: University of Oklahoma Press, 1991), p. 114.
15. Ronald Inglehart, *Cultural Shift in Advanced Industrial Society,* (Princeton: Princeton University Press, 1990), p. 314.
16. Robert W. Jacktmanm and Ross A. Miller, *A Renaissance of Political Culture: American Journal of Political Science*, Vol. 40, Issue 3, (Madison: University of Wiscosin System, August, 1996), pp. 632-659.
17. Robert Putnam, *Making Democracy Work,* (New Jersey: Princeton University Press, 1993), p. 240.
18. Pye, *op cit.*, f.n. No. 3, pp. 7-8.
19. Almond and Verba, *op cit.*, f.n. No. 4, p. 17.
20. *Ibid.*
21. *Ibid,* p. 12.
22. Sidney Verba, "Conclusion: Comparative Political Culture", *Political Culture and Political Development,* Pye and Verba (eds.), (New Jersey: Princeton University, 1989), pp. 512-560.
23. *Ibid,* p. 20.
24. Almond and Verba, *op cit.*, f.n. No. 4, pp. 17-20.
25. Morton R. Davies and Vaughan A. Lewis, *Models of Political*

*System*, (Delhi: Vikas Publications, 1971), p. 105.

26. *Ibid*, p. 116.
27. *Ibid*, p. 117.
28. Rod Hague, Martin Harrop and Shaven Brislin, *Comparative Government and Politics*, 3rd ed., (London: Macmillan, 1992), p. 136.
29. Meheran Kamrava, *Politics and Society in the Third World*, (London: New Fetterlane, 1993), p. 139.
30. Lok Raj Baral, "Jan Andolan, Sanskar Nirman Ra Rajnitik Prakriya," *Nepali Rajyako Naya Swroop Ra Charitra*," Krishna Hachethu (ed.), (Lalitpur: Nepal Centre for Contemporary Studies-NCCS, 2011), pp. 56-57.
31. Hague, Harrop and Brislin, *op cit.*, f.n. No. 28, p. 140.
32. Almond and Verba, *op cit.*, f.n. No. 4, p. 15.

# 2.

# Determining Factors of Nepal's Political Culture

Political culture, a term suitable for analyzing civic behaviour in the political area includes the real behaviour, the distinctive customs, skills and attitudes that individuals learn as the shared experience of their political system. Political culture, whether, heterogeneous or homogenous is a component of several interrelated factors-historical, geographical and socio-economic structures. So, it varies from state to state and region to region, as states develop themselves in spirit of ideas, which stood at their birth. Differences in political culture may emerge according to the level of education, ethnic composition, structure of social hierarchy and the style of political socialization. Accordingly, the connection between political culture and social context is seen as intimate, indeed inseparable. Hunt, a pioneer in the analysis of political culture of the French Revolution has reflected this idea:

> Revolutionary political culture cannot be deduced from social structures, social conflicts, or the social identity of revolutionaries. Political practices were not simply the expression of "underlying" economic and social interest. ...This is not to say, however, that the revolution was only intellectual or that politics has primacy over society rather than vice versa. The revolution in politics was an explosive interaction between ideas and reality, between intention and circumstance, between collective practices and social context. If revolutionary politics cannot be deduced from the social identity

of the revolutionaries, then neither can it be deduced from it; the revolution was made by people nor were some people more attracted than others to the politics of revolution.[1]

The above paraphrase acknowledges the inextricable and interactive connection among society, economy, polity and culture. While this political culture approach is still in its infancy in the contemporary Nepali studies field, its application to the study of political change elsewhere in the world is already well established. As French historian Baker puts it: political culture is a historical creation, subject to constant elaboration and development through the activities of the individuals and groups whose purpose it defines. As it sustains and gives meaning to political activity, so it is itself shaped and transformed in the course of that activity.[2] As formulated by Sidney Verba and developed by Almond and Verba, these values and beliefs can be classed as, 'cognitive,' 'affective,' and 'evaluative' orientation toward the system in general. In this context, Pye remarks that every community has a distinct political culture, which gives meaning, predictability to the political process that each individual in his own historical context learn his own personality, the knowledge, feelings about the politics of people and community.[3]

The variation in political culture is due to the historical, geographical, economical, cultural and religious factors present in the societies and nations. A multiplicity of races, ethnic and social groups, religion, allocation of resources, location of administrative centers and political movements and parties committed to furthering the cause of constituents further accentuate differences in political orientation, argues Rosenbaum.[4] In aggregate, political culture is the manifestation of people's orientation, their emotions, commitments, sentiments, basic values, norms and cognitions towards their system. All these statements clear that political culture is not static; it is a dynamic concept and responds to the needs generated within the political system. So, political culture is the product of history of a political system and also the life histories of the individuals who make up the system; and thus rooted equally in public events and private experiences. Alvares writes:

> the ideas, values, acts, even emotions of men like their nervous system, are cultural products, manufactured out of the capacities, tendencies and dispositions with which they are born; men, like their cathedrals or their temples, are cultural artifacts. ... Every culture has a system of technology and, therefore, also a history of technology.[5]

Every society has its own way of living artistic traditions, aesthetic appreciation and even styles of governmental performance. These ways and styles are deep rooted in the psyche of the people and soil of the country. With regard to the factors as the component of political culture, Tocqueville attributes the foundation of American political culture to its geography, and ecology, to its constitution or laws, but most important of all to its customs, by which he meant "the moral and intellectual characteristics of men in society." About the important foundation what he attaches to what we would call political culture today is the influence of practical experience, the habits, the opinions, in short, of the customs of the Americans upon this institution.[6]

The history of Nepal's ups and downs and challenges would naturally cover various aspects of culture, religion, society, politics economy, administration, religion, ethnicity, elites and many other factors. Against this background, this section, therefore tries to take stock of inquiry on Nepal's geography and geo-psychology, economy, ethnicity, religion as the major components of Nepal's political culture and concentrates on how Nepal's political culture remains dominated and interacted by these factors. It also attempts to explore how the factors including family, gender and education contribute to Nepali political attitudes and behaviours. These attitudes determine how Nepalis participate when they vote for and what political parties they support. So, my attempt here is to find out the solution of mainly two questions: What are the roots of Nepali political culture? What are the main features of political culture of Nepal? The roots of political culture of Nepal are deep and nourished in Nepali soil alien to the West; the flower is, therefore, strange that it possesses its own special feature.

**Geography and Geo Psychology: Formation and Interaction**

Political culture, the political psychology of a country or nation (or subgroup thereof) is the reflection of geo psychology which again is the reflection of geography, is rooted in history, culture and nationalism as well as in traditions and values of a society. The psyche of the people driven by geography and soil of the country is geo psychology. Psycho-cultural perceptions, the outcome of geo psychology form political attitudes of the people which cannot be separated from the geography, heritage, history, tradition, the ruling elites and subjects. Geo psychological paradigm is gradually acquiring significance in the fast globalizing world. Globalization and fragmentations are the fundamental qualities of human life in today's world. Due to globalization individual's encounters with different cultures, nations, and places are more frequent and our ability to face them more vital for our life. Geo psychology deals with such encounters, their impact on individual's psyche, and individual's ways and ability to respond to such encounters. Among central issues of geo psychology belong notions of home, genius loci, and individual's identity. It helps us to understand the dynamics of the post-Cold War international system given nontraditional threats such as separatist movements, religious radicalism and ethno-religious conflicts throughout the world, especially in the transitional societies.

Favourable location has helped British to meet foreign invasions successfully. The vast size and diversities have helped the Americans to accept the values of equality and freedom for all. Geography, as one of the main attributes in laying the foundation of political culture in Nepal, has played a significant role in shaping the course of its history and culture. Geo psychology of people, driven by Nepal's geographic set up has contributed in shaping knowledge, beliefs and behaviour of the people of Nepal. Owing to the mountainous environment, the people of Nepal became harsh and militant in character and preserved their traditional life style and cultures till recently without much change. Despite variegated conglomeration of races, castes and creeds, a deep unity among the people of Nepal existed in the past. Different religions and their followers, the kings in different periods, missionaries and pilgrims greatly fostered fundamental unity and created an exceptionally congenial environmental for the growth of a uniform civilization in the lap of the Himalaya. The great diversity in the physical features, the inaccessibility of its regions, intersected by mountains passes, deep rivers and impenetrable forest fostered a spirit of isolation and divided the country into small and mutually exclusive social units, whose divergences were accentuated by the infinite variety of local conditions. The long isolation also made the Nepalis introvert in thinking, so lacking in self-articulation, yet action oriented in behavior. The isolation, however, fostered internal interaction of people and helped to develop a number of common attributes and habits of mind and contributed to the formation of social and cultural existence among the people of diverse social origins.

Nepal's peculiar geographical position of being hemmed in by the two giant powers of Asia-India and China also dictated the policy of isolation. Prithivi Narayan Shah, the founder of modern Nepal, who laid the basis of this policy, pointed out that his kingdom was "sandwiched between two giant powers, and a "yam between two boulders,"[7] and advised his followers not to develop intimate relations with either of them.[8] The geographical isolation of Nepal until the 1950s served to keep the country rigidly shut from outside contacts. While the policy helped in preserving Nepal's independent entity, the forces of modernization, which became active in other parts of Asia, left her largely untouched until the middle of this century. Despite the proximity of Nepal to two great civilization systems- the Chinese and the South Asia- which have historically made it a main avenue for cultural synthesis, Nepal's greater geophysical exposure towards the south has made India an overbearing neighbour influencing its communication, circulation and acculturation process. It explains why Nepal located near the predominantly Hindu population centers of India has been moulded on the Hindu tradition and Hindu elites in Nepal often subscribe to the Sanskritic world view which is hierarchic and non-egalitarian of the Gangetic belt. The reassertion of this identity is manifested in the democratic constitution of 1990. Communism, Hinduism and Islamic fundamentalism flow to Nepal not from China but from India itself. Almost all the political parties of Nepal are affiliated with Indian political parties.

On the other side, Nepal's geographical feature has made the establishment of communication, circulation and transportation difficult. This variegated landscape encouraged the growth of diverse cultures, languages, values and institutions with the result that the mass culture of Nepal is extensively fragmented into region, religion, race, language, ethnicity, caste categories and to some extent inhibit an acculturation towards shared personal and social identity. The difficulties of intercommunication among various districts, zones and the regions retarded the growth of common national feeling among the people. In the absence of social interaction, inter-ethnic relationships are based on one group exploiting others. The culture of exploitation made the Brahmins and Kshettriya look as a superior caste with the responsibility of protecting the state. The culture of superiority again made certain ethnic groups see themselves as leaders of society and others as followers.

High caste groups, Brahmin and Kshettriya have traditionally dominated the composition of political leadership of Nepal. This is how the major political powers have been concentrated in Kshettriya and Brahmin groups for centuries in Nepal. The inadequate transport, communication, lack of social interaction among the ethnic groups, disparity in economic conditions among different regions have all contributed to a highly hierarchic centralized political culture in Nepal based on patron-client system. This is the reason why the history of Nepal during the advent of the Shah, the Ranas and later the Panchayat and even the present multi-party system has been dominated by the culture of centralization of power and authority. The over centralization has led to the culture of imbalance regional growth concentrated in Kathmandu only, which has been the nerve center of the country.

The diverse linguistic, religious, regional and cultural forces assume a transactional dimension-passing barrier to national integration and economic development for Nepal, where the sense of nationhood still struggles against loyalty and ethnic groups.[9] When such attributes allow developing a hostile alienated political culture, national integration is likely to suffer heavily and people in the name of different communities struggle for their separate identity instead of fighting for nationalism. As the hard reality, however is that, if democracy is lost, it can be gained as Nepalis regained in the nineties, but if nationalism is lost, the nation may be gone forever. But in the case of Nepal, the strong feeling of nationalism that is necessary for national integration seems to be challenged by the culture of communal feeling to a greater extent. The high mountains, the turbulent rivers and the dense forests not only confined the different ethnic groups into isolated habitats but also made extremely difficult for them to communicate with each other. The isolation of those groups produced a non-homogenous society with discreet sub-cultural identities contributing to a segmented political culture. Because of this Nepal does not symbolize the melting pot metaphor of culture homogenization.

In such a situation, the national government is scarcely perceived as an embodiment of the will of a united Nepali people; for feeling of solidarity among the people of Nepal are still very weak. Regional, ethnic and religious differences still remain the paramount foci of orientation for the vast majority of the population. Such differences are accentuated by the traditional notions of Nepali superiority and sense of exclusiveness. Such complexions and influences serve to increase the culture of fragmentation and alienation in Nepali political system.

Nepal's geo psychology is the reflection of her geographical position that accounts for her prolonged isolation, slow political progress, economic immobility and social backwardness, responsible for a diffused, alienated and heterogeneous political culture. But the fact that Nepal has been a non-colonial country distinguishes her from most other Asian and African nations. Nepalis do have neither the psychic scars nor the colonial experience that come from having grown up as an alien in one's own country. Rather, they enjoy a high degree of self-esteem and pride in their long tradition of independence. For Nepal, geography may not change but non-geographic political space and political culture can. But the change has to be planned and implemented consciously.

## Economy, Development and Cultural Variables

Every country has a political culture-a set of widely shared beliefs values and norms concerning the ways that political and economic life ought to be carried out. The political culture defines the relationship of citizens to the government, to one another, and to the economy. Inglehart's appraisal deserves particular mention in order to explore the linkage between economy and political culture. He says that economic development itself is influenced by cultural variables. The available evidence supports Weber's insight that culture is not just a consequence of economics; it can shape the basic nature of economic and political life.[10] Lipset, a pioneering social scientist did also elaborate on the correlation between the existence of democracy and such variables as per capita wealth industrialization, urbanization, and the level of education."[11] Based on it, the chapter seeks to answer a series of pertinent questions of intrinsic relevance to the theme. Inglehart's measures of culture are sensitive to short term fluctuations in economic growth rates.

The level of life satisfaction is systematically affected by economic growth rates. Can contemporary economic conditions in Nepal imply a better standard of living? Can it inculcate democratic culture in society to strengthen civic spirit? Does it reflect the aspirations to meet the needs of the people and how much people are initiated to democratic participation in the prevailing economic structure? The concern here is to focus on how poor and traditional economy is responsible for shaping the attitude, behaviour and orientation of citizens towards democratic values and norms in

Loctantrik Nepal. The chapter tries to answer the questions raised above from the following lenses: the socio-economic scenario, the culture of planning, impact of foreign aid and culture of democratic participation in the country.

***The Socio-economic Scenario***

Nepal's total population with 29 million with a growth rate of 2.2 percent at present is passing through low-level equilibrium trap characterized by poverty and stagnation and a very critical state of political transition. With a per capita income of $568 (by the middle of 2010 as estimated by the Central Bureau of Statistics), economic growth is 3.6 percent. With Human poverty index value 32.1 percent and power purchasing parity $1.25 a day, Nepal ranks 144$^{th}$ among 182 countries in Nepal Human Development Report 2009. Agriculture contributes 32.5 percent, industry 16.6 percent and service 50.9 percent to GDP with unemployment rate 46 percent. A recent UNDP/Oxford University report (2010) estimates that 65 percent of the population is below the poverty line. However, different sources of Nepal government claim that around 25 percent population is found to be below the national poverty level. Agriculture sector growth is 2.1 percent and non-agricultural sector 4.8 percent while the industrial production declined by 0.5 percent and inflation remained 13.2 percent. Tourism increased only by 1 percent. Although there is no growth in health sector, there is modest rise in education and road expansion.

The lack of investment, climate, poor capital expenditure, energy crisis, flood, labor disputes and round-the-year strikes, suppressed economic growth. Every year 350,000 youth enter into labor market and each day 750 people leave the country for job. About 3 million workers abroad and Gorkha soldiers in the UK and India send US $2833.88m and $50m remittance respectively which has reduced poverty to 32 percent. But, the global meltdown is likely to cut remittance flow and augment inequality in rural areas. Meanwhile, on the other front, the remittances that used to come from the Nepalis working in the Gulf countries have declined with the workers being displaced due to political volatility in the region. The warning signs are that depending on remittances is a folly.

Nepal has gone through several periodic development plans spanning a period of six decades already, these plans failed to make a significant change in the living standard of people. Nepal is finding extremely difficult to break away from the vicious grip of economic stagnation arising out of a primitive agrarian structure that distributes poverty, more than it generates socio-economic development. So poverty, unemployment, population growth and environment degradation are both the causes and consequences of underdevelopment reinforcing a crisis of social integration of the majority poor in the national society. In the same way, culture assertiveness and pride, one of the principal sources of individual self-respect and collective identity, have suffered because of rising unemployment, increasing inequality and economic impoverishment. A very large number of people cannot meet even the minimum necessities so are forced to live under the culture of deprivation, insecurity and self-denial. Dahal has commented that there is a yawning gap between the traditional and modern sector of the society especially in the areas of knowledge, technology, resources and power. This has unleashed economic dualism, feudalism and even an uneven acculturation process.[12] Besides that Nepal has superseded even Bhutan while incorporating herself in the list of poorest nations of the world.[13]

The structure of foreign aid in Nepal as at FY 2007/08 reflects that foreign grants constitute 61 percent, while foreign loan accounts for 39 percent of the total foreign aid during FY 2007/8. The extent of foreign aid comprising both grants and loan provided by ADB (21.9 percent), and IDA (22.9 percent) is the highest followed by education for all (EFA) - donors' organization (8.7 percent), Japan (8 percent), Germany (6.5percent) and India (6.2 percent). The contribution of DFID, UNDP, USAID, Denmark, Norway, Global Development Fund, IFAD, OPEC Fund, Saudi Development Fund, Swiss Development Cooperation, Finland, European Union (EU), and China ranges between 0.2 percent and 5.3 percent of total foreign aid available to Nepal. But it has been experienced that more foreign aid makes the country economically less free. World Economic Freedom report has ranked Nepal at 121 among the 141 global economies, i.e., the least free economy in the world. However, foreign loan has been playing a key role in the Nepali economy. The net outstanding foreign loan totaled Rs. 249,965.4 million in the fiscal year 2007-08 which further increased by 10.8 percent and reached Rs. 277,040.4 million in 2008-09. In the fiscal year 2007/08, 26.6 percent of total expenditure and almost 81.1 percent of Nepal's annual capital expenditure were borne by foreign aid.[14] A new dimension of foreign aid's contribution in Nepal has been on helping to restore and stabilize peace and democratic governance through peace-funding and other supporting activities in the aftermath of the decade-long (1996-2006) conflict.

The country currently faces a challenge of successfully coming out of the transition. Before 2002, aid related decisions were largely taken on an "ad-hoc" basis and on "good discretion." When aid policy came in 2002,[15] even then it could not incorporate aid into peace process and conflict dynamics. The need for effective aid policy is evident from Nepal's heavy reliance on foreign aid for the government-executed development and construction works. But the most disconcerting culture is that in Nepal, a government's success is measured by its ability to generate foreign aid. Governments have found it easier to convince donors than to exploit domestic sources. Why are we only creating dependency on aid and yet not making the effective use of aid is the discussion we carried out next. The gap between the increase of population (2.2 percent) and the rate of economic growth (3.5-5 percent) has not helped reduce poverty level of general people.

A sound growth in civic activities requires sustained development of the productive forces of society, so that civic participation could lead to the empowerment of citizens. Popular participation gives the citizens a sense of belonging to the polity and consequently, postpones apathy, alienation and rebellion. In a country like Nepal, where majority of people suffer from absolute poverty, inequality and dependency, civic activities alone do not ensure freedom to people unless they posses requisite resources to achieve liberation from docility and attain entitlements and social opportunities.

***Culture of Dependency***

How far has development aid in Nepal reduced aid dependency for its long-run sustainable development? The bigger and perhaps more important question is to reflect upon the efficacy of foreign aid in supporting the domestic economy over a longer horizon. Our documented evidence on foreign aid dates back to 1950s, with a growing influence in the later decades penetrating all aspect of the Nepali society, economy, culture and politics.

It is argued that foreign aid has reduced the pressures to generating its internal resources and become more accountable to its citizens. Foreign aid is the biggest single factor that is depriving Nepal of a sustainable independent future, because it discourages creativity and innovation in economic management. Nepal's dependency is exhibited not only in generating its own wealth but also in its dependency on policy formulation and resource utilization.

In one of the recent literatures published by Tufts University written by Gerald and Dorothy, it is shown that aid policies and the emergence of conflict are inextricably linked. They argue that aid can lead to conflict. This is why in Nepal and elsewhere the international community has not addressed this fundamental flaw in the development discourse. The role of aid on situation of conflict and prevailing peace has become very critical in recent times. With the end of the cold war, many countries are involved in civil conflict rather than inter-country wars. Nepal also saw a decade of violent civil conflict. While the conflict partly succeeded to mobilize as well as capitalize on the general grievances and frustrations of the Nepali people aspiring for a dignified living, the same period also provided an opportunity to check the relationship between conflict and aid.

The threat is not simply one of economic dependency, but of a form of ingrained social and psychological dependency as well. There increases the danger of developing a syndrome of being a "poor nation," so that the people fail to cultivate a sense of pride and confidence in themselves. Almost 81.1percent of Nepal's annual capital expenditure is dependent on foreign aid. Nepal's budget and financing requirement for the current phase of the Poverty Reduction Strategy Papers is only 20 percent with pledged donors amounting to almost 40 percent. This leaves a financing gap of between 40-50 percent for this programme period.[16] The other South Asian countries like Bangladesh, Pakistan and India etc, at least by Asian standards have very low dependency ratio. Unless we become committed to undergo a comprehensive programme to wean ourselves off of the permanent intoxication as a result of our addiction to foreign aid and be prepared to carry out the difficult economic reforms that will provide the platform for sustainable economic growth, we will remain stuck in this chronic dependency for a long time. Poverty Reduction Strategy Papers (PRSP) though well-intentioned, entrench this aid dependency culture. A western diplomat once said "we like it when they take ownership of the programmers but we mean our programmers. We don't like it if they start having their own ideas." In such a scenario, it is certainly difficult for the recipient countries to device their own policy and programs without any conditionality.

Several Nepali authors have reflected on the question of whether external assistance acted as catalyst to upgrade the living standards of the population, something that might not have been feasible for Nepal to achieve otherwise. There is no debate on whether Nepal needs foreign aid or not, the prime concern is of raising its productivity through effective utilization of foreign aid. What the critics of aid fail to appreciate, however, is that it is not principally the presence of foreign aid that is corrupting, but fatalism and assertive values. In recent years, the major issues like ownership of donor-driven projects in recipient countries, engagement of national experts in lieu of foreign consultants to ensure cost effectiveness, transparency, and aid conditional ties have dominated the center-stage of development drama orchestrated through foreign aid. Development, Pandey writes:

> ... is governed by two contradictory processes- the democratic process and the imperatives of foreign aid. The first requires development policies to be mandated by the people of Nepal; this is what the constitution of the land says. The latter is thus governed by the demands of the aid system as it operates domestically and internationally. The two processes are in conflict, causing many other contradictions and incongruities to emerge in the host country and aggravating progress in development management. In short, politics and programmes are not implementing a sustained manner. Resources are not used effectively and efficiently and corruption spreads.[17]

Foreign aid in Nepal does not have a strong positive relation to the alleviation of poverty, inequality and social evils. But it has become an obstacle to any indigenous development effort often leading to the co-modification of culture and people where the society is continually subordinated to either the economy or the state. It is also being used as an abrasive tool to hit public sector enterprises. As a result, citizen's loyalty to the political system is eroding with an economic crisis at hand and ethnic attention. In the past, the domain of recipient – donor interactions and engagements was limited to inter-state or governmental-international financial frameworks. Today, the rules of the game have undergone profound changes. The donors today take pride and satisfaction from their ability to work not only with the national government but also with the local communities in the districts and villages directly.

Aid money makes governments accountable to the donors than its people. On the other side, the political actors substantively interact with and depend more upon the donors than their domestic constituency. So in such a situation, where the donors not the state become the principal interlocutor of the civil society, the state becomes disabled. Civil society drawing its sustenance increasingly from foreign aid is also handicapped psychologically and morally.

In this sense, aid provides not just financial wherewithal but political legitimacy for the government. Political leaders lobby with the donor, not their government or political colleagues for projects that are of interest to them.[18]

It can be agreed that aid is not the prime mover of development. It has sometimes even been an impediment– but this need not be the case also. To use aid as a good reward for development may indeed be justified under certain circumstances, but often such circumstances itself can be met only with outside help. Aid, should, therefore, primarily be used as catalyst-sometimes to help generate other resources or gain access to them-sometime to help create domestic capacity or manage conflicts resulting from various forms of unsustainable development. At this juncture, what is required is special focus on aid policy which creates social harmony, political stability and peace-the preconditions for economic growth and development.

### *Culture of Planning: Policy Paradox*

Principally, a leader becomes transforming leader and a movement becomes successful, only when a qualitative change is brought about through the instrumentality of movement and actions. But in reality, both leaders and movements are far from this end. For most of the time, leaders are highly induced and dependent upon their political parties to create a constituency in support of their policy prescription which is detrimental to tap emotions and sentiments that can be calibrated behind or against a policy. The political leaders are hesitant to come forward and address demands generated by the critical mass whose perception of politics and policy is completely different from that of career politicians. Equally challenging for Nepali state is to come up with policies that can bridge the existing social, gender and intergenerational gaps. Although the political parties have spelt out their policies, the economic agenda of the New Nepal has not been taken up seriously by any of the stakeholders. For example, Maoists would like to have industrial capitalism, NC and CPN (UML) would like to adopt market economy.

Similarly, National People's front wanted to have mixed economy, Rastriya Prajatantra Party Nepal had said that it would adopt liberal economic policy whereas, as the ethnic and Madheshi's groups have expressed to adopt mixed economy. But how they are going to translate these policies in the actions have not been taken up seriously by any of the stakeholders. Nor has the establishment adopted any major steps to counter the challenges posed by the globalization and repercussions of economic slowdown. Nepal has completed its 11 plans and is entering into the next. How the planning process with its beginning in 1956 has succeeded to substantially transform the social and economic conditions of people needs an objective analysis. Started with NPR 21 cores, the first plan was more symbolic as it was just beginning of the planning process. However, the plans never played to give a sense of direction and coherence to multi-faceted development efforts.

It is observed that Nepali conflict was basically the manifestation of deep social and economic grievances produced and sustained by failed development. In this view, development fails, when planning and development become a bureaucratic ritual at the service of dominant interests at the center as opposed to the needs of people. Politics, its Nepali equivalent *rajniti,* as per *Chanakya* –the doyen of statecraft, theoretically is about-'to govern' and devise the rules for governance and policies (*niti nirman*) for the overall welfare of citizens. Politics therefore, has to be guided by the philosophy of generating stable governance, development, people friendly policies, investment in human capital in the country. Bhatta in this context has rightly argued that Nepali politics over the years has not been able to dispense noble goals of *rajniti* and *rajniti* seems to have been drifting away from its original stance of producing policies *(nitis)* keeping people in the centre, rather than politics and power.[19]

Nepal has gone through several development plans spanning a period of six decades. But those plans have not been successful to bring about a substantial change in the economic status of people. Although all the plans have included poverty alleviation as one of its prime objectives, why do a large proportion of people still live in absolute poverty? Why has the story of planning in Nepal become a story of unimplemented plethora of objectives and policies? Why the planners of Nepal could not make the people representative and participatory element? The reason behind is that culture of planning in Nepal has always remained top-down, paternalistic and centralized that has persistently discouraged local creativity and incentives for participation in development. A perspective reflection on the continuation of this trend as highlighted by Dahal deserves mention here- "a micro structural analysis of the planning process reveals the existence of a wide gap between official thinking and planning about development and ability to implement policies in the fact of citizens' ignorance, innovation and change. In the area of financial management, planning reveals a striking lack of success.[20] It shows a little relationship between planning and implementation. The greatest difficulty in planning lies not in policy but in implementation because each plan has shifted in its priority without meeting the targeted goals of the previous plan's goals. Pandey reflects this idea as he remarks that "development and planning have no direction in Nepal because it is going in a "circular fashion." ... When what needs to be done appears impossible to do. One ends up doing what appears possible but unnecessary and possibly harmful, from the society's point of view. Our inability to understand basic idea of development is the root cause of the present malaise."[21]

It is because of this working culture that Nepal's present political turmoil emanates from its political background, slow pace of its economic development and government's failure in fulfilling expectation of the people. Nepal lacks the political culture necessary for proper functioning of democracy as it is still in the process of evolution. So Bhattachan has commented that "the people's movement of 1990 had changed the actors but not the stage and drama of underdevelopment."[22] Dahal argues that "the rationality of planning in Nepal is rooted in a paternalistic approach, rather than entrepreneurial. The rationality acted on the doctrine that planners have all the knowledge (theoretical, empirical and practical), art and wisdom needed to catalyze the grassroots initiatives and creativity in the formulation and execution of development programmes."[23] So they only sought citizens' consent to the official decisions.

The tradition of planning in Nepal so far has only meant the control of national policy making and monopolizes resources. Development conceptualized by the planners in Nepal meant only the participation in market economy, not self reliant growth achieved through the participation of people in community property resources at the local level, acting on their own interests as they see them and under their own control. Dahal recognizes the validity to argue that "if plans are formulated by the NPC, executed by secretaries, financed and sustained by INGOs and NGOs, who are neither elected nor nominated by the people, how can such plans capture participatory, *Swadeshi,* and sustainable potentiality ? More importantly, how can it lead to the economic, political and cultural empowerment of the Nepalese people?"[24] In such a situation, the centralization of power is so entrenched and powerful that people are basically passive elements in the overall process of political change, devoid of any ownership over governance and developments. Can such a culture of planning be expected to be effective in changing the citizens' parochial and subject status to a participant political culture? It shows that the attitude and behaviour of planners and policy makers, therefore, do not generally contribute to the maintenance and growth of a participant culture in the country. They are either not thoroughly socialized in concrete forms of national life, or situated far apart from the historical time and space they are supposed to be in. Clearly they are not attuned to listen to the sub-cultures' world-views, multi-layered realities and the respective interest positions of the people of diverse social origins.

Development is an evolutionary policy instrument, which relies on the participant's knowledge of cause– effect and less on outside involvement unrelated to local incentives, norms and capacity. The efficacy of the plan, therefore involves the contextualization of the knowledge of planners, indigenization of the development, vision and implementation of the entire exercise by those affected by them. But a more plausible explanation is that they are obsessed with a culture of paternalism rooted in the monopolization of authority and knowledge, caught up in the network of governmental power with an eye on donor's money.

Generally, the established tendency is that who stands to benefit from the status quo resists any change. Those who are closer to the power centre or are in a position to capture power formulate slogans, arguments, emotions, claims, and even policies to mobilize the crowd either to resist change or to introduce necessary changes to meet their group interests. This approach is putting successive movements into the potholes and policies into paradox.[25] That is where the role of leaders and political parities becomes critical. This has partly been happening because those who make policies (either parliamentarian or member of planning commission or top bureaucrat for that matter) are also found to have been engaged in the private business such as in the operation of private schools, hospitals, transportation, NGOs, manpower agencies etc. So these people will never make policies that will jeopardize their own business interest. This class makes development projects, educational institutions, public contracts, licenses and public corporations new *birats* and *jagirs,* to be distributed among their *Affno Manchhe* according to political criteria. Policies would be formulated to support their business rather than interest of the common people as this class has no genuine stake in the nation's future. The members of this class educate their children abroad, seek medical treatment aboard, foster luxury consumption of goods, participate in the flight of capital and rely on external expert and advice. This results in the growth of distance between the culture of the experts and that of the larger public. A noted Nepali planner was of the view that implosion of ideas does become a matter of concern when one realizes the over exposure of Nepali intelligentsia to alien concepts in contrast to their ignorance of native reality.[26] The habitual dependence of planners, policy-makers and general intellectuals on outside has evoked self-doubt on their own self-confidence and lack of political will to develop the nation on its own resource and skills.

The lack of intimacy with local problems went to the extent that foreigner after a brief visit could consider themselves authorities on Nepali problems to be quoted in the words of Gurung– "the elite culture that separates itself from the life of ordinary citizens also expresses a lack of faith in the nation's plan."[27] The scramble of enthusiastic donors has been the most striking feature of the post-1990 Nepal. In Nepal, the restoration of multiparty system and the development of NGO and INGO culture are intertwined. As of October 2010, the Social Welfare Council has recorded 31,000 NGOs in addition to 25,000 not affiliated to it. The NGOs and INGOs seem to become powerful to influence the government. What is more amazing is that both the donors and foreign embassies dole out funds without being routed through the Government of Nepal. NGOs' role can be seen in the mobilization of people in many action–oriented projects especially at local development level. However, the state itself is increasingly becoming NGO-ized or INGO-ized as its own organs and agencies are dependent on foreign money.

It has been observed that government officials, advisors, planners, politicians, university professors and MPs are directly or indirectly linked to various NGOs and INGOs. This trend has contributed to making a new moneyed class widening the gap between a tiny privileged section and the general mass either by design or by default according to Baral.[28]

Recent unfolding of events in different areas such as education, (private versus public), health (private versus public), foreign policy (appointment of partisan versus professional ambassadors, and singing of treaties), employment (national versus foreign), land reform (modernization versus redistribution) and the governance crisis are the classic examples of manifestation of mismatch between politics, policies and development in the country. The Nepali establishment has not defined what type of education system, healthcare and economic system [29] wanted to have and overall who are going to be served and how, that is who are to be the real beneficiaries, whether we are targeting the urban idle class elites or ordinary citizens. A clear distinction has to be made. In a county like Nepal, state should act as a weapon of the weak rather than making polices for those who are already 'super rich'.

In the same vein, the urban political classes have floated land-reform agenda for more than half-a-century and many commissions have been formed. Yet, it has not been clear who are to be 'benefited' and how it is to be done. The top 5 percent of landlords own 27 percent of agricultural land, the bottom 44 percent occupies only 14 percent of the land. This makes land-reform essential for the Nepali mass to dismantle the multiple structures of the feudal system that still dominates the country. The policy paradox that exists in critical areas (health, education, employment youths and land reform) is immense and needs immediate policy intervention (affirmative) which, up till now, is heavily influenced by the utilitarian concept of 'power politics'– that makes few to enjoy benefit of change and forces rest to suffer as usual. This paradox, in fact, invites some fundamental questions as how we mobilize a leader or a government policy maker draw and implement policy perception in the best public interests in line with changed socio-political context? It can be only done by paying attention to what the people want, to what the people say and to what the people monitor for their own growth, says[30] Phrang Roy, IFAD's (International Fund for Agricultural Development) Director. He believes in listening to the poor people's need from their own mouth before directing any plan and programme for them from the center. But this has not been the case in Nepal.

The policies and programmes that the government brings in without consultation with the people will not only lose its validity but also fail to address their key problems. The regimes that come after the movements never attempted to craft people-centric economic policies that could divert and engage political crowds towards economic and state building activities rather than getting enmeshed in politics. But the culture of policy-making process basically involves the bureaucratic apparatus and is autonomous of either the dominant groups of society and political party or parties in power. The process, therefore, is highly politicized.[31] So there is constant error in policy formulation, because Nepali bureaucratic culture is driven more by a survival syndrome than a mission for socio-economic change. As a result, planners neither learn from the failure of previous policies nor adopt themselves to the vision of the people.

Political leaders make their own calculations based on their own personal and partisan interests. Nepali leaders neither use knowledge nor do they try to learn from the history and education, nor from institutional memory of social learning which would otherwise help them to address challenges generated by the timeframe in the history of the nation. If National Planning Commission (NPC) is to be used politically to meet the vested interest of ruling party, it does more harm than good. Until development plans and programmes are conceived and implemented without being influenced by trifle political interests, scarce resources will continue to be wasted.[32] It ultimately erodes the country's economic base. Arun III Hydropower Project and the Mahakali Integrated Development Treaty (MIDT) could be cited as cases that prove this. Arun III was finally scrapped and MIDT got through the ratification process in parliament with great difficulty. The Rastriya Prajatantrik Manch (National Democratic Front), a united group of several smaller parties, even did not hold an opposing view with regard to MIDT. This indicates something wrong in the culture of planning. With every change in government the vice-chairman and members of the NPC are replaced, whose ideology and allegiance lie with the party in power, which brings about in correspondingly changes in priorities and policies. Members of Planning Commission are generally inducted on the basis of their professional credential; although also on their appropriate political loyalty, and people, therefore, expect them to act as effective agents of change particularly for the cause of the poor and the disadvantaged in the country. But, in most cases their performance has systematically belied that expectation.

In a democratic culture, any change in the government should be treated as a regular process, not something that obstructs development. The rising budget deficits, spiraling inflation, declining tax revenues, shrinking job market (both intern and external) and prevalence of protest politics has threatened to destabilize democratic transition. Indeed, political transition has a great impact on the economic management and institutional capabilities of a regime and that in turn, determines the fate of a democratic transition.[33] Nepali policy makers have not realized the fact that political equality can only be achieved through economic and social equality. Scholars of the democracy point out that success of a political system's smooth transition to democracy depends on the strength of its national economy and ability of leaders to capture the golden mean of polity. It is argued that those with good economic performances provide with stable social support to the regime and give it strong institutional control over the democratization process and provide the regime with a better prospects to transform to some kind of stable democracy in the long run.

### *People's Participation: Application of Political Culture*

The socio-economic scenario of the nation and culture of planning together have effectively deterred the poor and the disadvantaged from participating in the affairs of the country. People's participation in the words of Lennan is the "direct application of political culture to a specific area of activity."[34]Any country whose democracy is installed without acquiring economic development is likely to risk falling prey to its enemies. Its worst enemies are increasing poverty and decreasing participation. Both of these factors are favourable to centralization of wealth and power. It is because of this situation that Nepal's present political turmoil emanates from its political background, slow pace of its economic development and government's failure in fulfilling legitimate expectations of the people. With the culture of centralized politics, administration and persistent socio-economic rigidities, the distribution of political participation in the country is most restrictive for a democracy. The style of government has not changed. Democracy has not trickled down to the villages, where 88 percent of the people live in rural areas. The attitude and behaviour of the people have not been changed towards their system and government. All these factors constitute a serious threat to young democracy. Lipset is correct while asserting that:

> … the more well-to-do- a nation, the greater the chances that it will sustain democracy. Democratic culture can survive in poorer countries if they generate economic growth, if they manage to generate development, if they reduce inequality and if they have parliamentary institutions. When poor countries stagnate, whatever, democracies happen to spring up tend to die quickly, poverty breeds poverty and dictatorship. Most countries, returning to democracy usually go back to whatever situation they had in the past.[35]

The above case is well fitted in the present context of Nepal where the opportunity for participation for many social groups still remains limited because of the concentration of political and economic power at the center. Dahal is right when he asserts that: "… when the state gives the vote to all and the economy gives the opportunity to only a few, conflicts become inevitable in state politics."[36] Conflicts are symptom of change. In theory people are the center of attention in any development activity. However, in reality it is not so in Nepal. If this is the case, little can be achieved in building a foundation for sustainable development. In a feudal and caste– ridden society, the ordinary people not belonging to the ruling classes have little opportunity to express themselves and participate in state affairs. The particular culture of participation underscores the short coming of a process where the elected officials are alienated from those who elect them and who, therefore, resort to non-acquiescent forms of expression.

Nepali political culture has remained dominated not only by traditionalism but also it is submissive in nature. That is the lack of hope but fatalism about the future. The feeling of powerlessness to change events also undermines the self-competence and self confidence, the "key political attitudes" for a citizen to be a democratic citizen according to Alamond and Verba."[37] Submissiveness gives rise to economic insecurity of the citizens which continues to hit their participation in public affairs affecting their behaviour and formation. So in such a situation they are compelled not to think beyond their stomach; so are preoccupied with their own survival and existence. This certainly leaves them in a culture of subject or parochial status, as reflected in Dahal's analysis that:

> Once people tolerate their vicarious existence as a part of their fate, they imbibe them into their norms, values, ideas, knowledge and beliefs. Political culture thus evolves as one aspect of the total culture of society. This is why two third of the Nepali citizens are terribly consigned into de-humanized life almost deprived of any opportunity to participate in public affairs. A lack of advances in functional literary, access to media and awareness of issues and events thus reflect an image of the photographic print of a social and economic negative.[38]

Under such conditions, feelings of psychological inferiority among the citizens have become intensely personal resulting in the formation of a 'culture of silence.[39] In this context, Nepali political culture can hardly be expected to achieve the level of desirable participation. So a participant political culture in Nepal is limited in quantity and manipulative in quality. With regard to the political participation in Nepal, rich people with high living standard do not show much interest in liberalizing the nature of existing politics. The political leaders coming from such group have shown least interest in bringing out change in the social structure. Their behaviour and attitude are ingrained with the traditional feudal order who, moreover try to retain their social prestige by maintaining status quo.[40] The continuity of this culture among the elites has preceded any move towards change and any kind of openness in the political process, with the result that they are no better than the poor who form majority in the society in remaining passive towards the political system. But the basic motive is different between these two classes. The poor remains passive due to ignorance, whereas, the rich do so to exploit the poor.

The other class of people in Nepal beside the rich and the poor is the middle class-the mediating agent of society, which has a considerable influence in the social and political development of the country. They are educated, conscious of their status and role in the society and are always eager to create distinct identity for themselves in the society. Sometime they move closer to the political system while other times they challenge the system. As a result, this class becomes the partner of the system either in support or in opposition. The current participation in politics in Nepal shows that the teachers, lawyers, medical professionals, engineers, professors and others belonging to middle class have been more active in Jan Andolan I and Jan Andolan II. Their role certainly is seen positive in the creation of a favourable political culture for the success of democracy. This is reflected by Huntington in The Third Wave; Democratization in the Late Twentieth Century in which he implies the correlation between wealth and democracy as shown below in (Figure 2.1) that transition to democracy should occur primarily in countries at the middle levels of economic development.[41] This view also corroborates with the growing literature on democracy that elaborates on the correlation between the existence of democracy and variables like per capita wealth, industrialization, urbanization and the level of education. In poor countries, democratization is unlikely; in rich countries it has already occurred. In between there is a political transition zone; countries in that particular economic stratum are most likely to transit to democracy and most countries that transit to democracy will be in that stratum. As countries develop economically and move into this zone, they become prospects for democratization. The movement of countries into the middle income ranges of the economic transition zone thus led to changes in social structures, beliefs and culture that were conducive to the emergence of democracy.

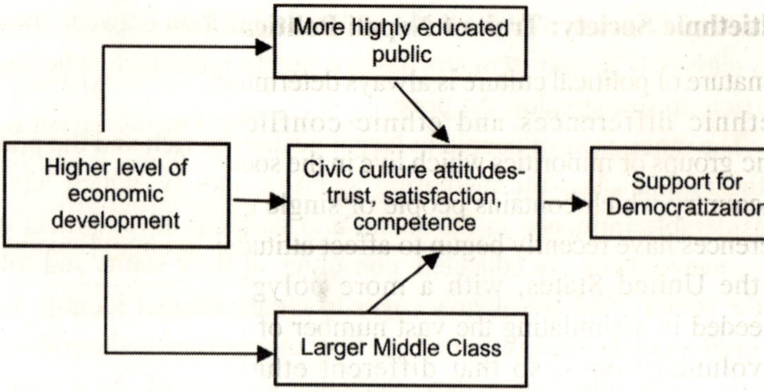


***Figure 2.1: Economic Development as a Factor in Democratization***

The above illustration shows an overall level of correlation that exists between the level of economic development and democracy. The future of democracy depends on the future of economic development.[42] Economic factors have significant impact on democratization although not determinative. There are studies, which have clearly brought into focus the correlation between such measures as trust, tolerance, efficacy and personal satisfaction and the per capita GNPs of the countries. Rapid industrial development certainly weakens traditionalism; raise standards of living, equitable distribution of resources, increases social trust and confidence in the political system. But the present economic condition and policies in present day Nepal hardly holds out any prospect of economic development and change in social structure and political culture.

The political culture in Nepal, therefore is barren of the very values, which are the crucial link between economic development and democracy. The lower level of socio-economic participation of the masses and culture of feudalism and fatalism that have prevailed in the society since long has threatened to destabilize democratic transition, subjecting the majority to subject and parochial political culture. So it is imperative to note that where people reject revolutionary changes, in favour of planned and evolutionary process, not only economic development occurs but democracy also remains stable and vibrant.

## Multiethnic Society: Trait of Nepali Political Culture

The nature of political culture is always determined by the existence of ethnic differences and ethnic conflicts among several ethnic groups or minorities which live in the society. There is hardly any country which contains people of single ethnic group. Ethnic differences have recently begun to affect attitudes in Great Britain. Yet the United States, with a more polyglot population has succeeded in assimilating the vast number of immigrants, at least the voluntary ones, so that different ethnic groups think of themselves primarily as Americans. Ethnic differences give rise to the emergence of sub-political cultures within the national political culture. The ethnic politics and the aphorism "Unity in Diversity" are the two unavoidable and acceptable formulas for social and political harmony and order in many countries. In the words of Kothari "ethnicity, which has gained increased currency in the contemporary international policies, has been variously expressed as assertions of cultures, communal upsurges, and revival of religious voices and movement of marginalized people, regions and nationalities. It represents the affirmation of diversity and indigenous identity of various people." [43]

Ethnic politics is gradually taking a volatile turn in many countries of South Asia in recent years. Nepal is also a part of global phenomenon of ethnic upheavals accompanying with the third wave of democracy. Parish has said that "caste and ethnicity have long been a central preoccupation- some should say: obsession - of anthropological studies of South Asian life. Caste is a social fact of the greatest significance for millions of people. It has saved their lives and fates."[44] Caste and ethnicity are living realities and form the major circle in an individual's widening social radius in Nepal. The caste system which has cultural, ethical and psychological basis cannot possibly be washed at will. A person's caste, ethnic origin and tribal relations have traditionally been crucial considerations in the Nepali political system. The history of Nepal shows that the caste-ridden society was characterized by a complete domination of higher castes over lower castes in social, political and economic fields.

There is no expectation to this tradition even in modern day political culture of Nepal. Caste that confers a certain social status has been one of the most powerful bases for socio-political stratification of Nepalese society.[45] A multiethnic society is the basic trait of the political culture of Nepal. The genuine trait of the culture is to maintain unity in diversity. The term ethnicity is generally used in a wider context encompassing race, language and other cultural characteristics.[46] Against this background, the paragraph highlights the prevailing reality of caste and its dominance in the social and political structures in the society. It concentrates on the social structure and social hierarchy, elite composition, culture and ethnic representation and their impact on the political culture of the nation.

***Social Structure and Hierarchy***

Social hierarchy is an important variable in making and unmaking the political culture of Nepal. Nepal is multi-structural society built on a caste system. Upon birth Nepalis obtain their castes from their parents. The tradition discriminates one man from another only on the basis of birth. Nepali society has traditionally been stratified into four broad casts– Brahmins (priests), Kshettriya (warriors) Vaisya (businessmen) and Sudra (artisans and untouchables) based on a vertical hierarchy, which also organized the production of material and spiritual life as well as the organization of political power. Control of land and high caste status has been the two basic criteria for participation in Nepali politics since long. Based on that only high castes like Brahmin and Kshettriya have dominated the Nepali political scene.

In the words of Gaige, they possess all four of the prerequisites for successful participation in Nepali national politics: control of economic resources, high-caste status, identification with the hill culture, and a high level of education attainment.[47] Although the above concept cannot be justified on the ground of humanity, justice and equality, social stratification in Nepal has been based on an unequal position for individuals in the society and bars board scale participation of people in major decision making affecting their lives. In a democratic system if all group representatives are not included in the decision making process, then those who are present will decide according to their needs and interests. The situation brings injustice to the excluded groups. It creates culture of exclusion which brings the culture of discrimination as embedded in the Nepali psyche which is a serious challenge to a rational civic culture.

After the advent of democracy in 1951, the government of Nepal had defined social relations and associated laws according to caste position. The social structure has evolved through everyday activities of the people. The average citizens belonging to the untouchables have neither the capacity nor knowledge nor allowed to have interest to mould their mind and character towards egalitarian politics and change their society in desirable direction. Illiterate, untouchable, devoid of political consciousness and resources to compete with other castes, people believe that their caste position is predetermined by *Karma*, meaning fate in the previous life and so unchangeable. A strong sense of fatalism has consigned them into an unequal environment for competition, resulting in their sullen passivity and extreme tolerance to authority with the result giving birth to the culture of submission and fatalism. The effects of the caste system on the social behaviour of lower castes are mainly social evasion, apathy, withdrawal and extreme conformity leading to a sense of powerlessness and pessimistic attitude towards their future. Proponents of the modernization theory believe that the archaic tradition of *Karma* stood in the way to Nepal's progress in science, industry and commerce. It is an accepted theory of democracy-embedded in the belief that citizens direct the course of events is simply misplaced.

### *Caste/Ethnicity and Regions*

The 2001 census recorded more than 100 ethnic and caste categories and 92 languages in Nepal.[48] The number of people comprising each of these groups ranges from 3.5 million to hardly a few hundred.[49] However, none of them makes a majority. The largest groups are Kshettriya and Brahmins, comprising 15.8 and 12.7 percent respectively, of the total population group belongs to the same ethnic and linguistic community. Hill Dalits also belong to this community. The hill caste groups, including Dalits, which are spread all over the country, make about 40 percent of the total population of Nepal. The ethnic groups in total make about 37 percent of the total and are very diverse. Each of them is a separate unit in terms of language, social system and culture. There are 59 officially identified indigenous ethnic groups, of whom only 42 are covered by the census report. The rest are unidentified and unreported. The major ethnic groups which make up to 5 percent of the population include Magar (7.14 percent), Tharu (6.75 percent), Tamang (5.46 percent) and Newar (5.48 percent). There are only 18 caste and ethnic groups which have population over 1 percent each. Out of 92 languages recorded by the 2001 census, only 12 have one percent speakers each. Nepali, which is spoken by 48.61 percent, is recognized as the official language. If we classify various population groups to their closest category, it may come up as shown in the following table:

- Ethnic people altogether make about 37 percent of the total population.
- There are more than 50 Hindu caste groups including Dalits, which make about 58 percent of the total.
- About 5 percent people belong to other religious minority groups, including Muslim.
- Madhesi people (other than the hill ones) make about 31 percent of the total.

**Table 2.1: HDI of caste/ethnicity and regions**

| *Caste/Ethnicity* | *Population* | *Percent* |
|---|---|---|
| **Hindu Caste Group** | | |
| Brahimin, Kshettriya Thakuri, Sanyasi | 7,023,220 | 30.9 |
| Hill Dalit | 1,615,577 | 7.1 |
| Madhesi Castes | 3,366,172 | 14.8 |
| Madhiesi Dalit | 1,059,605 | 4.7 |
| **Ethnic Groups** | | |
| Hill Ethnic | 6,485,013 | 28.5 |
| Terai Ethnic | 1,975,688 | 8.7 |
| **Religious Minorities** | | |
| Muslim | 9,75,949 | 4.3 |
| Others | 4,069 | 0.0 |
| Unidentified | 2,31,641 | 1.0 |
| Total: | 22,736,934 | 100 |

*Source:* CBS 2002: UNDP, RIPP/NTG, 2006.

The present state came into being as a result of the conquest by Prithivi Narayan Shah, the king of Gorkha some 250 years before. The territory that it comprises today has been historically settled by different caste and ethnic groups. Through King Prithivi Narayan shah described the newly founded kingdom as a garden of different castes and communities, it never evolved into a policy that provided equitable space for all the communities. Whether it was the Shah King or the Rana prime minister, each tried to homogenize it along the Hindu tradition, culture and Khas language, which is now characterized as the Nepali language. The power elite were confined to a few privileged families of Brahmin, Kshettriya and Newar. Others, including the women remained marginalized. The pattern of development in Nepal could not remain unaffected from this trend. The centrality of Kathmandu is the most distinguishable pattern of the development over centuries. Other areas remained overlooked and peripheral. There has been uneven development as per caste/ethnicity as well as region. Nepal Human development reports on Nepal illustrate such an uneven state of development both in terms of region and communities. Compared to the whole of Nepal, the hill districts of far-west and mid- west regions' are behind the national average. The national HDI is 0.509, whereas, these regions' HDI is between 0.436 and 0.448 only. Likewise, the Terai region is also behind compared to the hills in general. HDI for Terai district is 0.494 on an average against 0.543 for hill districts including the Kathmandu valley.

**Table 2.2: HDI of caste/ethnicity and regions**

| *Caste/Ethnicity* | *HDI* | *Region* | *HDI* |
|---|---|---|---|
| All Brahmin/ Kshettriya | 0.552 | Mountain Hill | 0.436 |
| Madhesi Brahmin/ Kshettriya | 0.625 | with Kathmandu | 0.543 |
| Hill Brahmin | 0.612 | Hill without | 0.504 |
| Hill Kshettriya | 0.514 | Kathmandu | 0.494 |
| Other Madhesi Caste | 0.450 | Terai | |
| Newar | 0.616 | | |
| Ethnic groups other than Newar | 0.494 | | |
| Hill Ethnic Groups | 0.507 | | |
| Terai Ethnic Groups | 0.470 | | |
| Dalit in General | 0.424 | | |
| Madhesi Dalit | 0.383 | | |
| Muslim | 0.401 | | |
| Nepal | 0.509 | | |

***Source:*** UNDP, 2009.

In most parts of the country, population settlement is highly mixed. For long, the country adopted a highly centralized and unitary polity governed from Kathmandu, the capital city. Nepali language, Hindu cultural ethos, monarchical supremacy and Brahmin- Kshettriya-Newar elitism overwhelmingly prevailed in overall national affairs. There were some attempts of decentralization and policy of cultural diversity but it could not devolve power nor satisfy the people's aspiration for identity and their culture as well as ethnic rights. This ultimately pushed to the demands for proportional representation, reservation of seats in administration, education, job etc. and federalization of the state.

After the restoration of democracy in1990 some ethno-regional political parties and ethnic activities have raised the voice for the recognition of ethnic rights and autonomy. Some of them even aired the opinion for federalism. Nepal Sadbhabana Party and some other hill-based ethnic parties have called for federal system but these parties could neither mobilize sizeable electoral support nor influence the public opinion in an environment of democracy and political freedom. In the post -1990 politics, various ethnic groups were organized and articulated their demands and collaborated on common ethnic agenda. To begin with, the agenda comprised on such demands as secularism, inclusion, multilingualism, proportional representation, reservation of seats in the administration, education, job etc. This was more a reaction to the dominance of certain caste and cultural groups mainly Brahmin, Kshettriya and Newar in overall state affairs rather than well argued rationale for federalism. The recognition of identity, autonomy and inclusion was accepted when political parties had to mobilize popular support against autocratic monarchical regime.

The agenda for change is popularly phrased as *Rajyako Punarsamrachana* (restructuring of the state). Therefore, restructuring the Nepali state, understandably with a provision for federalism became one of the major banner headings of Jan Andolan II. Henceforth, the state has entered into several agreements and understanding with concerned groups, such as Nepal Federation of Indigenous Nationalities (NEFIN), Madhesi Janadhikar Forum etc. assuring federal state with autonomous self-governing units. As per the provision of the Interim Constitution a high state restructuring commission has been established in November 2011 to work out the details of structuring and make recommendations to this effect.

### *Elite vs. Mass Culture*

A national political culture consists of both an elite and mass culture. There are some differences between the political orientations of those who have responsibility for decisions and those who are only observers or participating citizens. The relationship between the two is a critical factor determining the performance of the political system. But the mass political culture in Nepal is elusive. Available data suggests that the political culture is not properly socialized. The immobile people inhabiting the rural areas lack the communicative channel of political socialization and political culture. How do the people understand democracy to be a better system in the absence of required socialization is a pertinent question? In most traditional and transitional system especially as in Nepal, one tends to have quite different career lines and receives quite different social experiences from the society.

The very base of legitimacy of the leaders and decision-makers rest on the popular belief that they are men inherently set apart from others at birth. So, about political culture in the context, one would observe that people's orientation of problem solving is absolutely insignificant. Hence, it is very difficult to understand, whether they are pragmatic or rationalistic. In the state of communicative immobility for reasons underlined above, people's orientation to collective action is apparently insignificant. To categorize and understand their co-operative or non-cooperative motive is also very much difficult as the mass political culture is elusive. There exists a milieu for indeterminate people's behaviour in the political system which means an indeterminate mass political culture. Moreover, a vast gap exists between the urban and rural mass political culture. It is obvious that urban living necessarily change a mass conception of his physical and spatial surroundings. In addition, new and different associative patterns are encouraged which inevitably impinge on parochial and traditional values and attitudes.

Politics is associated with power and, therefore, dominated by the influential elites. Political elite means those persons who direct the state apparatus, bureaucracy and elected representatives. In Nepal, these elites are called *Thalus*, an influential section of the society, consisting of leaders, planners and key decision makers in the rural area. These elites continue to play major role in the life of the state and society; no matter, whether or not they are elected. They are, in fact, symbolically and functionally shapers of the value patterns of a society. Nepal's political culture is so deeply rooted in the local cultural context that the society spontaneously produces its own distinct and persistent form of political elites. As a separate group, political elites hold inordinate power, wealth and authority relative to the larger section of people,[50] who are powerless disorganized and marginalized. Even the modern educated elites have not been able to challenge the conservative concepts of traditional elites. Today, these new "political elites" can be seen not only in school, colleges, universities, students' unions, but have also become a force in the professional unions and constitute a strong pressure group in the local village and district development committees. As the power structure maintains hierarchy, these new elites find no place within the structure and the result is conflict and frustration, leading to the creation of new castes, ethnic, linguistic and religious associates and organizations to vent their frustrations and oppose the existing political structure. The modern educated elite, as Shaha points out:

> They have not been able to withstand either the strain of poverty or that of prosperity. They have developed a split mentality which is the worst enemy of national character and which can be cured only by an intensified effort on their part to coordinate their belief and action. Their education in Western values has made the elite neglect traditional value themselves cut off from the mainstream of national life and culture with the result that they can fit it nowhere.[51]

### *Politics: Preserve of Political Elites*

In Nepal, politics has been the preserve of the political elites. Nepal's political culture remains dominated by elite culture, since the political culture of dominant elites composed of Brahmin,

Kshettriya, Thakuri, Rana, Newar, Rajput is caste–based and hierarchic. The traditional elite castes Brahmin, Kshettriya and Newar have monopolized education, business, and public institutions, so dominate political power. The so-called elites are taking advantages of stagnant society. Social norms, traditions and even the supposedly neutral rules and standards favour the social dominant groups. The elite culture has thus delayed the social advancement of the people of other classes.

The gazetted civil service posts are seen virtually the fiefdom of Brahmin, Kshettriya and Newar as shown in the following Table:

**Table 2.3: Ethnic Representative (in percentage)**

| *Ethnic/Caste Group* | *Section Secre.* | *Asst. Officers* | *Deputy Secre.* | *Joint Secre.* | *Additional Secre.* | *Secre.* |
|---|---|---|---|---|---|---|
| Brahmin | 62.1 | 54.5 | 45.6 | 54.9 | 46.2 | 31.3 |
| Kshetriya | 9.5 | 11.2 | 13.4 | 17.1 | 15.4 | 31.3 |
| Newar | 21.0 | 26.6 | 29.9 | 22.5 | 34.6 | 25.0 |
| Hill Ethnics | 2.0 | 0.9 | 2.1 | - | 3.1 | - |
| Terai Group | 4.2 | 5.2 | 7.9 | 5.4 | - | 9.4 |
| Muslim | 0.3 | 0.3 | - | - | - | - |
| Unstated/Other | 0.8 | 1.3 | 0.9 | - | - | - |

*Source:* Ministry of General Administration, quoted in *Development Research for a Democratic Nepal (DREFDEN),* 1992, pp. 4-6.

The above Table shows that Brahmins dominance ranges from 31.3 percent at the secretary level to 62.1 percent at section officers level. The Newar ranges from 21.0 percent at section officer to 34.6 percent at additional secretary level. The only other with some representation are the Terai group and a few hill ethnics. Of those at the highest level (secretary), nearly two-third is Kshettriya–Brahmin a quarter Newar and about one-tenth is Terai group. It indicates that in course of time the bureaucracy will be monopolized by the Brahmins and Kshettriyas. It may cause much dissatisfaction. Being placed in the position of decision-making, they have and are misusing their authority in favour of their castes and kins. The same example of increment list position is revealed in a recent Human Development Report of Nepal, which states,

> The composition of leadership in the state bureaucracy mirrors the condition in the political sphere. ... There is an astonishing continuity in the predominance of the high caste and specific ethnic groups in state administration since the formation of the Nepali state more than two centuries and a quarter ago, which appear to have occupied 98 percent of the total civil service posts in 1854. More than one century later, in 1969, this percentage came down only marginally, to 93 percent. At present, of the 454 top-level civil (special class and first class) positions, 417 (92 percent) are still occupied by the same groups. Similarly, only about 5 percent of high civil service positions are held by women.[52]

It implies that the Bahun-Kshettriyas took 144 years to come down from 98 percent to 92 percent (24 years for 1 percent) and if they should follow this rate of descent it will take 1,488 years to come to their current real size, that is about 30 percent according to *Mithyanka* (cooked data) of the census. It shows elites influence and exercise political power disproportionate to their size and contribution to the modernization of society. It can be through informal channels of access as well as formal structure of political institutions. These traditional elite groups dominate the legislature both through election and nomination. During the Panchayat period, the National Panchayat used to be the preserve of traditional elites, mostly elected indirectly. When the election was through direct voting in 1981, after the 1980 referendum, although some educated youths were elected, these were also drawn from traditional elite castes.[53]

The 1990 people's movement was a major political upheaval but it has had a very little impact on the country's ethnic equation and that the dominant classes-mainly the Brahmins and Kshettriyas still continue to enjoy the prominent position in the society. The effects of all major political changes– be it during the 104-year Rana rule or the Panchayat – have been confined in favour of the ruling Brahmins and Kshettriyas only. This is exactly why none of the political change has really altered the brutal fact that majority of total population of Nepal compromising indigenous ethnic groups Dalits, Madhesis, Muslims and others have been suppressed, oppressed, depressed, exploited, subjugated and discriminated by the ruling elites.

The culture of inequality which has given the opportunity only to a small area of the country cannot be said to be consistent with the modernization goals of the rational civic culture. The result is that this has led Nepal to the participatory crisis which ultimately led the country to political imbalance. This imbalance has resulted into an authoritarian nature of decision-making process which has developed the elite influence at a high level. Similarly due to ethnic and regional politics i.e. what is being called identity politics now also has become a serious threat for national security and integrity ahead. If the state does not scientifically and democratically address the demand sand grievances of Janjati and Madheshis in the process of state restructurings, Nepal will sooner or later encounter ethnic insurgencies.

Now, the emerging global paradigm of ethnicity has created a tension in Nepali society. In this context Bhattachan critically analyses:

> Indigenous ethnic groups are federating themselves to challenge continuing monopoly of the ruling class in national, political, social and economic resources. Madhesiyas are raising their voice against the hill people's domination and the Dalits are fighting against continuing social discrimination by high caste groups. High caste and low caste groups, and Madhesiyas have recently started to claim themselves as Janjati ethnic groups. Given the continuing and rising social and economic inequality, the Nepalese people now fear that Nepal may be on the verge of witnessing ethnic conflicts in near future as a part of the process of globalization.[54]

Out of 110 major armed conflicts recorded in a period between 1989and 1999,103 took place within states, mostly focused around identity issues.[55] Nepal is still exempted from ethnic war if the ethnic content of the Maoist insurgency and sporadic armed rides in Madhesh are not counted. Inter-ethnic relation in Nepal largely appears none-antagonistic, so some see it as harmonious and free of violence. Up to the present time fortunately there is no immediate confrontation among ethnic groups in Nepal as with its neighbors, such as India, Sri Lanka, and Pakistan. The social fabric of Nepal is not fragile as many tend to judge against the rise of parochial trends. Political upheavals, ethnic and regional demands have not shattered the solid foundation of society. Yet the question arises, how long can such a foundation continue to absorb the invading negative trends manifest in political sphere? If politics continues to be fragmented and parochial, its impacts on disturbing social harmony may be strong and insurmountable. As Gaize and Scholz have rightly pointed out:

> As in Eastern Europe, the authorization system in Nepal had managed to submerge, rather than resolve, the regional and ethnic animosities in an ethnically diverse population. The new found political freedom in post – 1990 Nepal led to the expression of pent-up frustration that expressed to threaten the national existence, particularly since ethnic and regional identities could be exploited by candidate competing for voting blocs. Fortunately, Nepal's political constitutions again demonstrated sufficient capability to integrate the mosaic of ethnic groups and defend potentially explosive ethnic issues.[56]

Over the time, ethnic relation has been changing rapidly towards the greater degree of discord, conflict and tension since the rise of ethnic movements in aftermath of the restoration of democracy in 1990.Owing to better education, increased means of communications and improved transport network, political consciousness grew amongst Nepal's ethnic groups. Democratization speeded this process, since the transition to democracy, ethnic groups from the hills and the peoples of the Terai have found a new voice. A provision has been made to maintain the cultural diversity of the country and to promote healthy and cordial social relations among the various religions, castes, tribes and communities and linguistic groups by aiding their languages, literatures, scripts, arts and culture.[57] But those arguing for greater recognition of Nepal's multi-linguistic and culturally pluralistic population insisted that the monopolization of politics and economic life by high caste people have rendered the promises of the constitution an empty gesture only. The accommodation and liberal approach of the high caste people and assertive activity of the ignored group must go side by side on the process of nation building and state building. Those victims of Nepali society increasingly view that constitutionalization of society may tantamount to status quo and consequently serve as reflected in Sidney Verba's statement. Verba writes:

> The way in which demands for participation are met plays a major role in the development of attitudes toward political participation and integration. If the new groups demanding a voice in politics are welcomed by those who hold political power, the integration of the political system is likely to be maintained. ... On the other hand, if the incumbent elites do not accept the new participatory demands as legitimate, those who demand this participation are likely to conceive of such participation as requiring the overthrow of the older authority structure in order to be effective. Participation will be through of as involving a conflict with other authority structures. Rather than there being belief structure that facilitates the sharing of political power and that incorporates older more deferential political beliefs with the beliefs supporting political participation, there will be a sharp break in the development of the political culture. The new values of political participation will replace and destroy older attitudes supporting political deference.[58]

Loktantra in Nepal must recognize the collective orientation of the people. Ultimate authority in Nepal must reside with a power which can recognize both the needs and can be committed to the genuine interests of the people. No sensible person would deny that the most important aspect of democratic culture is equality in opportunity and rights. However, the constitutional choices are not free from the country's distinctive history, political culture and character of the population. Federal constitution cannot be free from the positive and negative reflection of the prior constitution. Nepal's constitutional experience has always been unitary one and the political and administrative mind set of the ruling elite is very much based on unitarianism.

Federalism in Nepal's present context is also not founded on well argued philosophical base, but is a product of reaction and resentment to hill Brahmin/Kshettriya domination on one hand and populist mobilization of ethnic issues by some political parties, on the other. When the time to transform the country into federal structure came nearer, the leaders were expected to rise above the sloganeering phase of federalism and translate it into political reality. But they failed to moderate their stands. We know federalism has a potentiality to produce ethnic harmony as well as ethnic conflict. The constitution-makers and the advocates of federalism in Nepal with sufficient preparations need to take into consideration of the ethnic, linguistic, and cultural homogeneity of population along with geographic contiguity, natural resources and economic viability, administrative feasibility and mutual interdependence for a federal system. This also requires immense homework with sound technical back up.

Ethnic assertion, which has become a crucial facet of national life has to be managed with proper understanding to avoid further social distress and possible ethnic insurgency. Social inclusion, therefore, has become the imperatives of the state, an absence of which could only drive a wedge between the state and society resulting into further weakening of the state with increasing social alienation. The Nepali state, therefore, requires playing a constructive role of mutual empowerment rather than mutual apprehension in the society.

Now, Nepal is faced simultaneously with problems of nation building and of state building. The crisis of nation-building is felt since Nepali state is struggling to maintain the common national identity. State is now fragmented across ethnic, religious, linguistic and religion lines. The problem of state building has come about because state institutions are not in a position to deliver services. By contrast, the state building process is deeply preoccupied with political, social, cultural, regional, economic, religious and external factors.

In the process of transformation, Nepal has discarded number of factors of the past- single official language, a national anthem and a national code of dress. Nonetheless, all its citizens have common fights and obligations that can eventually contribute sense of national identity and cohesion in tandem with the preservation of cultural diversity. Moreover, the making of the constitution offers the possibility of influencing the nation building process towards establishing a set of common ideas, values and institutions that will serve vital elements of the burgeoning of a collective national identity. Cultural differences can trigger violent conflicts when state policies are discriminatory. But there does not need to be a trade-off between diversity and unity, nor between peace and respect for diversity. Both can move together well if one respects the others' sentiment and culture under multi-cultural policies of the state. Only a strong state can control and mediate among diverse social groups and create culture for political stability, undertaking the reconstruction of the country's political, economic and social fabric.

The model of a successful democracy requires that all citizens be involved and active in politics and this participation be informed, analytic and rational. The civic culture of rational model of democratic citizenship is one component of the civic culture when combined in some sense with its opposites of passivity trust and deference to authority and competence. Jaitly has said: "It is not caste per so that is essentially harmful. It is its alliance with the opposite categories of politics that poses greater challenges to social cohesion" [59] Theories of comparative politics suggest that the more the sources of power and position are concentrated in the few elite groups, the more troublesome it becomes to institutionalize democracy. How to bring the non-participant non-represented and non-elite social and ethnic groups in the political process has become a major challenge to Nepali democratic culture under the present structure of values and institution. Is a person likely to be discriminated because that, he is a Brahmin or Sudra, a Kshettriya or Newar, a Pahari or a Madhesiya? Inequality is the result of social policies rather than human nature and intelligence. So, the only path to improve the status of disadvantaged groups in Nepal is the adoption of affirmative action based on egalitarian principles. A progressive alternative would be to provide politically disadvantage groups higher representation. Otherwise, in such circumstances, one cannot expect to find a rather subject – participant political culture for the success of Loktantra in Nepal.

The result is the emergence of diverse ethnic sub-cultures, which is a serious threat to national integration. Survey's findings (conducted over a period of three years, (first in 2004 and the second in 2007) show that people's preference to ethnic regional identity is on rise and identification with national identity is down from 58 to 43 per cent.[60] On emergence of ethnicity and regionalism as a dominant part of the Nepali political culture, a foreign expert on Nepali society and politics observed "if the period of 1960 to 1990 was one of nation –building, the 17 years since then has been a time of ethnicity- building."[61] The pity of this situation is that it has an effect exactly opposite to the cultural construction of the nation state as provided by renowned Nepali historian Acharya in *Nepalko Sanskrit Parampara.*[62] (Nepal's Cultural Tradition) in which he draws every Nepali into the sphere of a nation – state and collective participation in the formation of a single identity Nepal.

My strong observation is, only a strong state can control and mediate among diverse social groups and create conditions for political stability, undertaking the reconstruction of the country's political, economic and social fabric. The basis of the state or of the power structure is the nation. Therefore, a state can be strong when it has a strong nation, however diverse its peoples. Democracy is nationalism with collective sentiments and collective mission of the good of people. If a state becomes parochial by adhering to a particular ethnicity, religion, language or culture, it naturally becomes prejudiced to a particular group or religion thus violating the very foundation of democracy, nationalism and civic culture.

## Religion: Reflection in People's Thought and Action

Religion, which has been treated as obsession neurosis by psychoanalysts and opium by Marxist is one of the oldest psychic creations of human kind. Politics and religion are pervasive as these affect not only the life of an individual and society, but also of a nation. These two differ in how they affect as religion affects the individual first and then society and the nation, whereas, politics affects a nation first and then the society and individuals. As in most countries of Asia, in Nepal too religion has played a vital force in the people's thought and action. There is no aspect that religion does not touch or affect in the people's day-to-day living.[63] For South Asian Nations, the complex relationship between religion and politics indeed remains a perennial dilemma for both, the democratic secular states as well as the non-secular ones. The rise in the assertions of ethnic and primordial identities in most of the multi-religious societies has become a growing feature for the contemporary world politics. Most of the countries in South Asia are inhabited by diverse ethnic and religious groups.

Nepal is a home to a number of ethnic, caste groups with different languages, religions and cultural traditions. The numerical and percentage distribution of the population by religion over the last four decades is given in the Table below.

Table shows that three major religious groups live side by in Nepal- Hindu, Buddhist and Islam. The 1991 census has identified "Kirat religion" a local animistic tradition whose followers are mostly the Rais and Limbus of Eastern Nepal. The other "Minor" religious, groups are Jain, Christian and others. However, the Hindus are overwhelmingly represented. In 1952/54, 88.9 percent of the total population was Hindus and this came down to 86.5 percent in 1991, a moderate percentage decline over the last four decades. But the absolute number of Hindu has more than doubled in the period. 7,318,392 in 1952/54 to 15,996,953 in 1991, an absolute increase of 8,678,561 people in 40 years. The only religious group whose percentage as well as population is constantly increasing

**Table 2.4: Population Percentage by Religion in Censuses**

| *Religion* | *1952/54* | *%* | *1961* | *%* | *1971* | *%* | *1981* | *%* | *1991* | *%* |
|---|---|---|---|---|---|---|---|---|---|---|
| Hindu | 7318392 | 88.87 | 8254403 | 87.69 | 10330009 | 89.39 | 14335787 | 89.50 | 15996953 | 86.51 |
| Buddhist | 707104 | 8.59 | 870991 | 9.25 | 866411 | 7.50 | 799081 | 5.32 | 1439142 | 7.78 |
| Islam | 208899 | 2.54 | 280597 | 2.98 | 351186 | 3.04 | 399197 | 2.66 | 653218 | 3.53 |
| Kirat | | | | | | | | | 318389 | 1.72 |
| Jain | | | 831 | 0.01 | 5836 | 0.05 | 9438 | 0.06 | 7561 | 0.04 |
| Christian | | | 458 | | 2541 | 0.02 | 3891 | 0.03 | 31280 | 0.17 |
| Other | 684 | 0.01 | | | | | 365445 | 2.43 | 26416 | 0.14 |
| Unstated | | | 5716 | 0.06 | | | | | 18138 | 0.10 |
| Total | 8235079 | 100.00 | 9412996 | 100.00 | 11555983 | 100.00 | 15022839 | 100.00 | 18491097 | 100.00 |

*Sources:* *CBS*, 1958, *Population Census*, 1952/54.
*CBS*, 1968, *Population Census*, 1961.
*CBS*, 1975, *Population Census*, 1971.
*CBS*, 1977, *The Analysis of the Population Statistics of Nepal*, p. 42.
*CBS*, 1984, *Population Census*, 1981, Vol. 1, Part III.
CBS, 1993, Population Census, 1991.
*CBS*/Nepal (*Central Bureau of Statistics*), (Kathmandu: CBS, 1993).

over the last four decades is the Muslims. The Muslims have tripled during the period from 208.899 in 1992/54 to 653,218 in 1991.

**Table 2.5: Religious diversity in1952/54 -2001**
**(Increased Assertion of various Religious Groups)**

| Religion | Census | 1952/54 | 1961 | 1971 | 1981 | 1991 | 2001 |
|---|---|---|---|---|---|---|---|
| Hindu | 1952/54 | 88.9 | 87.7 | 89.4 | 89.5 | 86.5 | 80.6 |
| Buddhist | 1952/54 | 8.6 | 9.6 | 7.5 | 5.3 | 7.8 | 10.7 |
| Muslim | 1952/54 | 2.5 | 3.0 | 3.0 | 2.7 | 3.5 | 4.2 |
| Christian | 1961 | - | - | - | - | 0.2 | 0.5 |

*Source:* Population Census of 2001, CBS.

The statistical data of Hindu population reached to 89.5 percent in 1981, and declined in the 1991 census with a recording of 86.5 percent. In 2001, it further declined to 80.6 percent. The average percentage of Buddhists and Muslims during the Panchayat period surprisingly increased since 1991. The 1991 census also observed the recording of Christians (0.2 percent) for the first time, which later increased two fold in 2001 census (0.5 percent). This trend clearly reflects the increased assertion of various religious groups since the introduction of multiparty democracy in 1990.

The majority are Hindus in Nepal by religion. Since the unification days to the downfall of the Rana regime in 1950, Hindu-Buddhist religions, Nepali language, the caste system and partilineality have been applied to institutionalize the social life in Nepal and achieve value integration.[64] Hindu rulers of Nepal had been generally tolerant in behaviour towards these religions and had done nothing to hinder their practice. There had been a regular attempt by the Nepali rulers to develop a homogenous Nepali culture within the frame of Hindu political ideas without seriously considering the diversity and complicity of Nepali culture within the frame of Hindu political ideals. Dahal writes that, the self-consciously Hindu Shah and Rana rulers rationalized these elements as being essential to contain foreign threats, preserve the social order at home and secure external markets. He further writes the Sanskritization, socialization and civilization of dozens of inarticulate tribal, ethnic and indigenous people and cultures along dominant norms did produce a semblance of social stability. The societal process in Nepal was such that Hinduism did not proselytize. In this context, Sanwal makes clearer that the geopolitical situation in the kingdom reinforced the Hindu concept of law and imposed on the king and his administrators concern for local customs and traditions, acceptance of them, and even sanctions customs that were at variance with the religious ideas that motivated the state.[65]

Until Nepal moved to secularism subsequent to the fall of monarchy had always been recognized as a Hindu state. Despite the politicization of religion as a major cause of concern in South Asia which eventually invites regular clashes between Hindus and Muslims, violence against Christians, higher communal tensions in India, various cases of attacks on Hindus in Bangladesh and Bhutan, Shia-Sunni clashes in Pakistan, and Buddhist intolerance in Sri Lanka, Nepal as a Hindu state comparably remained unscathed by such inauspicious events and essentially enjoyed total harmony between religious faiths in the past.

Historically, Nepal has not encountered a great deal of conflict between various religious communities, though in different interval of time there have been few instances of communal tension especially between Hindus and Muslims. From the very beginning of the formation of modern Nepal, state responded hastily by not paying attention to the demands of non-Hindu religious minorities groups, and later enforcing its religious character even in the democratic constitution of 1990 (Article 4(1) of the 1990 constitution). In this regard it can be pointed out that since the position of Hindu king was safeguarded in article (27(1), there was no reason for the constitution to call Nepal a Hindu state in Article 4(1). This provision not only disappointed Nepal's vast indigenous (Janajati) population along with Buddhist, Muslim and Christian minorities, but is equally contrastive to other constitutional provisions, such as Article 2, which states that Nepal as a nation is constituted by Nepali people, irrespective of religion. Similarly, article 11(2), ensures that state should not discriminate against any of its citizens, on the basic of religion, race, sex, caste, tribe, or ideology. Sushil Shashank, as the tribal culture scholar opined that the hegemony of Hindu religion has overruled the psyche of Nepali population since long. Such claims correspond to the fact that a state religion means dominion of a culture, a language, and some castes, which goes against the potential of a society arising out of its pluralism. This is one of the major reasons, why our country passed through conflicts and violence.

Until 1950s missionaries were barely tolerated in Nepal. The practice of conversion was considered illegal, and several episodes of arrest were made for various acts of proselytism until 1990s. But there existed absolutely no animosity between Hindus and Christian Missionaries. For instance, schools like St Xavier's and St Mary's were allowed to be opened in the 1950s, and are still regarded as the respected institutions of learning. Various minority groups in Nepal, however felt that the majority, monolithic state-backed Hindu elites, who speak the Nepali language and wore the Nepali national dress, were knowingly curbing their culture, religion and language. Minorities regarded such phenomenon as a restriction imposed on them, where they would not be able to contest with the centralized political structure due to dominance endowed upon by the Hindu religion, Nepali language and caste hierarchy. Therefore, they deliberately desired Nepal to become a ''secular state'' so that country could observe inclusiveness.

Now, the conversion from one religion to another is not considered as illegal since religious institutions are made free to exercise their religious mission in Nepal. FM station 10.5 MHz was established by the Christian missionary in order to spread religious message. Remarkably, since 2008, the government of Nepal has announced national holidays on the major festivals of various ethnic and religious minorities.

### *Culture of Religious Diversity*

With the advent of democracy and lifting of ban on party-politics in Nepal, issues of language, religion and ethnic conflict came to the forefront. Numerous ethnic and regional parties appeared on the scene claiming to fight the political and economic domination by the high caste Hindus. In reality, it is natural that Nepal's ethnic and religious diversity should be reflected in the democratic system. Nepali intellectuals while supporting this trend came out with the opinion that democracy will not be democracy if it continues to satisfy the demands of only one segment of the population, even if that segment comprises the majority. They argue that the state cannot patronize one religious system. In a multi-lingual country like Nepal, ethnic and religious identities are bound to emerge with the growth in education and human right. So, it is remarked that religion in Nepal provides an opportunity for individuals and groups to project their identity.

A caste, a tribal, a linguistic or a religious group can be major on one dimension but a minor on other dimension. In general, the so-called "minority-groups" of Nepal regard themselves to be socially, economically and politically disadvantaged and believe that the state is unfair to them and they suffer serious discrimination in every field of life. Many of them also feel their cultural identity is getting gradually displaced from the national mainstream and the government is not serious about it. Such awareness and feeling have become a ubiquitous aspect of political culture in Nepal even after democracy. The culture of religion stipulated the practice of caste system and untouchability since time immemorial in Nepal. But the trend has not been able to reflect better expressions of the time, but has been holding the entrusted traditions of the past still now. As a result, the Nepali people of the lower caste have had to sufferer set-backs on so many places. They are deprived of the right to equal opportunity guaranteed by the constitution; rather they are being cheated on so many areas only because of the religion. It is not unnatural that so many elites, including the political leaders have started to raise voices against this concept.

***State Secularization: Changing Dynamics***

Religious tolerance, peoples' adoptability and resilience are some of the strongest bonds of social harmony and secularization. One of the glaring examples of such resiliency is the peaceful change of Nepal from a Hindu state into a secular state after the parliament and later the CA made the decision unanimously in 2008. The popular uprising of April 2006 overthrew the absolute monarchical system, and it took no less time for the re-instated parliament and the government of Nepal to declare the country as a 'Secular State' on 18 May 2006 instead of a Hindu Kingdom. All citizens, regardless of religion would have equal rights afterward. Nepali people of diverse religious faiths, particularly religious minorities, developed a sense of dignity and inclusiveness, guaranteed to them by the state. Consequently, various ethnic and religious minorities, Christian missionaries, hailed the instated parliament's decision by saying that it ensured justice against the domination by a particular religion.

The online free Encyclopedia defines the concept of secularism as a secular state, whereby a state or country is officially neutral in matter of religion, neither supporting nor opposing any particular religious beliefs or practices. A secular state also treats its entire citizen from a particular religion over other religions. The secularization thesis is based on the theory that as societies industrialize, they become more rational, scientific and specialist; and thus traditional values, beliefs and practices decline. The Nepali translation of the word 'secular' has been stated as *dharma Nirapeksha*, which has brought a false meaning among the people that their government has now turned atheist instead of being uniform or equal to all.

Deriving benefits from such ill-favored situations, different radical groups have been conveying wrong information to the people that secularism implies to be 'anti-Hindu'. Hindu activists have continuously protested against the government decision to declare Nepal a 'secular state'. Some demonstrations were observed in Kathmandu, and the most critical situation was reported in the South, on May 25, 2006, when around 10,000 pro-Hindu protesters spilled into the streets of the industrial city of Birgunj. They waved tridents and saffron flags and shouted slogans against pro-democracy parties. The rally that embraced Hindu leaders and demonstrators protested with a motto that interim government's decision had betrayed the expectation of 80 percent of people. As a reaction to the declaration of Nepal as a secular state, a new Hindu fundamentalist organization known as NDA (Nepal Defense Army) was formed with an extremist intention to restore Hindu Kingdom in Nepal. This organization has repeatedly asserted its violent beliefs against the ongoing Christian missionaries in Nepal. If millions of Christians dwelling in Nepal did not relinquish their mission of conversion from any religion to Christianity and lastly abandon Nepal, millions of bombs would be sited in various churches across the country. Many riots, communal violence, and attacks in Lalitpur, on May 23, 2009 were the first attack in Hill area by the NDA. Most of the riots in the past were observed between Hindu, Muslims, but since the last some years or so, Hindu-Christian conflict is clearly visible. Availability of firearm including bombs and explosives has intensified militancy among the fundamental groups. Bombs blast in the Assumption Church of Lalitpur and the Mosque in Morang are the two instances that provide evidence to the argument. Fundamentalist organizations like NDA have warned numerously to terminate all church activities concerning issues of conversion (which is no more illegal), and have threatened entire Christian communities of Nepal to leave the country.

It shows religious conflicts are rising in Nepal. The secularization of state has led to unhealthy competition among major religions in New Nepal. The unhealthy trend of inter-religious competition has been introduced through the state secularization, and the state power does not seem to have the essential capacity to check and control violent activities of different groups. The culture of inter-religious conflict is likely to continue as a potential challenge to social harmony in future. It must be clearly understood that a political leader can be religious but his politics cannot and also be clearly understood that secularism does not stand for neglecting religion but for respecting all religions equally. If a nation adopts any religion and gives preferential treatments to its adherents, it entails the culture of injustice to the believers of other religions.

It is well observed that political attitude and belief of the people are influenced to a greater extent from history, tradition, the ruling elites and subjects of the nation. People inherit their behaviour and values from their soil and climate, habitat and heritage. Nepal's political system is perpetuated by its political culture and structure based on geography, economy, pyramidal social structure and social stratification, and religious ethos. The democratic values in Nepali society have been greatly diluted by the existence of poor economy fortified by an extremely stratified hereditary hierarchical society with increasing social alienation. Various aspects of socio-economic structures ranging from the cultural patterns and social behaviour to the feudal socio-economic relations are generally observed as constraints to democratic culture in Nepal.

## NOTES

1. Lynn Hunt, *Politics, Culture and Class in the French Revolution,* (Berkeley: University of California Press, 1984), pp. 12-13.
2. Keith Michael Baker, *The Political Culture of the Old Regime,* (Oxford: Pergamon, 1987), p. xii.
3. Lucian W. Pye, "Introduction," *Political Culture and Political Development*, (New Jersey: Princeton University Press, 1965), p. 7.
4. Walter Rosenbaum, *Political Culture,* (New York: Praeger, 1975), p. 41.
5. Claude Alvares and Homo Faber, *Technology and Culture in India, China and the West, 1800 to the Present Days,* (Bombay: Allied Publishers, 1979), p. 27.
6. Alexis de Tocqueville, *Democracy in America*, (New York: Alford A. Knopf, 1945), p. 299.
7. Yogi Naraharinath and Baburam Acharya (eds.), *Rastrapita Shri 5 Bada Maharajh Prithivi Narayan Shah Dev Ko Diviya Upadesh,*

(Kathmandu: Prithvi Jayanti Samaroha Samiti, 2010 BS), p. 15.

8. *Ibid,* pp. 18-19
9. Dev Raj Dahal, "Geopolitics of Nepal: Survival Strategies of a Small State", *The Political Economy of Small State*, Anand Aditya, (ed.) (Kathmandu: NEFAS-FES, 1997), pp. 25-46.
10. Ronald Inglehart, "Culture Shift in Advanced Industrial Society", Princeton: Prinction University Press, 1990, quoted in Robent W. Jackman, Ross A Miller, *A Renaissance of Political Culture? American Journal of Political Science*, Vol. 40, Issue 3, (Madison: University of Wisconsin System, August, 1996), pp. 632-659.
11. Seymour Martin Lipset, Some Social Requisites for Democracy: Economic Development and political Legitimacy, American Political Science Review, 53, i:1959, pp. 69-105. As mentioned in Lok Raj Baral, *Nepal-Nation-State in the Wilderness: Managing State, Democracy and Geopolitics,* (New Delhi: Sage Publication, 2012), pp. 166-167.
12. Dev Raj Dahal, *The Challenges of Good Governance: Decentralization and Development in Nepal,* (Kathmandu: Centre for Governance and Development Studies, 1996), p. 32.
13. CCASS, *Abadharana and Karyakram*, (Kathmandu: Centre for Civil Awareness and Social Studies-CCASS, 2055 BS), p. 3.
14. Madhab Ghimire and Samesh Adhikari, "Foreign Aid and its Dynamics in Nepal: Lessons from the Future", *Sangam Journal Quarterly,* Vol. 1, Issue 1, (Kathmandu: Publication of Sangam Institute for Policy Analysis and Strategic Studies 2009), p. 9.
15. *Foreign Aid Policy,* (Kathmandu: Ministry of Finance, Government of Nepal, 2002).
16. *World Development Report- 2006,* (Kathmandu: The World Bank, 2006).
17. Devendra Raj Pandey, "Matching Democracy and Development Policymaking in an Aid-Dependent Country: An Illustration from Nepal," *Harvard Asia Quarterly,* (USA: Harvard University, 1999-2002), p. 1.
18. *Ibid.*
19. Chandra Dev Bhatta, *Challenges of State Building in Nepal* (Kathmandu: Friedrich-Ebert-Stiftung (FES), 2008), p. 102.

20. Dev Raj Dahal, The State, Society and Development in Nepal, paper submitted to IIDS, Centre for Governance and Development Studies (GDS), (Kathmandu: Jan. 31, 1998), p. 42.
21. Pandey, *op cit.*, f.n. No. 17.
22. Krishna B. Bhattachan, "Nepal in 1993: Business as Usual," *Asian Survey*, Vol. 34, No. 2, (Berkeley: University of California Press, 1994), p. 175.
23. Dahal, *op cit.*, f.n. No. 20, p. 41.
24. *Ibid.* p. 42.
25. Bhatta, *op cit.*, f.n. No. 19, p. 103.
26. Harka, Gurung, *Nepal: Dimensions of Development*, (Kathmandu: Awarta Press, 1989), p. 293.
27. *Ibid,* p. 118.
28. Lok Raj Baral, *Nepal-Nation–State in the Wilderness: Managing State, Democracy and Geopolitics,* (New Delhi: Sage Publication, 2012), p. 72.
29. Currently, we are producing two-types of polices one for the urban elites and another for the rural poor. The private-public dichotomy is the classic example to this end.
30. *The Kathmandu Post*, (Kathmandu: Kantipur Publication, August 8, 1997).
31. Dwarika Dhungel, "The Nepalese Administrative System", *Contemporary Nepal,* Pashupati S.J.B. Rana and Dwarika Dhungel (eds.), (New Delhi: Vikas Publishing House, 1997), p. 134.
32. *The Kathmandu Post,* (Kathmandu: Kantipur Publication, August 7, 1997).
33. Ganga B. Thapa, *Nepal: From Authoritarinism to Democracy in Navnita,* Chadha Behera (ed.), (New Delhi: International Relations in South Asia, 2008), p. 156.
34. Mc. Lennan and Barbara N., *Comparative Political Systems,* (Massachusetts: Duxbury Press, 1975), p. 142.
35. Seymour Martin Lipset, *Political Man: The Social Bases of Politics,* (Baltimore: John Hopkins University Press, 1981), p. 140.
36. Dahal, *op cit.,* f.n. No. 20, p. 35.
37. Gabriel A. Almond and Sideny Verba, *The Civic Culture: Political Attitudes and Democracy in Five Nations,* (Princeton: V.J. Princeton University Press, 1963), p. 257.

38. Dahal, *op cit.,* f.n. No. 20.
39. *Ibid.*
40. Rabindra Khanal, Political Institutionalization and Political Culture in Nepal, paper presented to National Seminar Organized by Department of Political Science, T.U., in corporation with FES, (1998), p. 8.
41. Samuel P. Huntingtio, *The Third Wave; Democratization in the Late Twentieth Century,* (New Delhi: Adarsh Books, 2010), pp. 60-69.
42. *Ibid,*
43. Rajani Kothari, *Rethinking Development,* (Delhi: Vikas Publishing House, 1988), p. 191.
44. Steven M. Parish, *Hierarchy and its Discontents– Culture and the Politics of Consciousness in Caste Society*, (Oxford: Oxford University Press, 1997), pp. 6-9.
45. Suresh C. Chalise, *Sociology of the Legislative Elite in a Developing Society,* (Kathmandu: NEFAS, 1995), pp. 20-21.
46. Harka Gurung, *NEPAL: Social Demography and Expressions,* (Kathmandu: New Era, 1998), p. 129.
47. F.M. Gaige, *Regionalism and National Unity in Nepal,* (Los Angeles: University of California Press, 1975), p. 195.
48. CBS, *National Population Census 2001,* (Kathmandu: Central Bureau of Statistics, 2002), pp. 40-42.
49. 2001 Census has reported 101 caste/ethnic groups in Nepal. There are five such groups whose population is less than one thousand and an ethnic group called *Kusunda* has only 164 persons (CBS).
50. *Ibid.* p. 2.
51. Rishikesh Shaha, *Nepali Politics: Retrospect and Prospect*, II ed., (Oxford: Oxford University Press, 1978), p. 4.
52. *Nepal: Human Development Report*, (Kathmandu: Nepal South Asia Centre- NESAC, 1994), pp. 145-46.
53. Gurung, *op cit.,* f.n. No. 46, p. 122
54. Krishna B. Bhattachan, "Globolizattion and Its Impact on Nepalese Society and Culture", *Impact of Globalization in Nepal,* Madan Kumar Dahal (ed.), (Kathmandu: Nepal Foundation for Advanced Studies (NEFAS) Friedrich– Ebert - Stiftung (FES), 1999), p. 92.

55. Benjamin Reilly, *Democracy in Divided Societies: Electoral Engineering for Conflict Management*, (Cambridge: Cambridge University Press, 2001), p. 2.
56. Fred Gaize and John Scholz, *The 1991 Parliamentary Elections in Nepal, Asian Survey,* Vol. XI, (California: University of California, Nov., 1991), p. 1054.
57. HMG/Nepal, *The constitution of the Kingdom of Nepal 2047 B.S. (1990),* (Kathmandu: Ministry of Law, Justice and Parliamentary Affair, His Majesty's Government of Nepal, 1990), p. 15.
58. Sidney Verba, "Comparative Political Culture," *Political Culture and Political Development,* Lucian W. Pye and Sidney Verba (eds.), (USA: Princeton University Press, 1989), p. 557.
59. Anam Jaitly, *India's Political Culture– In search of a Frame Work,* (Jaipur: Aalekh Publication, 1991), p. 200.
60. Krishna Hachhethu, *State of Democracy in Nepal: Survey Report*, (Kathmandu: SDSA/Nand International IDEA), 2004.
61. David N. Gellner "Ethnicity and Nationalism in the World's only Hindu State," *Nationalism and Ethnicity in a Hindu Kingdom: The Politics of Culture in Contemporary Nepal*, David N. Gellner et al. (eds.), (Amsterdam: Harwood Academic Publishers, 1997).
62. Baburam Acharya, *Nepalko Sanskritic Parampara,* (Kathmandu: Kathmandu Printing Press, 2054 BS), p. 59.
63. Prayag Raj Sharma, "Nepali Culture and Society: Reflection on some Historical Currents", *Nepal: Perspective on Continuity and Change*, K.P. Malla (ed.), (Kathmandu: CNAS, 1989), pp. 139-165.
64. S.J. Stiller and Ludwig F., "The Silent Cry: The People of Nepal 1816-1839" (Kathmandu: Sahayogi Prakashan, 1976), pp. 153-178, quoted in Dev Ral Dahal, *The State Society and Development in Nepal,* (Kathmandu: GDS, Jan 31, 1998), p. 5.
65. B.D. Sanwal, *Social and Political History of Nepal,* (New Delhi: Monohar Publication, 1993), p. 25.

# 3.

# Political Culture and Political Socialization: Interaction and Traits in Nepal

Political socialization is a process of acquisition of political culture and changes in the patterns of political culture come about through political socialization since political socialization is defined as a process by which "political cultures are maintained and changed."[1] The socialization process by which one is exposed to particular culture and trained to be useful member of the society in course of time acquires conscious and subconscious experiences about politics which has a profound influence in the shaping of one's basic personality structure. The individuals are trained and prepared in a way that they become well functioning members of a political community. It has peculiarly a psychological dimension in the sense that it is the gradual learning of the norms, attitudes and behaviors acceptable to an on-going political system.

## Political Socialization and Political Culture

The literature on political culture and political socialization suggests that political systems work best when they are underwritten by a robust set of belief values and norms. Political socialization concerns how and when human beings learn about politics. Political culture asks what it is that they learn when they are socialized. The process works at individual as well as community level. It is one of the important functions of the political system. Political socialization and political culture are thus interrelated areas in modern political analysis. Political culture embraces not only what people are taught about politics but also concerns what they come to feel about politics in which they live. Political culture is the set of values, beliefs and attitudes within which a political system operates. Gabriel Almond and Sidney Verba in their major work *The Civic Culture* wrote on political culture as the "pattern of orientations to political objects among the members of the nation."[2] Political culture is not simply to do with what we believe, but is also bound up with the ways in which we behave politically. So political culture can also be understood in terms of the political practices and ritual of a given community. Kavanagh preferred political culture as a short hand expression to denote the set of values within which a political system operates. It is something between the state of public opinion and an individual's personality characteristics.[3]

If political culture suffers to the complex of values, beliefs altitudes that define the rules of the game in a political system, political socialization seeks to inculcate those norms and orientations in the minds of the individual. With that they develop trust in their political system, thereby keep themselves like well functioning citizens and leave their indelible imprints on the minds of their successors. Socialization may thus be defined as the process by which an individual becomes acquainted with the political system which determines her/his relations to political phenomena. Political socialization determines, what the individual feels towards the system, how one views other persons and actors in the political process, the variations and its government institutions, how one participates or does not participate in politically relevant activities and the kind of self image one develops about place and role in the political system. The nature of political socialization helps to define the limits to set the parameters within which political orientation, behaviour, attitudes and norms of an individual evolve. Moreover, the approach assumes that the make-up of a political culture influences patterns of political behaviour within a political system and that these behavioural patterns, in turn, have a major influence on the stability of a regime. It shows that individuals who are socialized into a political culture undergo a learning process that provides them with the resources, knowledge, skills, attitudes and beliefs- to function as reasonably competent political actors within that milieu.

In shaping the political culture, political socialization process operates in terms of various socializing agents. Some of these agents, such as the family tend to be prominent at the early phase of the socialization process and the influences are mostly related to personality characteristics fundamental to the political culture. Other socialization agents, such as the mass media and political parties tend to be more critical at later stage and thus are primarily involved in influencing the more cognitive aspects of the political culture. The concern in the chapter is to concentrate on how the agents of political socialization in Nepal have shaped moulded and maintained Nepal's political culture. It will be centered on these dimensions –family, educational institutions, authoritarian culture, gender socialization and the culture of Black Science *(tantrism),*

**The Familial Core**

The most dominant influences of childhood political socialization are the family, school, and media. Of these, the family generally exerts the most significant and long lasting influence on political attitudes, behaviour and belief of a person. Basic political attitudes and values tend to be formed early in childhood that relatively continue throughout life. The family is the direct political socialization tool of the state. It has been proved that early orientations proved to have strong and lasting effects.[4] In this view, primary socialization experiences tend to produce persistent effects, which are only marginally influenced by later socialization experiences.[5] Moore has critically examined that "the impact of direct experience on behaviour is severely constrained by norms passed across generations through early socialization."[6] The social scientists have established that the foundation of one's personality is laid in the first five years of one's coming. They also accept the view that core values are imprinted at an early age. That is why, the child's early family environment is important because "early impressions tend to coalesce into a natural view of the world. All the later experiences then tend to receive their meaning from this original set."[7] So it is an accepted fact that political socialization is a continuous process beginning in the early childhood that continues throughout adolescence and adulthood.[8] Family is the most powerful medium through which value systems develop and which wields a profound influence on the growth of attitudes and interests of an individual.

Family is thus the single most important channel through which values considered conducive to individual and social good could be cultivated.[9] The UN Secretary General Kofi Annan in his message given on the occasion of the International Day of Families, 15th May 2000 has rightly emphasized the crucial role of family. He stated that, "it is within the family that children can learn positive values that will guide them for the rest of their lives, and it is within the family that people can learn key lessons about equality, tolerance and shared responsibility." He further said in his message that families can be real bastion of human values and human progress. Let us do our utmost to create conditions family need to fully realize their potential."[10]

The latent and manifest influences inculcated at the early stages in life have powerful and lasting influence. Among the many important latent influences, perhaps the most distinctive is the shaping of attitudes towards authority. The family provides the major means of transforming the mentally naked infant organism into adult. The family makes collective decisions: and for the child these decisions are authoritative. An early experience with participation in decision making can increase the child's sense of political competence, provide him with skills for political interactions and thus enhance the probability of active participation in the political system when becomes adult. The family according to Hymen, is peculiarly potent in the United States, determining party loyalties and vital in producing commitment to democratic values. [11]

Studies show that families are generally the first and often the most enduring influence on young people's developing political opinions. It is also observed that as people grow older other influences crisscross the family and naturally their attitudes tend to diverge from those of their parents. However, the influence skill remains. Logically, the more politically active the family, the more likely one is to hold the same beliefs. Although this relationship may be less strong on specific issues, they hold the same general political views. Despite family disagreements and generation gaps, children tend to grow up and vote the way their parents do.

***Family Structure: Psychological Root of Attitude***

Family authority is hierarchically structured, descending from the male parent to the oldest male sibling and so on down through the entire family membership. One general culture of Nepali habit says Nepali Poet Lekh Nath- *Badale je garyo kam huncha tyo sarba sammat* (whatever the senior does is right and be accepted). The writ of the head of the family, whether he is the grandfather, father or eldest brother runs supreme in the management of the family's property or earnings. His precepts have to be carried out in every case, since the extended family has hardly tradition of solving problems through discussion in a spirit of mutual accommodation. It is something bound by the traditional culture, high religious faith and inscriptive values of the society. So the psychological root of attitude towards authority lies, of course in the family structure. The experience in the family is continuous and consistent with the rest of Nepali culture.

In the case of Nepal, there are three generations under one family living at the same time. Citizens belonging to the older are more traditional and conservative. They are more personal and deeply inculcated in the individual and retain the stamp of parochialism. Middle aged members in the family are generally involved in politics than youths and old persons in the present day Nepal. Most of these middle aged members accept and attempt to encourage the spread of modernization in its economic and social aspect, but they are not yet completely aware of the implications of participation in the determination of government policy. So they are sometimes compelled to accept the limitations of the subject and sometimes they adopt an authoritarian attitude. So their participant norms are not in the ascendancy. They are still not in a position to demand such a development. In the words of Khanal they are a kind of pendulum in between the old and the new, as a result, they are weak, corrupt and confused. [12]

The blend of old and new is typical of a culture in transition that reflects the considerable socio-economic change undergone by the society. The co-existence of the political beliefs of an older era with the new orientation is explainable in parts by generation change, the passing away of older cohorts of voters and the entry on the political scene of new generations of political actors. These new generations are socialized under rather different political circumstances from those of their elders. They are better educated and have higher expectations. They are politically more aware and more inclined to get involved in political action because of improved media of communication. So a marked cultural division occurs between the older and new generation– the traditional and modern sub-cultures.

The phenomenon is evident in many of the newer nations, where new generation of people have been modernized and socialized in a specific, universalistic and pragmatic orientation, which typify modern culture, while the older generation remains tied to the rigid, diffused and astrictive patterns of tradition and socialization. Modern political science has demonstrated the continuing prevalence of traditional elements in all modern societies. The nature of individual socialization makes the duality of cultural style inevitable. Some empirical research in the 1970s appeared to confirm a definite value difference between generations. Older generations seem to be more firmly embedded in a structure of materialistic values, while younger generations are clearly more amenable to post-materialist concerns. Westerners may claim that the extended family operates as a conservative force and has become a barrier for democratic culture. Young people are prepared to try innovations but usually receive little more support from their older members of the family with who they are in constant touch. Their motivation systems are both consciously and unconsciously rooted in the old habits and culture. Nepali family both in urban and rural being organized around the central idea that children must accord unquestioning obedience to respect for parents and grandparents is fundamentally authoritarian in character. Doesn't this cultural environment contradict the very essence of Loktantrik culture where decisions are rarely taken on a democratic basis? Children are not expected to participate in decisions concerning themselves, nor are they often permitted even to complain about actions they consider basically unfair. But it does not mean that Nepali family socialization is not encouraging for the evolution of a healthy and vigorous Loktantrik Nepal as what Almond and Verba call the "civic culture in the western context."

In the west duty is the derivative of individual rights, while in the *Vedic* tradition the dharma-mediated ethical system embedded individuals in a web of moral and social duties and relationship. It was designed to beef up the ideal potential of the order of creation. A duty-based society naturally fosters co-dependency and minimizes the potential for conflict as it does in the right-based societies of the west. So the fragmented, isolated and alienated political culture which currently characterizes Nepal does not grow out of experiences in the family only. It cannot be said that the structure and style of Nepali family fails to provide its members with a coherent view of the national political system or with a sense of effectual involvement concerning it. The socialization process and family experiences no doubt prepare adult Nepalis to accept and support authoritarian culture rather than democratic culture. But not only independence and freedom of will are important values that parents should transmit in the socialization of their children. The values of love, affection, cooperation, brotherhood, collective action, work ethics and overall the culture of morality are equally important that are inherited from family socialization. Nepali family does not encourage being egoistic and selfish, which serve to increase the amount of parochialism in Nepali political culture. Many examples of brave Nepali heroes in support of their own family have sacrificed their lives for the sake of people and country. Family relation and political assertion are entirely different aspects. So the children should be assertive against the parents in order to be autonomous according to western view is something doubtful in this context.

### *Family Dynastic Rule in Nepal*

Family relations have a crucial role in the Nepali political system. With regard to the role of family in political socialization in Nepal, Shaha explains:

> Nepali politics and society have always had a pronounced familial core. The extended family has been the primary agent of education and the center of social action for the child. Nepali citizens owe their knowledge of Nepali religion, economics, politics, castes and class to the family, who's several and various kinships are often today in the same household patterns as in the past. In this system, the child is made to accept uncritically the precepts of the all-powerful family. The members of the extended family do not posses freedom of initiative in any matter, not even in the choice of profession.[13]

In reality, the family dynastic rule is popular throughout South Asia and Nepal is no exception. Under democracy in Nepal in the 1990s, the particular Koirala family and their alliances, many of them are inept in most of the positions, have become ubiquitous in all aspects of Nepali social, economic and political life. Starting from Girija Prasad Koirala, Sushil Koirala, Nona Koirala, Sujata Koirala, and their alliances such as Sailaja Acharya, Mahesh Acharya and Chakra Prasad Bastola, and to name a few, who have become the new Ranas for the ordinary Nepali people. Likewise, if we turn over to Ganesh Man Singh, who gave his life for democracy in Nepal, was also cashed heavily by his own family members such as Durgesh Man Singh, P.L. Singh, Prakash Man Singh and others. The story of the UML, the ML and the RPP leaders is also basically the same. When the UML government was in power, all the cadres of UML Party occupied key positions in all the government offices and technical skill. Even the prestigious academic positions such as the Vice Chancellor, the Rector, the Registrar, Deans, and Executive Directors of Research Centers were divided on the basis of family and party lines. When comrade Madan Bhandari died, his wife Vidya Bhandari was picked up as the member of the Parliament and eventually given the position of the Minister. Likewise, when comrade Pushpalal died, Sahana was chosen automatically to replace his position and this type of family connection goes on and on in to hold positions in Nepali social and political life. It shows the social position in Nepal is mostly ascribed and not achieved up to now. Proper family ties and kinship in appropriate place have continued to play dominant role in the culture of politics in Nepal.

***Impact of Globalization on Family and Society***

The fever of globalization in Nepal, a recent development has become a new religion in which life within societies is increasingly affected by international influences. Globalization may be homogenizing the world, but it is also throwing into question traditional ideas about home, national identity, social justice and political freedom. With regard to the impact of globalization on Nepali society, Bhattachan remarks that positive impact of globalization, such as the benefits of modern science and technology, better health care, transportation and communication education and foreign consumer products can be seen in Nepal, but such benefits are the exclusive "privilege" of the elite class. The overwhelming majority of Nepali people are actually experiencing all possible kinds of negative impacts. [14] The negative impacts on the process of globalization on Nepali society, as Bhattachan points out are the development of "West is the best psyche, pacification, increasing rich– poor divide, rising individualism, marginalization of women and children, loss of sovereignty and criminalization of politics, brain drain and muscle exchange.[15] The impact has been more intense and deep on the younger generation than the older. Another related impact is the change in native societal norms and values by Western norms and values. Those younger generations are discovering that alien culture that promotes individualism is good but communitarian is bad. A new process of individualism has begun in working pattern, life style, culture and politics which is less characterized by the traditional notion of public and political life. So collective life and community feelings are deteriorating. Indigenous social, culture, religious, political and judicial institutions are disappearing rapidly. Many youths emigrate to the Gulf and South East Asian Countries in search of manual labour jobs, whereas, at the national level elected political leaders, civil servants are busy in self gratification instead of doing something for the common good. Social consciousness and the responsibility among the younger generations are increasingly deteriorating. So, a perception is growing among the Nepali people that if the negative impacts of globalization are not checked, the sentiments of nationalism, patriotism would become weak.

## Authoritarian Culture

Nepal has been an authoritarian state based on traditional sources of legitimacy. Since the unification of Nepal in 1769 AD, Nepal had been governed by *Hukumi Sashan*, an arbitrary and authoritative command of the Rana and Shah Kings. The family reign during the period depended essentially on a depoliticized genteel population, the traditional army and external support. The tradition of authoritarian political power in Nepal has remained so strong that centralized authority and initiative are still taken as a way out. The Nepali propensity to centralization that has a familial and cultural background has continued to penetrate the decision making structure at the higher level since the *Vedic* age, the age of knowledge and enlightenment.

A traditional authoritarian system is characterized by a single leader or small group of leaders, no party or weak party, no mass mobilization, weak ideological constraints on elite decision-making and the frequently arbitrary exercise of power by a single leader or small group with limited and not responsible government. These specific forms of nondemocratic or authoritarian regimes are referred to as one party system, totalitarian systems, personal dictatorships, military regime, and the like. Almond and Verba conceptualized authoritarianism as a personality syndrome characterized by implicit antidemocratic tendencies. These features are deeply embedded in the Nepali political culture which serves to reinforce and legitimize the authoritarian features.

Nepal is carrying both an authoritarian tradition and subject political culture along with some political elements of a politicking society-whereby a perfect willingness to obey orders from above and an unquestioning attitude to the authority exists.[16] One familiar paradox of the Nepali political culture is that constitutionally political sovereignty rests with the people but practically it rests with the super-ordinate political authority and trickles top-down. Traditional Nepali culture had been built on the concept of duties of the subjects to the monarch, tenants to the landlords, children to their parents and pupils to their teachers. Although their relationship is based on mutual trust, a personal code of honour, discipline and personal identification, these values cannot be considered to be the necessary values for democratic culture because socialization within authority structures provides an inadequate training for the performance of civic activities.

The salient feature of Nepali political culture is that it is highly allergic to the pluralization of power. The net result of democratic experiment has been the growth of vertical power structure with a rigidly centralized authority placed tightly on the top. Why Nepal has centralization of power and authority despite its liberal policy? Is it because of the centralizing traits more rooted in Nepali soil? Nepal has always maintained a rigidly centralized authority. The tradition has been carried over by the ruling elite even in post-independent Nepal. While doing so, they conveniently overlooked its incongruence with the emerging democratic political culture of the country. In fact, it acquired greater complexities. Granted that the ruling elite wanted to preserve their legacy of acquiring control over man and resources, but the moot point is, why and how could the tradition legitimize in the nation? Richard Burghart, in this regard points out that Hindu kingship was important as a way of constituting relations of intrinsic loyalty between a king and his subjects by virtue of their common religion bond. Furthermore, Hindu kingship enabled Nepal to claim a source of authority that was uniquely Nepalese.[17] Moreover, the source of tradition of centralized authority is traceable within the cultural setting of Nepal. The setting has been historically plagued by a peculiar authorization docility arising out of feudal Nepali tradition of subservience, hierarchization of the society, dependency, the joint family system, division of labour and other social control mechanism. It is not specific to Nepal only but is the general tendencies of all the Asian states. And Nepal's political and cultural history is impregnated with reference to sub-continental influences, which contributed to shaping their knowledge, beliefs and behaviours by means of centralization of power.

A purposive social, political transformation could have ended the rigid authoritarianism of the transitional society. But that precisely did not materialize during the Rana and Panchayat rules. Instead of catering to the exigencies of economic transformation and development, they chose to forestall it since their driving motive was the extraction of surpluses, levies etc. for benefiting the rulers and privileged classes. Even with the restoration of democracy, the process of transferring power to the people is incomplete. Democratic consolidation has not brought significant progress in transferring the authoritarian political practice to a democratic one in the mind of public. The government apparatus continues its tradition of centralization and remains far too remote from the people. The state is equated with central government and the central government with the executive. The executive in turn is no more than a few "like-minded" ministers and associates exercising power as the executive committee of the parliament. The government is often run without a democratic dispensation.

A political analyst recognizes the validity of this argument when he says that the centralization process no longer meets the needs of a diverse population. This is the reason; there is a high segmentation of the political culture and less differentiation of roles in Nepali politics. This segmentation is pervasive even at the micro-level where social pluralism has facilitated a greater scope for adversarial elite politics rather than govern ability.[18] Civil servants exercise their delegated authority, *Adhikar Pratyayojan,* in a chain of top-down hierarchy. Junior officials, therefore, do not feel strong enough to withstand pressures from the *Aadesh.* Command of ministry as a clear division of responsibilities does not exist. With each change of government which has happened so frequently, Civil Service Acts and Regulations continue to be bypassed while transferring and deputing civil servants. It has injected a culture of crisis of confidence among them resulting in increasing culture of indiscipline. Traditionalism, parochialism and patriarchalism revolving around the authoritarian culture are still the dominant trends in Nepali political culture. Political loyalties to family, cast/ethnic groups, region, religion and faction still remain exceedingly high hindering democratic consolidation.

A tradition that encourages accountability to upward *Adesh* (command of patrons) discourages the growth of vibrant, impartial and politically neutral bureaucracy capable of standing above caste, class and ethnic considerations which serve public interests. By adopting the highly authoritarian, particularistic, and inscriptive and patronage based political culture, Nepali political elites have weakened the process of democratic consolidation. So, Nepal has a political culture yoked with an unmodernized and authoritarian style. The political culture of this sort has led to a strange situation where power structure is democratic but power pattern offends all democratic norms. Thus, the traditional emphasis upon the authoritarian style has become difficult to support with democratic culture.

The legacy of the past authoritarian regime is the most difficult obstacle for a smooth democratization in Nepal. Especially in the field of public administration, a majority of high posts have been occupied by those who were socialized and trained by the previous authoritarian regime and, therefore, appear loyal to them rather than the democratic dispensation of today. The authoritarian culture based on hierarchical principles has made Nepali political culture a monologue, with no voice from below. It helped Nepali elites to inherit feudal features into their political culture. The feudal culture is, by nature, rigid in caste and class stratification as well as hereditary in the transmission of status and authority within a few social groups.

Even after the restoration of democracy the leaders of political parties who used to comment that the political opportunity was exploited only by a few caste groups, the same political culture rather more individualist in practice is being nurtured by the leaders. The political parties are more individual leader oriented than group or common objective oriented. Authoritarian nostalgia as conceived by the scholars as mentality rather than an ideology could conceivably pave the way for the slow death of a democratic regime, with the military or other authoritarian forces resuming power.[19] By 1990 at least two third wave democracies had reverted to authoritarian rule. The problems of consolidation could lead to further reversions in countries where the conditions for sustaining democracy were weak and during which most regime changes throughout the world were from democracy to authoritarianism. The weakness of democratic values among key elite group and the general public, economic crisis or collapse that intensified social conflict, the breakdown of law and order resulting from insurgency and the determination of conservative middle and upper class groups to exclude populist movements contribute to the causes of shifts from democratic to authoritarian political systems.[20] Yet sustained inability to provide welfare, prosperity, equity, justice, domestic order, or external security could over time undermine the legitimacy of even democratic governments. As the memories of authoritarian failures fade, an irritation with democratic failures is likely to increase.[21]

## Gender and Civic Culture

Gender is a key focus of the cultural structure in Nepal. Nepal's political culture remains dominated by male culture. While the constructions of gender and gender relations vary to some extent by age, life-cycle, related positions within the family, caste, ethnicity, class, region etc. patrilineality and partrilocality contribute to an extremely unequal level of life opportunities and attainments between men and women. The high ritual and other values attached to sons as against daughter pronounce emphasis on gender-specific socialization. The highly gender—segregated access to household productive resources, income, house-hold decision-making, schooling, paid-economic participation, unequal access to public decision-making structures and public facilities are the manifestations of disparity.

In the social system, however, the position of women exhibited a gap between theory and practice. Religion, tradition, culture, social norms and values that govern the communities and families are itself gender discriminatory. In spite of women's projection as the goddesses "*Durga*" and "*Kali*" as symbols of power and goddess "*Saraswati*" as a symbol of learning, religion treats woman inhumanely and derogatorily as non-human objects. Hindu scripture treats women as a source of power (*Sakti*). The spiritual reverence would always be commanded by the mothers, daughters, and sisters. But socially and legally they are not treated as equal to male members. This shows the culture of contradiction between religion and spiritual feelings and the practice.

Women of Nepal are subjected to work in a patrimonial model of society enshrined inequality. Such a situation unlocks special paradoxes. The subordinate status of females is in non-political and non-monetized spheres. The females are made committed to home and family life only. Consequently, women are found in an absolutely marginal position in the political and pubic spheres. In

Nepal, wives almost automatically share many important personal and social values of their husbands and agree on many questions. Logically enough, a woman's political identity is subsumed in that of the man. Women's access to knowledge, skill and independent political activity is limited. The result is the recharged domestic ideology of masculine privilege.

The Constitution of the kingdom of Nepal 1990 had made several provisions for the empowerment of women. For election to *Pratinidhi Sabha*, the lower house of Parliament, at least five percent of the seats should be allocated to women candidates by all parties. For the election of *Rastriya Sabha,* the Upper House of Parliament, three women must be elected by the *Pratividhi Sabha.* In spite of the constitutional provision the political parties have not done justice to the females. Three parliamentary elections have taken place after 1990. But none of the political parties nominated more than 5 percent female candidates provided by the constitution. The percentage of female MPs is even lower. Only twelve females have been elected in 1999, five more than in 1994 which hardly reflect genuine representation of participatory politics for women. It shows the new democratic system having a mandatory constitutional provision for at least five - percent women participation has not substantially improved the situation as compared to the previous regime. There are many male MPs who even openly reject the legal, social and economic equality of women. In the 60-seat National Assembly the member of female MPs rose from 5 to 9 in 1999, which was also still less than 10 percent?[22] The under representation of female in leadership position shows the continued culture of social disparity in the country's politics.

A sociological study has thus shown the great disparity existing between the male and female representational pattern in the Nepali politics. It states that under the party less Panchayat polity, for instance, in the 1981 elections, out of a total of 1,096 candidates, there were 34 female contestants in the fray which constituted 3.1 percent of the total, out of which only 2 (5.8 percent) got elected. That meant a mere 1.7 percent representation in the 112-member unicameral legislature. But that figure increased in 1986 elections as a total of 70 women candidates contested the polls 4.5 percent of the total contestants (1,548) but only two (2.6 percent) could win the election.[23]

Compared to the previous regime, the new democratic system having a mandatory constitutional provision for at least five percent women participation did not substantially improve the situation. Although at least five percent women should be enlisted as participants in all layers of elections, the political parties seem to make it more ritualistic by trying only to fulfill such a constitutional provision failing to encourage more women participation in all units- village, city/town and national parliament. The result is that, the leadership role of women is negligible, that contrasts with the spirit of the constitution. In the general elections of May 1991, out of 1,345 candidates for the House of Representatives (Lower House), only 79 candidates (5.87 percent) were female. The party wise break up of candidates was as follows: The Nepali Congress had 11 female candidates out of 193, CPN-UML had 9 out of 168, RPPs had 17 out of 301, Minor Left parties had 25 female out of 186 and others had 12 out of 348 candidates. Altogether only eight candidates could get into the House of Representatives, among who five were from the NC and three from the CPN-UML thus amounting to 3.9 percent. The National Assembly (Upper House), a house of 60 members, had three female members.[24]

***Women in Constituent Assembly (CA)***

Six major political parties and leaders of the Maoist movement brought an end to 10 years of armed conflict and committing themselves to a democratic process by signing a Comprehensive Peace Agreement (CPA). The CPA includes a commitment to June 2007 elections for a Constituent Assembly that should be elected through a mixed first-past-the-post (FPTP) and proportional system (PR) and be charged with deciding the future of the country. According to Election Commission (EC), 54 political parties had fielded a total of 6,000 candidates to contest the election. 335 seats were allotted under the (PR) Proportional Representation. The Election Commission had published a list of 3,131 candidates for FPTP electoral system from 54 political parties in which only 322 (or 10.28 percent) candidates were women. The Constituent Assembly had 32.8 percent women representatives which is a record high in any political institutions of Nepal. It means a considerable member of women from the grassroots have reached the constitution drafting body. May be they are not well educated but with their experiences and responsibilities, they understand well the real needs of the people at the grassroots, so can raise the voice of the people of the classes they represent.

### *First-Past-the Post (FPTP)*

In CA election, of the 30 female members who won the CA elections through the FPTP electoral system, 24 were from the CPN-Maoist Party; the highest among the parties that fielded female candidates. Two female candidates from the Nepali Congress and one from the CPN-UML had won the election under the direct system. They had fielded 42, 26 and 27 female candidates under the FPTP system respectively. Two female candidates of the Madhesi Janadhikar Forum and one from the Terai Madhes Loktantrik Party also won under the FPTP lot. They had fielded 3 and 4 female candidates respectively. Similarly, one female had been elected from the Terai Madhes Loktantrik Party.

### *Proportional Representation (PR) Based Electoral System*

Under the proportional system, the CPN-Maoist had provided the highest number of seats to women representatives. Out of the 100 members, 50 were women. Of these, 10 were from the Terai community, 14 from indigenous groups, 5 from the marginalized group, 5 from Terai indigenous groups, 2 from the backward group, while 14 were from other groups. Similarly, the Nepali Congress nominated 36 women out of the 73 seats that were allocated to it. Among the 36 women representatives, 10 were from the indigenous, 6 are Madhesis, 1 was a Madhesi Dalit, and 1 represents the community and 3 from the Terai indigenous groups. Similarly, 4 were Dalits backward community while 11 were from other groups. Out of the 67 seats, the CPN-UML nominated 35 women representatives. Among them, 8 were from the Madhesi community, 10 from the indigenous group, 3 were Dalits, 1 was a Madhesi Janajati, 1 was a Madhesi Dalit 1 came from the backward community while the remaining 11 were from other groups. Madhesi Janadhikar Forum nominated 11 women representatives out of the 22 seats allocated to it. Among them, 6 were Madhesis, 3 Madhesi Dalits and 2 from Madhesi Janajati group. Terai Madhes Loktantrik Party selected 3 women out of the 11 seats, and all the 3 women were from the Madhesi community. Similarly, Rastriya Prajatantra Party chose 3women out of the 6 seats allocated to the party. Among them, 1came from the indigenous group, 1 from the indigenous group of the Terai while 1represented another group. As the Interim Constitution of Nepal 2007 has the provision for 33 percent representation of women in all the state agencies, the Election Commission had made it mandatory for all the political parties to have 10.5 percent of women candidates for the direct election and 22.5 percent under the proportional representation in the CA. However, the NC had fielded only 9 percent women candidates for the direct election to the CA. The CPN-UML had fielded 10 percent and the CPN-Maoist 18 percent.

Despite concerns before the election that women members might not reach the 33 percent ratio stipulated by the Interim Constitution, 30 (12.5 percent) women won seats via the first-past-the post ballot. The proportional representation ballot allocated 161 (48.1 percent) seats for women and 6 (23.1 percent) were nominated making the total number 197 which is 32.8 percent of the 575 elected representatives although it was extremely hard for some sections of our patriarchal society to accept that women were on the frontline. This was a great accomplishment for all Nepali women says Sarala Lama of Sa-Shakti Nepal, a women's party that contested the election. In the CA, 73 women candidates were from the Communist Party of Nepal (Maoist), 39 from the Nepali Congress (NC), 36 from the Communist Party of Nepal-United Marxist Leninist (CPN-UML) and 13 from the Terai-based Madhesi Janadhikar Forum (MJF).

It is observed in this election that people voted for transformation. So it was not surprising that Maoist women had defeated veteran politicians like Chirianjibi Wagle and Bam Dev Gautam in constituencies like Gorkha-1 and Bardiya-1. It shows how Nepalis were desperate for change and was tired of the same old politicians in power. Voters across Nepal who wanted change made women win. It was the inability of the old and male politicians to not realize that brought about their downfall. Sarita Giri of Nepal Sadbhavana Party (Anandidebi) was to right observe that "women were elected because people trust them to be good leaders." In the same way, Maoist representative from Rolpa, Jayapuri Gharti Magar, beat her Nepali Congress counterpart by more than 22,000 votes. Magar says that "Constituent Assembly is special because groups- that have hitherto been oppressed are represented in CA." There was a time when only women from high caste could be MPs; the CA election changed that concept. It was up to the 197 women of various castes, groups, ethnicities in the CA to ensure that their rights would be protected.

This phenomenon can be observed as an impact of democratization on the political participation of women who control into the structures and processes of political direction. Although having 33 percent women in the assembly has been a great victory for them, the pressure of women is still scant. So they are demanding 50 percent representation. Sapana Pradhan Malla, who had been nominated by the UML to the CA, says that "a large number of women in the parliament will not really make a difference if women-friendly policies are not made. Our movement is not against men, it is against the oppressive behaviour of Nepali patriarchal society which may not change even if we have 300 women in the parliament." She says that "the women representatives and women's movement should not press for not just gender sensitive policies but also lobby so that they are actually implemented."

Importance of women's political participation in socio-political and economic development is not generally recognized by our patriarchal society. That is why they have to struggle for a longer period even to get 33 percent reservation. It is seen that women have low political status as compared to men. Low participation results from low socio-economic status stemming from social norms from a male–dominated socialization. But it is seen that although in the process of political socialization the opportunity to acquire knowledge of the political process is not readily available for Nepali women, they are developing in themselves a sense of self–awareness and national consciousness and accordingly claiming an equal status with men. A positive change is being developed in their behaviour and outlook. That is, there is a change in their political life style over periods of time.

There is an increased political awakening among women. They have pleaded that women should not merely be considered housewives and mothers but also citizens and active participants in the country's social, economic and political life. Today, women across Nepal are contributing to build New Nepal by participating actively in the constitution making process to ensure that the constitution not only promotes and protects gender equality but also enables them to achieve equality. We acknowledge the progress made so far. It is also to be recognized that there is still a long way to go to achieve true equality. It is true that the issue of gender is highlighted more by the Maoists than by other parties

The main reason for the low political participation of women in politics is the outcome of the patriarchal structure and ethos of the Nepali society. The conflicting interpretations of the women participation handed down to the present also put women at inferior category. The tradition and culture are against the active role of women, although no legal constraints are in existence for greater women participation. In a patriarchal and male-dominated society, the inadequate and unfair representation in politics has been a historical hard reality. So the principle of inequality exerts its influence in the society and socialization process. Although the

Nepali family system, the primary unit of socialization is moving forward as the wave of democracy swings across the global and carries the message of gender equality, women in Nepal substantially rank lower than men on all the indices of political attitudes and activities associated with the civic culture. Although, women make up more than fifty percent of Nepal's population, they do not have an adequate role in the political decision-making. Lack of education opportunities provided to women and mentality have worked as stumbling blocks for leadership of women. If democracy excludes half of human kind, the political culture is not a civic culture; so cannot be a democratic culture as it reverses the central focus of democracy.

Why is there such a discrimination and inequality between men and women? Why Nepali women are bound to suffer from the culture of domination, exploitation, suppression, subordination and silence by their men counterpart? This can in part be inequality by the differing socialization of men and women within the family, community and society, which is imprinted in religion and psyche. Women are less likely than men to participate in the family and at school. They are less likely to go on to higher education. When they enter the paid labours force, they are less likely to have higher status jobs and experience of work-place participation.

Social norms thus have put women in inferior position in many situations although the religious norms define women as pure forms that have to be protected from being defiled essentially restricting their independence. Biology is not and should not be the destiny. In practice the male– centered process of socialization such as conditioning, indoctrination and imitation under patriarchy continue to reproduce these ugly relationships between men and women that make belief that biology is the destiny in Nepal. Such a male centered biased and controlled process of socialization results in the homo-social reproduction of existing discriminatory and exploitative relationship between men and women. Gender–Sensitive Development Indexes (GDI) and Gender Report 1997 reveal that women's situation in Nepal is very frustrating. Both

GDI and Gender Empowerment Measure (GEM) value of Nepal are three times lower than that of the GDI for the developed/industrialized countries.[25] This is because woman and domestic sphere in Nepal are viewed as inferior to the male-dominated public world of civil society and its culture, property, social power, reason and freedom.

Women's civil position is inscriptive, defined by the natural particularity of being women. Patriarchal subordination is socially and legally upheld throughout civic life, in production and citizenship as well in the family. Thus to explore the subjection of women is also to explore the fraternity of men. These interrelated socialization processes have dominated Nepal's political culture since long. The imperfect socialization is a serious threat to national integration. So, when the balance of the civic culture is based on gender, the civic culture is a male culture. Women tend to be on the inactive side of the civic balance. When the civic culture remains imbalance in gender, it poses a problem. Obviously, active women are needed just as some active men are required, if there is to be a balanced civic culture. This is also reflected in Almond and Verba's analysis that competent, aware and active women seem to be an essential component of the civic culture.[26] The lack of congruence and coherence in socialization process has had a trend of masculine political culture, based on still a traditional early socialization process. So there is a constant place for particularism for diffuse identification and for attaching importance to gender and place of birth in Nepali political culture.

Nepal's civil society has been constructed through the exclusion of women, whereas a properly democratic society includes women not only as full citizen but also an active member. The most complex problem for political theory and practice is how the two bodies of human kind-feminine and masculine individuality can be fully incorporated into one political life by decreeing the level of the culture of discrimination, the culture of exclusion and the culture of imbalance.

## Education and Location

Formal education, the door to innovative ideas and actions is an important variable for political culture.[27] There is an urge of civic education worldwide. Civic education is a key to democracy. The primary concern of civic education is to create a vibrant civic culture committed to deepen democracy in public and private life to citizens. The three essential circles of civic education are: Socialization of people and making them aware of undertaking social responsibility. Humanization of citizens, so that they are capable of understanding the international obligations arising out of the nation's relation beyond borders and finally, continuous participation of citizens in the public or political life seeking social transformation. It is a process of transforming the subjects' *praja* into the citizens' *nagarika* and the citizens into a public *chetansil barga*. Only a strong civic sense among the people helps foster the base of nationalism, the ideology of the state and democracy.

The survey reports all over the world on education and democracy show that people with better education are more often able to understand and appreciate the complexities of politics. They have greater confidence in their ability to be effective citizens and as a result, they respond to political events more intelligently. In such a case, the average citizens develop subject-participant orientation, because they know that they must be active and are participant.

The concern is to focus on how educational system and location have been socializing the younger generation and political leaders prepare them for a homogenous political culture in the country. In a politically transitional country like Nepal, the role of political education in shaping the attitudes, behaviour and orientation of citizens and their leaders towards the values and institutions of democracy is highly significant. It helps the citizens learn the structure of government, the system, the input and output process, the feedback. It also helps the citizens learn the art of articulation, aggregation, communication of their interest and solve problems.

The crucial issue of political education is to train people, so that they can become conversant in the ideas and practice of citizenship, whereby political ideas and values of equality and participation are encouraged and citizens develop a sense of trust in their leaders. Hence, political education of young people and political leaders provides them with knowledge about the formation of political culture, their conception about their role in the polity and exercise of democratic liberties. It is the preparation of the people and leader for democratic citizenship.

The educational preparation of at least sizeable segments of a population is a basic factor in the modernization of political culture. As literacy spreads, an increasing specificity of orientation is likely to spread also. But illiteracy and ignorance offered a little opportunity to be so in Nepal. Nearly 80 percent of the population is functionally illiterate in Nepal, despite official claims that 40 percent Nepalese are literate.[28] Low educational attainment tends to constitute subject and parochial sub-culture, whereas the educated classes posses the key to political participation and involvement that is a participant culture. Illiteracy and cycle of poverty in Nepal are automatically concerned with the immediate problems of survival and adjustment. This is not surprising. Since people are poorly educated and often illiterate in Nepal, the combination of poverty and illiteracy have led people to think that their fate is responsible for their misfortune and accept their status in the society as predetermined by their *Karma*, with a belief that one has no control over the divine arrangement. The individuals are readily induced to accept powerful external forces as prime movers in the world.[29]

The culture of fatalism still exists in Nepal, which does not encourage people to work hard or to believe in self-promotion by means of personal industry. This kind of attitude has not only created a passive notion about the system but also has given chance to the exploiters in exploiting the natural apathy of the poor and illiterate. As a result, the culture of active participation of people in the political process in any form is unimaginable. Because an acceleration of the process of poverty, disease, ignorance, and a number of human induced misfortunes continue to overwhelm their socio-economic participation, security, national pride and self dignity. The precarious existence of the citizens has an effect exactly opposite to the one intended for the modern vision of democracy and human rights.

Educational institutions have been playing a critical role as a tool for political mobilization. With the dawn of democracy in Nepal, the importance of civic education has increased. Yet, there are no curricula or schools to teach people about the complexity of democracy, for example, infrastructure of democracy, its socialization pattern, rights and duties of citizens, role occupancy, and the process of democratic transfer of power. As a result, despite the proliferation of several educational institutions and universities, the Nepali educational system is wandering aimlessly. Political education in Nepal is not providing the young people and leader with knowledge about the formation of political culture, their conception about their role in the polity and exercise of democratic liberties. Without a wide spread system of education, the attitude towards the political system and the actors within it will continue to be based on parochial values and on perception of the nature of government born of centuries of maltreatment and exploitations. The result is slow and painful process of political and cultural modernization of the nation.

Modern education in Nepal began with the establishment of the first school in 1853 which was only for the members of the ruling families and their courtiers. Schooling for the general people began only after 1951 when a popular movement ended the autocratic Rana family regime and initiated a democratic system. In the past 50 years, there has been a dramatic expansion of education facilities in the country. As a result, adult literacy (age 15+) of the country was reported to be 48.2 percent (female: 34.6 percent, male: 62.2 percent) in the Population Census, 2001, up from about 5percent in 1952–54. Beginning from about 300 schools and two colleges with about 10,000 students in 1951, there now are 49,000 schools (including higher secondary), 415 colleges, nine universities, and two academies of higher studies. Altogether 7.2 million students are enrolled in those schools and colleges who are served by more than 222,000 teachers. Despite such examples of success, there are problems and challenges. Education management, quality, relevance, and access are some of the critical issues of education in Nepal. Societal disparities based on gender, ethnicity, location, economic class, etc. are yet to be eliminated. Resource crunch has always been a problem in education. These problems have made the goal of education for all a challenge for the country.[30] Although the total number of students in higher education of Tribhuvan University, Private colleges, Kathmandu University and Mahendra Sanskrit University combined as of 1997 are 133,680,[31] these institutions have not been able to induce the expected socialization of people making them aware of undertaking social responsibility.

The influence of partisan politics is increasing in the management of education, teaching, research and administration. The frequent changes of government have resulted in constant change in educational sector resulting in ambivalent and disrupted programming. The younger generation of thoughtful and responsible citizens in Nepal has been expressing their conscience through educational institutions. The college students both female/male get heavily involved in political activities. They are divided into several factors and are affiliated to one of the political parties or their sister organizations. They are funded and nurtured by the politicians. Each political party has its own student wing which is very active during the election period. In fact, most of today's political leaders once were the leaders of student wings. This means, they are indoctrinated by the political parties into their respective political ideologies and are engaged to pursue their political ambitions. Given below is list of some of the important political parties and their student wings active in defending their own political parties.

**Table 3.1: Political Party and Student Wing**

| *S.N.* | *Political Party* | *Student Wing* |
|---|---|---|
| 1. | Nepali Congress | *Nepali Vidyarthi Sangh* |
| 2. | CPN-UML | *Akhil Nepal Rastriya Swantantra Vidyarhti Union* |
| 3. | RPP | *Prajantantrik Vidyarthi Samuha* |
| 4. | NSP | *Nepal Sadvabana Vidyarthi Samuha* |
| 5. | UCPN-Maoist | *Akhil Nepal Rastriya Swatnatra Vidyarthi Union (Krantikari)* |

The student wings can be very useful in the socialization process if the political parties stop using them to fulfill the individual political leader's ambition. But this is not the culture going. The political leaders are often heard saying that educational institutions should be made zone of peace. However, the victims of their petty interest have been the students. The political leaders see no places other than the academic institutions for their dirty politics. Neither are they found striving to improve the ever deterioration quality of their own educational institutions nor are they concerned about the injustice meted out by the state to its people. So where are they heading? This has been a crucial question. They have become main flag bearers of the leaders of the political parties. Their colour is no more academic than of partisan politics. Since the country counts on the youths to take the country forward on the path of development and prosperity, playing with the future of students does not befit responsible politicians. It would be better if politics was kept away from the campuses and academic establishments and focus was laid on matters of academic nature, i.e. improving the quality of education and dealing with problems faced by students peculiar to them. So the FSU polls should be understood in the way that there are no winners or losers but a victory for all students. As such, the FSU should not be taken as a prestige issue by the leaders of the political parties.

The Free Students' Union (FSU) polls held on March 2009 were regarded by some as a popularity test for the various political parties after the historic elections to the Constitution Assembly in which the UCPN- Maoists had won the largest number of seats enabling it to lead the government. Politicians were seen directly involved in campaigning. It was observed that particular poll was much more politicized than in the past, as was evident during the campaigning.[32] The campaigns were so intense that ugly violence between rival student unions was witnessed and many students were injured and one killed, apart from resulting in the destruction of the property and infrastructure of the campuses.

Too much politics has also spoiled the careers and futures of hundreds and thousands of students because poor education has held them back in life's competition. The problem is also that the various student unions are wings of the political parties and many student leaders are building up their political careers there, with the ambition of going on to hold respectable party positions. That is why we see the same persons renewing their enrollments in the same level at TU for years on end, just to indulge in student politics.[33] It is time the student unions put politics on the back burner and rise up to mount pressure on the government, the political parties, the TU authorities and the teachers to improve the things soon. Political parties have also divided teachers and administrative staff along party lines which has resulted in the increasing undermine of their professionalism.

Another manifestation of the new political culture in Nepal is interference in the affairs of the students, who are weaned away from studies and other constructive activities in the name of electioneering. And, poor student leaders act as mere pawns in the hands of unscrupulous politicians and their cohorts. Instead of channelizing the dormant energies and talents of students towards nation building activities, these leaders turn them into anti-social elements. As a result, academic indiscipline is on the increase leading to a decline in the quality of secular and civic education.

Political education in Nepal has not been much effective in changing the citizen's parochial and subject status to a participant political culture even after so many years of experience with multi-party democracy. Nepali people are even unaware about how social dynamic affects the agencies and the actors of democracy, how economy, leadership and civil society are related to these processes and how particular political culture is needed for the democratic transformation. The world wide scenario tells us that the attitude of leaders is responsible in developing human resources required for country. Countries having educated political leaders always led the development of their country through the production of competent human resources.

An international research carried out by analyzing more than 30 years' data, whether the educational and professional background of political leaders matter, data was collected from 500 political leaders from 73 countries. A research article in the journal of Comparative Economics in 2009 concluded that leaders who were entrepreneurs, professional scientists and trained economists focused national education towards development reform orientation. Contrary to this, they also found that leaders who were just union executives in the past were impeding reforms. There is a significant implication of this result in Nepali society. It is a pity when former Prime Minister of Nepal and the leader of the biggest party UCPN-M Prachanda announced to transform the university into military barracks. All political leaders have the same syndrome like Prachanda regarding education and development of the country. This is not their fault, it is the fault of the kind of education they have had and the kind of capability they posses, says Wagly, the renowned educationist in Nepal.[34] He says "as members of the academia it is our duty to educate them and to warn them against such move in Nepal.[35] Nelson Mandela spoke of the centrality of education in recreating the nation in 1997 that, "our own reconstruction and development effort, the renaissance of the entire continent and our successful interaction in the global village depend largely on the process we make in educating our population." He realized the potential of educated youth in the country and reminded his country people that "the power of education extends beyond the development of skills we need for economic success." Moreover, he saw the importance of education in nation–building and reconciliation.

In 2006, then UN Secretary General Kofe Annan spoke of the role of education in reducing conflict and terrorism, stating "I believe, it is imperative to work on both fronts at once-seeking both to improve social and cultural understanding between peoples and at the same time to resolve political conflicts." "Any strategy to build bridges must depend heavily on education." It is imperative that our political leaders must prepare themselves to develop nation through education, transforming its human resources into competent technicians and scientists required for the 21st century, not by turning them into militants. Education in Nepal according to Dahal appears "de-contextualized" despite a number of reform initiatives. He further remarks that the negative impact of regular strikes and the lack of credibility in the examination system in the Tribhuvan University and its affiliated Colleges are increasingly losing relevance and led the upper class people including a majority of politicians, businessmen and civil servants to send their children abroad for higher education.[36]

Without the knowledge and wisdom of family tradition shaped by historical experience and national culture, does the style of education shaped in the image of alien culture help produce the citizen suitable to the national culture? In such a situation, education offers not secular consciousness but a false consciousness and a distancing from their indigenous social roots. There are others who think that once democratic culture is full-grown, the socialization process will catch up with the cultural possessions of the nation. There is a preformed connection between the content of education and political will formation for social change and national development. But the diverse school system in Nepal has resulted in sharp contrast between the socialization behaviours of the students of public and private schools in the country, as well as, those abroad concerning their civic sense and national responsibility.

Location plays an important role for civic education which is a key to democracy. As an urbanite, one should become a more frequent consumer of the mass media and should finally engage in more meaningful participation in the political process. So, the major factor strongly affecting Nepali political culture is the striking difference between the rural and urban area. People living in the urban areas have access to the better facilities in life. They get the privilege of education, employment, information, and communications. As a result their dependence on government grows and awareness of their political interest increase. The growth in awareness of self interest leads in turn to placing greater demands on government and to higher levels of popular political involvement and participation which ultimately leads them to expose a participant political culture. But in the case of Nepal out of total 18.5 million populations, 16.2 million (87.6 percent) are living in rural area while remaining 2.3 million (12.4 percent) are living in urban areas.[37]In the total population about 49.9 percent are male and 50.1 percent female. About 6.4 percent male and 6.0 percent female are living in urban centers, whereas, remaining 43.5 percent male and 44.1 percent female are in rural areas.[38] Household and community solidarities are vital forces in the villages and they carry with them a set of political attitudes and behaviour patterns which are concerning and traditional in tendency. The traditional forms of social organization have been less rapidly and extensively affected by the forces of modernization in these areas. The existing family system operating in relatively isolated agricultural communities furnished an environment favourable to the survival of the traditional social order and the complex of political attitudes associated with it. They do not even know the very existence of government. They have no idea what the government is.

Certainly, this is not the case in every part of the country but it is still so in many rural areas where there is no facility for transport and communication. The political importance of rural life is often highly exaggerated by the politicians especially at the time of election but their promises are immediately forgotten after election. The rural mass is very much ignorant who have not developed stake on democracy. This is because opportunities for involvement in most types of politically relevant organization, parties, labour unions, community action groups, etc. are also relatively more numerous in urban areas. The urban dweller is likely to be much better endowed with the opportunities and resources which translate into political involvement than in his rural counterpart.

Owing to the much greater visibility of political and governmental activities in urban areas, the urban dweller is better able to distinguish among political parties, governmental agencies and incumbents of certain political roles. The sense of political efficacy, image and evaluations of the government differ significantly. The nature of this sort of socialization makes duality of culture inevitable. As a result, the rural masses produce party functionaries while urban produce elites, the leaders, decision-makers and managers. So the image of the rural mass is not one of assertive discourse communicating with the urban elite in a dialogue of equals. The dimension of intellectual professionals and political classes remains to be participant while the bulk of the silent mass of the rural areas forms the sub and parochial political cultures respectively depending on civic capacities, knowledge and exposure.

Urbanization makes the individuals less parochial, lassitude to traditional institutions such as the family, villages, community and neighborhood. So being male of middle or upper-class background and residing in an urban area contribute powerfully to educational advantage in Nepal. The advantage has repercussions on political culture as the growing gap between rural and urban areas is becoming quite acute. The diverse system in Nepal has resulted in a sharp contrast between the socialization behaviour of the students of public and private schools in the country, as well as those trained abroad, concerning their civic sense and national responsibility. The cognitive gap that separates the urban from the rural students according to Dahal has produced a dualistic political culture. He further remarks that,

> on one side are modernizers, with their total belief in science, rationality and individualism. On the other are the defenders of the faith, nationalism and moral certainty of their stand. They mirror a divergent response to references regarding the principles and values of democracy. This has driven our socialization process into an imperfect track.[39]

The public educational institutions in which more than 70 percent of people are to be socialized, suffer from neglect, lack of equipment and enabling environment. On the other side, private ones are thriving, although they are beyond the reach of 70 percent of people, who live below the poverty lines. The social repercussion is that this has made the circulation of elites and social mobility difficult for the artisan and ethnic groups. As a result, the media, NGOs, Human Rights Organizations, Trade Unions, Women's Organization, Students Union, and Teachers' Union etc. are dominated by the traditionally privileged elite class.

Educational attainments have become a source of power to claim elite status in the society. The present dual system of education-private and public in schools, colleges and university is based on that economic model which does not reflect the bed rock beliefs and aspirations of the larger section of the society. As a result, the majority of the powerless citizen feels a loss of their civic power and increasingly question, whether their civic competence affects the functioning of government they elected. In such a situation, how do majority of the Nepali youths and actors socialized in public schools and colleges become a part of national culture? How do the rural youths feel that they have an equal opportunity to development as their urban counterpart? In circumstances of this sort, political culture arises out of incomplete and misdirected political socialization. It also disturbs the coherence of cultural norms and upsets the uniformity of political culture. James S. Coleman rightly argues that "right from the time of Plato and Aristotle, political philosophers affirmed that quality of school determines the quality of the state." In other words, "what you want in state you must put into the school."[40] Keeping this in mind, political parties and academicians should be able to bridge the gaps that exist between the public and private educational institutions through their political programmes. Educational system has to be so altered that every citizen fully recognizes her/his role in the total political system.

The orientation of every Nepali towards the polity is a product of one's whole life experience- the style of political socialization, traditional concept of legitimacy, the familial core of politics, gender, and authoritarian trend. Nepal's political culture thus has remained dominated by these factors. Since induction into the political culture is a psychological process, the political memories passed from generation to generation and the ways these memories are formed are crucial. The basic norms supplied by early socialization in family, educational institutions, continue to resemble values, beliefs and symbols appropriate to a more diffused parochial political culture. In a transitional culture like Nepal, it is essentially an unplanned and implicit process and there is no single set of accepted norms of political realities. So the democratic norms in Nepali society have been greatly diluted by the existence of an authoritarian, assertive allegiance and gender bias culture. In seeking the roots of political culture, one must look beyond the direct political experience of the individual.

## Culture of Black Science (*Tantrism*): Source of Power

The political structure and the system have been changing faster in Nepal over the last six decades. i.e. from Rana oligarchy to democracy (1846-1950), multiparty party efforts (1951-1960) to party less Panchayat system (1962-90), and constitutional monarchial system to republican set up. Famous playwright George Benard Shaw says in his *Play, Arms and Man* that,

> everything has its own rate of change. Fashions change more quickly than manners, manners more quickly than morals, morals more

quickly than passion and in general the conscious, reasonable, intellectual life more quickly than the instinctive, willful, affectionate one.[41]

Politics and governments change still faster than the political culture. In this juncture, Nepalis have to learn to shoulder responsibility, develop a culture to respect each other as equals and help bring about a change in their basic attitude and perception, so that they have an appreciation of the fact that things change only as a result of hard and determined individual action. All of these factors help to constitute a special feature of Nepal's political culture responsible for a culture with a parochial– subject orientation into existence.

Since Nepal's social and citizenry concept have been developed under feudalism, the political and social life has also been inspired by blind power rather than modern values, commitment, science and technology. It is true that a political leader cannot be different from his social surroundings. This is why even after the change of the political system through people's mandate, the political culture has not changed. Kinship and family structure have still remained core factors in Nepal's political culture that have remained prominent to occupy key positions even in Loktantrik Nepal. The recent democratic political structure that gives reflection of the past legacy has become even worse in sharing the power of resources among the ordinary people. It has not been able to dismantle the older social stratification, the traditional structures of power and authority. Despite the democratic constitution, Nepali political culture in the twenty first century still operates on the blank adherence to black science (*Tantrism),* as source of power handed down from religion (*dharma*) and custom.

The Nepali word for religion is *Dharma*, which means duty, ethics, morality, rule, merit and pious acts. But it is experienced and observed that Nepali leaders and masses are still used to strange and superstitious religious practices established over the centuries by religious usage without bothering to understand the philosophical aspects of the religious system. The tendency of Nepali traditions to overemphasize spiritual and magical concerns has not encouraged a rational confrontation of the worldly problems of time, space and matter. Because of such orientations of the people towards religion, Nepali people enjoy enormous authority and power in the name of religion. So such beliefs and faiths have become an indivisible aspect of Nepali political culture since long. Hinduism and Buddhism have made great integration or fusion with diverse local beliefs and faiths of the people practices in the land.

The tradition-oriented people of Nepal still are no longer in a mood to discard their own beliefs and faiths, which to some extent, are of amusing nature. The assimilation of these cults made both Hinduism and Buddhism to bring an offshoot known as *Tantrism* that gave rise to a religion of animistic nature practicing miracle and magic. The trend is to propitiate local divinities by offering food and sacrifices in the name of religion and utilize them for the sake of one's own benefit. It is widely experienced and observed as a custom among the ordinary people as well the leaders of Nepal that they still equate injustice with fate and show allegiance to God for good fortune by making lavish offering at holy shrines.

Even the most democratic leaders like Comrade Man Mohan Adhikari and Prime Minister Sher Bahadur Deuwa, Unified Maoists' Party Chief Pushpa Kamal Dahal 'Prachanda' have not been able to discard this trend. As regards such practices pursued on by the Communist Prime Minister Comrade Manmohan Adhikari, the *Saptahik Vimarsha* mentions:

It was a matter of Wednesday (31$^{st}$ November, 1994), when Man Mohan Adhikari, the leader of UML, was administrated oath of office as the Prime Minister of the Communist party. On that very night, when he was about to enter the Prime Minister's residence, he sacrificed a black goat at the poll of the residence where the flag had been hoisted. The blood of the sacrificed goat was sprinkled on every nook and corner of the residence and Adhikari entered into the residence by stepping on the blood with the conviction that it will make the Prime Minister bold and confident while running the country.[42]

Generally, communist leaders are not supposed to believe in religion and do not follow traditions and cultures based on religion. But worshipping a buffalo to appease the planets to ward off negative effects of *Shani* (the planet of bad luck), visiting a prophet, and announcing that religion and astrology has a scientific basis is a new dimension in communism in Nepal. When astrologers discovered scientific facts about the UCPN-Maoist Chairman, Pushpa Kamal Dahal Prachanda being under the negative influence of Saturn, buffalo worship by him has raised a lot of eyebrows in the country from academicians to the laymen. Prachanda is reported to worship buffalo as a symbol of planet Saturn in a ceremony at Chatara Sunsari along with Congress leaders Arjun Narshing KC and Sujata Koirala on February 12, 2010. The same leader writes in the *Nepali Times* on February 13, 2010 that:

> who had ordered his cadre to slaughter cows and forced people to eat beef during the conflict. He doesn't seem to see the irony in worshipping a buffalo now. Those who slaughtered cows were given a couple of thousand rupees and sent home. In the presence of their revered leaders, the combatants were declared disqualified in front of the Nepali people, political parties and the UN. It is because they survived the war. Had they been killed, they would have been declared great martyrs?

The *Nepali Times* also reports Senior Maoists leaders hobnobbing with many holy men lately: the high priest of Gorakhnath, Manakamana Mata, Pilot Baba, Yogi Kamalnayanacharya, Chandra Swami. If only Babaji and Swami Maharajas would indoctrinate the disqualified and qualified combatants, it would be a fusion of spiritualism and materialism assuring the great leap forward in the revolution.[43]

These are few among the series of the incidents that has raised a big question mark on the moral and beliefs of Maoist top leaders in Nepal who often self describe as the ideal change makers of the 21st century new democracy. Karl Marx said religion was the opiate of the masses. These are some of the glaring examples to show how the Maoists were inspired by Marx, but they forgot to take into account that there should be a different political system in a multi-lingual, multi-religious, multi-cultural and multi-ethnic country like Nepal.

It shows that people and leaders of Nepal are still used to black science fiction or black speculation fiction which is an umbrella term that covers an activity of using science, technology, and science fiction as means of exploring the black experience. The Nepali people are living in this way under the influence of the traditional local cult and superstitious beliefs as handed down to them by their forefathers. The crown and palace in Nepal enjoyed enormous authority in the name of religion. The reason behind it was that the Hindus served the king as the incarnation of Lord Vishnu, while the Buddhists referred him as the *Avalokijeshwara*, one who always looked for the deliverance of all the suffering beings, or *Bodhisatwa* (future Buddha). As regards the inheritance of this tradition and ethos, King Birendra had expressed the following words to an *American Weekly* in September 1973:

> In Nepal, the monarch and his subjects have been governed by *dharma*, a system drawn from the Hindu religion. The King cannot change this value system. Therefore, he too is governed by the ethical code. According to this code the King lives to protect the people, to dispense justice to them and punish the wrong doers. Indeed the king embodies the collective identity of the people and as desired by the people, it is he who grants and amends the constitution.[44]

In answer to a question, 'How do you feel about being looked upon as god? He further added,

> It is not a question of how I feel about it. These are local customs and traditions. This relates to our religious background. I have responsibility (under the *Vedic* scriptures) to protect the people against injustice. The concept of God is there among the people.[45]

Such religion propagating tradition was imposed for the first time in Nepal during king Jayasthiti Malla's period. It was consolidated further more by the Gorkha King, Prithvi Narayan Shah, after the conquest of the Kathmandu valley. The religion got deeply rooted in the kingdom after the unification of Nepal by his successors. The same trend was pursued by the Rana Prime Ministers too. The result was that the laws of the state were governed by Hindu scriptures and interpreted by the *Dharmadhikar* or *Rajguru* (royal priest). Nepal has been inheriting still now the same political culture in the name of religion and Nepali people are not yet free from feudalistic outlook. The activities spread in the name of religion too have left the most significant imprints in the mind and psyche of people. The new trend could not bring any new reformation in the traditional society as it helped to turn Nepal into a class ridden society, where the Brahmins and Kshattriyas overruled others. If it is making blind adherence to primitive and animistic beliefs, can the civic society with civic culture go with the democratic ideas like non discrimination and equality? The process of human development is fostering cultural changes toward greater individual autonomy, erosion of traditional religious values and beliefs opening the possibility of democratic political culture based on equality and justice.

One lives today in two such worlds at the same time, a world of ideas which we share with the rest of the civilized world, and another world of one's own which have been inherited from the past. As a consequence, while one believes in the progressive social principles, busy in introducing new reforms in the social structure, at the same time the other is making blind adherence to primitive and animistic beliefs. A stress is laid on personal liberty on one side but a passive tribute is being paid to astrology on the other with the belief that planetary influence determines the course of life and politics. How such practice still continues even among the Maoist supreme leaders of Nepal in the 21$^{st}$ century can be evidenced from the following efforts:

*Telegraph Nepal* reports that:

> astrologers have suggested the Unified Maoists' Party Chief Pushpa Kamal Dahal 'Prachanda' to move together in the future with his party's deputy, Dr. Babu Ram Bhattarai. The radical Communist Leader who arrived in Chatara of Sunsari District along with his

party leaders C.P. Gajurel and Hari Bol Gajurel, February 12, 2010, was suggested to forget his animosity with Dr. Bhattarai when he met with astrologer Swami Krishna Das Maharaj. In fact, after Prachanda made public that India had pushed Dr. Bhattarai's name as the country's next Prime Minister addressing a program in the capital, the two top Maoist leaders had not been in friendly relations. Dr. Bhattarai then refuted Prachanda's allegation by terming it a conspiracy hatched by the Royalists in the Maoists' camp against him. Prachanda also presented his Janma Kundali (*Vedic* Birth Chart) to the Swami ji. Another astrologer, Madhu Sudan Rijal told Prachanda that his Rashi (Zodiac) is being heavily influenced by negative effects of the Shani-the Saturn planet. He thus suggested the atheist communist leader to perform Griha Shanti Puja of Shani planet (worship of Saturn).It is believed in Hindu religion that worshipping Shani will ward off some doshas (negative effects).The astrologers were of the opinion that since the birth charts of Dr. Babu Ram and Prachanda showed good relations between the two personalities, it would be in the benefit of the nation that the two leaders unite. Then Prachanda was told to perform Griha Shanti Puja right at the venue. He was also told to chant some Vedic mantras…which he spelt out beamingly.[46]

*Jana Austha* weekly reported:

> Nepal's embattled king Gynendra, whose centuries-old dynasty faces its end within weeks, made a ritual animal sacrifice with a belief that the ritual worship increases the strength and power of the worshipper and saps the power of his foes. The 58-year-old king, known for his obsession with making sacrifices to propitiate the gods and consulting astrologers before undertaking any new venture, offered panchabali-five sacrifices to Kali, the Hindu goddess of power, in Kathmandu Dakshinkali temple.[47]

In the same way, while an emphasis is laid upon actions and effort, one talks of fate too and regard as destiny's puppets. Even when casteism is not to be believed, most of the social performances are based on caste *sanskars*. Likewise, it is preferred to follow ancient ceremonies for the marriage purpose, though believed in civil marriage. The acceptance of these contradictory ideas at the same time presents an atmosphere of vagueness to the worsening situation of Nepal. These are some of the glaring examples to show how Nepali political culture still operates within the twin-light zone of democratic governance and culture of Black Science (*Tantrism*) as source of power. Because of such culture, beliefs and superstitions towards power and politics, the rigid, ascribed, parochial culture have not come to be overridden by a set of codified and universalistic rules. The result is that the sentiments, attitudes and behaviours of the people and rulers instilled by various institutions of traditional society born of centuries deep and nourished in Nepali soil make economic, social, political and socialization process change extremely difficult.

The norms and values of a democratic society is that a responsible government seeks suggestion from the people rather than from astrologers and prophets. For internalizing universal norms and values, political socialization is the basic imperative. Our country needs nurturance of rational mind, which indeed is lacking due to lack of universalistic pattern of socialization, where power is thought to be derived still from *trantrism.* For such a rational strategy to emerge, the political culture has to be changed from superstitious traditional patronage-based to a modern civic one based on people's opinion, support and strength.

The need of the hour is to be aware of the contemporary realities of Nepal and then to give up much of what the forefathers held to be sacred and which by a curious process has been identified with Nepal itself. It is time to show that the politicians have learned the hard way and have grown in mind with a sense of responsibility and can be responsible. It cannot be believed that the new life in New Nepal can develop only by holding to encrusted tradition and by hugging with affection every relic of the past as being a part of Nepali culture. Social tradition representing custom and conventions is undoubtedly of immense value because it ensures continuity and carryover of national individuality. But if they become the cause of vague yearning of the undefined past by withdrawing unto ourselves from the better future to come, they are to be rooted out.

Nepal is making a momentous transition from a society which determined population by caste/ethnicity, region, gender, religion and black science to one that stresses reality, human dignity and equality as the main motto of New Nepal. So at this juncture, family, educational institutions, political parties, law, media as the major agents of political socialization have to play a duel role. They have to dissocialize women and men form old values, attitudes, knowledge, and information. Then, they must re socialize them, so that they emerge not as passive recipients but active participants shaping their own destinies given the opportunities open to them.

## NOTES

1. D. Kavanagh, *Political Science and Political Behaviour,* (London: Unwin Hyman, 1983), p. 49.
2. G.A. Almond and S. Verba, *The Civic Culture: Political Attitudes and Democracy in Five Nations,* (Princeton: Princeton University Press, 1963), p. 15.
3. Kavanagh, *op cit.*, f.n. No. 1, p. 49.
4. Ventura, R., "Family Political Socialization in Multiparty Systems," *Comparative Political Studies,* 34(6), 2001, pp. 666-691.
5. Green, D., Palmquist, B. and E. Schickler, *Partisan Hearts and Minds, Political Parties and the Social Identity of Voters,* (New Haven: Yale University Press, 2002), p. 46.
6. Barrington Moore, *Social Origins of Dictatorship and Democracy,* (Boston: Beacon Press, 1966), p. 60.
7. Kavanagh, *op cit.*, f.n. No. 1, p. 45.
8. Fred I. Green Stein, *Children and Politics,* (New Haven, Conn: Yale University Press, 1965), p. 81.
9. R. Indra, *Socio-cultural Basis of Value Development; Chapter in Education in Values-* A Source Book, (Kathmandu: NCERT, 1992), p. 13.
10. *UNICEF/Press Release/27-2000,* (New Delhi: 11th May 2000).
11. Herbert H. Hyman, "Political Socialization: A Study in the Psychology of Political Behaviour," (Glencoc: Free Press, 1959), quoted in *International Encyclopedia of the Social Sciences,* Vol.

II, (New York: The Macmillan Company and the Free Press, 1972), p. 220.

12. Rabindra Khanal, *Political Institutionalization and Political Culture in Nepal*, paper presented to National Seminar, organized by Department of Political Science, TU in corporation with FES, 1998, p. 8.
13. Rishikesh Shaha, *Nepali Politics: Retrospect and Prospect,* 11 ed., (Oxford: Oxford University Press, 1978), p. 28.
14. Krishna B. Bhattachan, "Nepal in 1993: Business as Usual," *Asian Survey,* Vol. 34, No. 2, (Berkeley: University of California Press, 1994), p. 88.
15. *Ibid,* p. 89.
16. Lok Raj Baral, "Political Culture and Political Process in Nepal," *Nepal: Perspectives on Continuity and Change,* K.P. Malla (ed.), (Kathmandu: CNAS, 1989), p. 330.
17. Richard Burghart, "The Political Culture of Panchayat Democracy," *Nepal in the Nineties*, Michel Hutt (ed.), (Oxford: Oxford University Press, 1993), p. 6.
18. Dev Raj Dahal, *The Challenges of Good Governance: Decentralization and Development in Nepal,* (Kathmandu: Centre for Governance and Development Studies, 1996), p. 32.
19. Guillermo O' Donnel, "Challenges to Democratization in Brazil," *World Policy Journal 5,* (Spring 1988), pp. 281-300.
20. Samuel P. Huntington, *The Third Wave: Democratization in the Late Twentieth Century*, (University of Oklahoma, Norman, 2010), pp. 290-91.
21. *Ibid,* p. 292.
22. INSEC Nepal, *Human Right Year Book,* (Kathmandu: Informal Sector Service Center, INSEC, 2000), p. 46.
23. Suresh C. Chalise, *Sociology of the Legislative Elite in A Developing Society,* (Kathmandu: Nepal Foundation for Advanced Studies, 1995), p. 60.
24. *Ibid,* p. 62.
25. Laxmi Keshari Manandhar and Krishna B. Bhattachan (eds.), *Gender and Democracy in Nepal,* (Kirtipur: Central Department of Home Science Women's Studies Program, 2001), p. 78.

26. Gabriel A. Almond and Sidney Verba, *The Civic Culture Revisited*, (USA: Sage Publication, 1989), p. 78.
27. Tirtha B. Shrestha, *Education Development, Population and Literacy, in Population Monograph of Nepal* by CBS, (Kathmandu: CBS, 1995), p. 375.
28. NESAC, *NEPAL: Human Development Report*, (Kathmandu: Nepal South Asia Centre-NESAC, 1998), p 13.
29. Dor Bahadur Bista, *Fatalism and Development: Nepal's Struggle for Modernization,* (Calcutta: Orient Longman, 1991), p. 77.
30. *http://en.wikipedia.org/wiki/Education_in_Nepal*
31. Central Bureau of Statistics/Nepal (CBS), *Population Census-1991,* Vol. 1, Part II, IV, VI, VII, VIII and IX, (Kathmandu: CBS, 1993).
32. *The Himalayan Times*, March 23, 2009.
33. *The Himalayan Times,* August, 2008.
34. Mana Prasad Wagly, "Political Leaders' Accountability in Education: What a Pity in Nepal," *The Himalayan Times*, (December 24, 2010).
35. *Ibid.*
36. Dev Raj Dahal, *Challenge to Good Governnamce in Nepal*, paper submitted to International Institute for Electoral and Democratic Assistance, (Stockholm: Sweden, Oct. 2, 1997), p. 48.
37. Central Bureau of Statistics /Nepal (CBS), *Population Census-1991* Vol. 1, Part 11, 1V, V1 V11, V111 and IX, (Kathmandu: CBS, 1993).
38. *Ibid.*
39. Dev Raj Dahal, "Political Socialization and Democracy in Nepal", Mohan P. *His Majesty King Birendra: Multi Dimensional Personality,* Lohani and Bikas Lohani (eds.), (Kathmandu: Silver Jubilee Celebrator Committee, 1997), pp. 38-45.
40. J.S. Coleman (eds.) *Educational and Political Development,* (Princeton: New Princeton University Press, 1968), p. 6.
41. George Bernard Shaw, *Arms and the Man,* (New Delhi: Orient Longman, 1979), quoted in Prem Sharma, "Changing Political Culture and its Impact on Nepalese Society", *Sangam Journal*, Vol. 1, Issue 1, (December 2009), p. 60.
42. *Saptahik Vimarsha*, (Kathmandu: December 2, 1994).
43. *http://www.nepalitimes.com.np/issue/2010/02/26/* from the Nepali Press/16841.

44. Quoted in S.D. Muni, *India and Nepal: A Changing Relationship*, (Delhi: Konark Publishers Pvt. Ltd., 1992), p. 18.
45. *Ibid*, p. 19.
46. *http://www.telegraphnepal.com/backup/telegraph/news_det.php?news_id=7171.*
47. *http://www.indianmuslims.info/book/export/html/348.*

# 4.

# Political Culture of Nepal: A Historical Perspective

> People without a past will be without a name and identity, a rope of sand. It makes a man think, feel and desire in forms that have prevailed in the human environment for centuries.[1]

> Culture, as immersed in our tradition, is in this sense dialectic between the classical and the folk, the past and present, the dead and the living. It is this gift to tradition which imparts a cultural continuity that enhances the possibilities of a better life on the criteria of a more meaningful and purposive living.[2]

Political culture is the product of many inter-related factors, traditional as well as modern elements. Changes in political culture come under the influence of these factors. A study of these factors is essential for an understanding of the political culture. History plays an important role in the making and evolution of political culture. Historical events always influence the shaping of political culture in a big way. In the case of British political culture, the signing of Magna Carta, 1215, Petition of Rights, 1628, and the 17th century struggle between the King and the Parliament over the issue of sovereignty, the Glorious Revolution of 1688 etc. have all played a deterministic role. Likewise, the American Declaration of Independence, the war of Independence and the civil war of mid 19th century exercised a big influence upon the American political culture. Indian political culture bears the influence of events of the freedom struggle and the contact with western civilization and culture. As such the political culture of each society is greatly influenced by the historical events. Knowledge about attitude and behaviour of the people towards political institution during different historical periods provides one with insight on the extent to which individuals are informed about political institutions and political processes. It also provides knowledge, whether people are reasonably satisfied or not with the efficacy of various institutions and processes. So a discussion of political culture of Nepal will not be clear until it is looked back into ancient period.

## Tradition of Civility: The Nepali Legacy

Nepal is perhaps the only great historical civilization that has maintained its cultural integrity without identifying itself with a particular political centre. The essential identity of Nepal has not been political but cultural. Nepalis have felt themselves to be Nepalis are not political but cultural. Civic life in Nepal had grown with the *vedic*[3] age (around 2000 BC), the age of knowledge and enlightenment. Nepal's history treasures the importance given by the society to civic institutions, knowledge, skills and spirits. Civic life with civic culture had grown with the *vedic* age when *dharma* (institutional duties and role), *shastras* (moral and legal treaties) and *shastartha* (philosophical discourses) shaped the cognition and character of the subjects and monarchs, defined the governing norms of the society and polity according to *barnashram dharma* and oriented them towards public welfare. The emergence of civil society is historically linked with the rise of the notion of public space, a space rationally governed by the interest of the public. During the age, the *rishis* and *munies* upheld the capacity for oversight of governance, performed the functions of interpreting *dharma* and *shastras* and instilled duties of monarch and subjects towards the promotion of collective good, such as virtuous conduct, promotion of *sanatan dharma* (eternal moral duty) and culture, loyalty to the state and attain the knowledge of the cosmic order.

The Hindu treatise *Bhagawad Gita* states that those who are actively engaged in the welfare of all beings attain the Brahman or *mokchha.* The Buddha's teachings of *Pancha Sheela* that evolved around 2,500 years ago laid down the five rules of life-refrain from killing, stealing, adultery, alcohol drinking and lies which corresponds to the great five sins of the Hindus. The Hindu-Buddhist religion that grew in the cultural repository of dharma emphasized the need to dissolve personal ego for enlightenment. Buddhist by *nirvana* from the wheel of existence-birth, disease, decay, old age death and Hindu by attaining Brahman or *mokchha,* both denote salvation of life. Both the religions claim that no one can attain salvation without performing virtuous and supreme conducts in his/her life. Each is based on the theory of *Karma*, denoting that good action lays positive results while bad action negative.

The *Karma* principle is based on the simple theory of cause and effect. Civic life of the then settlements also drew its legacy from Rajarshi Janak of Mithila whose scholarship and statecraft were primarily devoted to *dharma*-care, justice, and righteousness of all human beings. Lumbini in the southern part, Gandak region and Kathmandu valley in the north are often regarded as the cradle of Nepali civilization that emerged much earlier than the founding of the Lichchhvi state.[4] Several religious and social cults, including the *deos* cult, founded around temples and monasteries have formed a widely known public space for rational contest of ideas and action. Buddhists *bihars* (monasteries) and *sangha* (mass organization), Hindu temples, *gurukuls* (voluntary schools run by the community) and the *panchali pratha* (local arbitration system) were the fountains of reason, lore, culture and civilization. As these ambient factors were embedded in the cognition of citizens of those days, the socialization and acculturation process was spontaneous and sustainable. It made life flourish together with civility and civic culture in Nepal. This sort of civic life reflects the clue of liberal political culture. This indicates that the tradition of civility, civic life and civic culture that existed since time immemorial is not an alien concept in Nepal, rather the Nepali legacy.

## Pre-Rana Period (1769-1846 AD)

The political culture of people gives an orientation towards their polity and its operation procedures. Against this background, the chapter concentrates on the content and trend of Nepal's political culture during the pre-Rana period i.e., the ancient, medieval and modern period. It includes the Kirat, Licchavi, Malla and Shah Dynasties in general. Any political culture is highly influenced by traditions, socio-cultural values and beliefs of a society. It is safe to presume that the pre-Rana political culture was influenced by the traditions, socio-cultural values and beliefs of the society. The inter-play between the government and society helps in shaping the political culture of that period. The orientations towards the political institutions-monarchy, the divine character of the kingship, relationship between king and people, public opinion and participation and bureaucracy in general give the clue of political culture of pre-Rana period of Nepal.

Ancient Nepal has set a kind of standard in all spheres of life of the Nepalis, be it the political culture or social, religious, economic, or artistic standards. The pattern of life, their orientation towards socio-cultural values commenced by the Kirats, Licchavi is even today alive in Nepal. It is still influencing the life of the individuals and of the society with some changes only owing to the modernization of the country.

Paucity of sources comes in the way in dealing with the orientation and behaviour of the people towards their system, but the available sources, mainly the inscriptions and the chronicles give some glimpses of the past. The chronicles mention that the then Kathmandu Valley was a big lake from where water was drained by Manjusri. The chronicles trace the founder of Nepal as a sage or *Muni* named *Ne.* As the country was sustained by the sage *Ne,* it got the name Nepal. More reliable version about the nomenclature of Nepal is that the country got its name after the group of cowherds named *Nepa* i.e. area inhabited by *Nepa* people.

The successors of *Ne* were called *Gopalas* (Cowherd). This cowherd dynasty was followed by the rulers of *Mahispalas* (buffalo herds), also knows as *Abhiras* or *Ahirs.* Defeating the *Ahirs,* the Kirats appeared on the political horizon of Nepal, who ruled over Nepal for 32 generations i.e. about eight hundred years. But the evidence of recorded history of Nepal begins with Licchavi dynasty which coincided with the beginning of Christian era and ruled the country to 879 AD, known as Licchavi period.

Among the various other communities of the ancient Nepal, the Kirats were one of the prominent groups of people, who settled in the Kathmandu Valley and ruled Nepal from about 4th century BC. When the Kirat dynasty was defeated by the Licchavis, the Kirats fled towards the Kosi region in the eastern Nepal. The Kirats are still survived in eastern Nepal hills and are called the Rais and the Limbus. They developed a well-organized society and spread themselves in and around the valley with their own way of life and maintained their own language entirely different from Sanskrit. Moreover, they organized a well-developed social life, administrative system and the economy.[5] Shaha also mentions that the Kirats find their mention in the well-known Hindu epic of *Mahabharat,* as a hill tribe with a remarkable skill in archery and warfare.[6]

The concept of state and statesmanship was not developed, and people were socially and culturally disorganized and living neolithic pattern of life. However, Kirats are credited for converting ancient Nepal into a monarchical kingdom. Since then monarchy existed in Nepal till the unitary state transformed into a federal one with the abolition of monarchy following the success of the historic Jan Andolan II in April 2006.

*Kuthera Adhikaran* (an office dealing with the taxation), lingual (an office dealing with water supply for drinking and irrigation), *solla* or sulli (judicial office dealing with crimes) and *Mapchok* (an office dealing with divorce cases) were the Kirat legacy during the Licchavi period.[7] The peculiar culture of Kirat civil society was the equal status of people irrespective of caste and creed. Nowhere do we find the chronicles of Nepal mentioning the social stratification during that period as in the later periods. The society was not divided into class and castes. From this evidence it can be said that all enjoyed equal civic rights. As a consequence, this type of value orientation among the Kirats must have encouraged a liberal policy, which gives the flavour of what is called today the trend of democratic culture. This is in sharp contrast to the later periods which consciously lived on ethnic and cultural superiority based on Hindu religion. An equal civic footing of all the subjects respecting their just sentiments can be taken as the determining feature of Kirat political culture.

When the Licchavis, who are believed to have migrated to Nepal from Vaisali, North India succeeded the Kirats, the historic period began in Nepal. As they had been living under a confederation called *Vriji Sangh* with a republican form of government in India before their migration, by orientation and background, they had been republicans. But they adopted the local monarchical form of government with the king at the apex of entire politic– administrative system recasting their own political system to suit the local needs. The aboriginals of the land did not possess adequate political consciousness required for a republican system of government. Moreover, they had have feared that the adoption of political system unknown to the original people of the land would have created the bitter feeling of victors and vanquished. So they adopted the customs and tradition of the local people by assimilating with them. That value orientation proves that the ideal Licchavi rulers always thought and even vexed themselves with the thought of providing happiness and stability to the countrymen. They were more responsive than responsible in administration. It was that socio-political ethos which enabled them to wield power and wrest command in an alien setting. Supuspa, the founder ruler is mentioned to have ruled the country in a righteous ways according to *Aryamaryada*[8] as the state's policy and developed Hinduism through the implementation of *Varnavyastha.* The latter rulers like Amsuvarma, Shivadev and others took pride in their successful implementation of the principles of *Aryamaryada* based on Hinduism which was the basis of the socio-political culture of ancient Nepal. The culture of that period arose and proliferated on the foundations of *dharma* and the traditions thereof.[9] The age "saw spring time efflorescence in all spheres of life. It is on this account that it is commonly known as "the golden age" of Nepali history.

The medieval era had its beginning after the termination of the Licchavi rule in Nepal. The advent of the era is marked by the rule of a Thakuri dynasty. With the start of *Nepal Sambat* in AD 879, the medieval history of Nepal begins. Raghavadewa, who is given credit of initiating the *Nepal Sambat,* was the first king of the period. The absence of sufficient number of inscriptions has made it very difficult to give a clear picture of the political situation obtaining in that period. But still the available historical materials and the stray inscriptions found in temples, inns and water spouts, manuscript colophons and the chronicles such as *Gopalaraj Vamsavali* guide to the medieval history.

Among the various administrative cultures prevailing down from the ancient times, dual administration was one. That was called joint administrative system where the joint rule between the father and son, the brothers and nephews was likely. Whereas, in the monarchical system only one incumbent was entitled to the throne, administration was centralized. It appears, therefore that the political culture of the medieval period was dominated by joint rule or pluralistic rule. Because of joint rule, the political culture of medieval Nepal gives reflection of both positive as well as negative side. The strong sense of collective feeling and sharing of burdens of state affairs as one of the causes resulting in the strong entrenchment of joint rule give the positive picture of the then political culture. On the other side, the joint rule also sowed the seeds of dissension among the members of the ruling families, thereby weakening the political unity. Although the political fiber during the early part of medieval period was fragile, the kingdom of Nepal was not divided.

The advent of Jayasthiti Malla (1380 AD) marked the codification of a stable social life in Nepal which was defined by caste ordering. The Malla Kings had extensive interest in promoting literary societies constructing roads, arts and aesthetics, temples, *pati pauwas* (resting places), irrigation works public *dharas* (water sprouts) which provided a powerful spiritual basis for social and cultural sentiment. In the 12th century, the culture of Nepali politics took a new direction. The division of the center into three petty kingdoms viz. Bhaktapur, Kantipur and Lalitpur after the demise of King Yaksha Malla in 1482 weakened Nepal in regard to its position and strength in the first half of the medieval period. Though the center prospered economically and culturally, the culture of clash, attack and internal disputes with one another made them weaker from the military and security point of view. Because the rulers of the center had become weak, they simply paid attention to self-protection and seek help from the third kingdom. On the contrary, the newly established kingdoms like Khas Kingdom in the Karnali region, the Doya Kingdom of Tirhut in the Terai and Malla at the center were becoming stronger.

It was a tragedy for the later Malla rule that not a single king lineage in the political scenario to thread the divided kingdoms appeared again into one single state. The Malla kings are taken as the last rulers of medieval Nepal. Taking advantage of the culture of feud among these three kingdoms, the kingdom of Gorkha made many attacks to secure the coveted throne of Nepal. Although the attacks proved failure in the beginning, fortune favoured the king of Gorkha, Prithvi Narayan Shah in the year 1769 AD, when he could annex these kingdoms within the Gorkha state. He laid the foundation of greater Nepal, to say in other words, "Greater Gorkha".[10] After Prithivi Narayan Shah unified the country into a modern nation- state, Nepal in 1769, he articulated the pluralist social space of the nation– "Nepal *char jat chhatis barnako phulbari* ho," in his state- craft as imagined in his *dibya upadesh*. This marked the end of medieval period and the dawn of modern age which is also the starting point of Pre-Rana period (1769-1846 AD) in

Nepal's history. In this philosophy of governance he not only preached the highest standards of purity in life and private conduct but also accepted the cultural autonomy and ideas of all social and cultural organizations.

***People's Orientation towards Monarchy***

Placed at the apex of politico-administrative hierarchy of the country, the king during the Kirat and Licchavi Nepal was the source of all state power and controlled all socio-cultural affairs of the society as its religious leader, fusing political, religion and administration at his hand. King was the head of the executive, judiciary, legislative and military organs of the state. Based on Kingship, Malla polity in medieval Nepal had made him the fulcrum of entire politico-administrative system. During pre-Rana period too, king was the source of all power. Pre-Rana period was the government by the will of the monarch, the rule by '*Hukum*' or peremptory command. The political culture of that sort gives reflection of an intermittent political system. It had no set of roles, separation of power, and no specialized political structure which was specialized for political purpose. They were loosely articulated on with the other by bonds of mutual and moral obligation. It was a patrimonial system in which there was an administrative staff, specialized roles, but was directly controlled by the ruler.

In a modern civic sense the king could be regarded as a dictator exercising legislative, executive, judicial power. But in practice his dictatorship during that period was a benevolent one because it was dedicated to the welfare of the people. They did not tinker with the existing social beliefs, traditions and arrangements but set out to internalize their rule through symbolic gestures of tolerance and benevolence, the peculiar political culture upon which the system was founded. It was essentially rooted in the noble character of the rulers. With regard to it some evidences can be cited here. Licchavi king Amsuvarma considered promotion of people's welfare as his main duty. He said- "How will my people be happy?"[11] Narendra Dev had declared that people's welfare would be taken into consideration. They ruled the country in accordance with the laws based on the Hindu religious scriptures. The first instance of the promulgation of a written law annexed at the recommendation of the people or the prominent officials are found during the Licchavi period.[12]

We have an example of a Malla king undertaking a great risk for the welfare of his subjects. In 1657 AD, there was a great drought in the valley. Pratap Malla, the then king of Kantipur entered into Shantipur to bring out a book so that it would cause the rainfalls.[13] The king was fully aware that in case of his failure to protect the people there won't be any security in the life and properties of the subjects. Why have such orientation and attitude developed? That is because of traditions and ancestral edicts that deserved a great importance during the period and king could hardly go against that. Although he had the power to issue orders, changing an existing social customs, values, sentiments and beliefs prevailing in the society was not an easy job. Nowhere is that more true than in medieval Nepal where it was impossible to overestimate the force of traditions. Vaidya in this regard has rightly commented that: "... The kings and people of the Malla period were highly religious minded and God-fearing. So, they could not do anything against the religions and religious beliefs."[14]

A new dimension of Nepal's political culture appeared during pre-Rana period after Prithivi Narayan Shah and Pratap Singh Shah. The political fortune fluctuated widely from the culture of absolute authority to political impotency. King became simply cipher and real powers were exercised by queen mother, royal family members or by queen themselves[15] or by prime minister (entitled *Mukthiyar*-). [16] As they clashed with one another, the nobles also got divided into two parties to the support of their respective leaders. It ensured a frantic struggle for power among various factions of the nobility led mainly by the Pandes and Thapas. The culture of extra monarchial rule emerged not only because of the minority of the reigning monarch and his non-assertive and weak nature but also because of the traditionally power orientated attitude and behaviour of the people. The persons in power – King, Queen, Royal family member, Prime Minister would be praised and worshipped by the society, most of whom also made substantial contribution on the promotion of the national interest. But militarization in every sphere during the period had crippled down people's role in administration and polity; so turned the citizens into passive subjects.

***The Divine Right Theory***

Mass political socialization in Nepal is influenced more by the religious epics than by political literature. The great Hindu epics, *Ramayana* and *Mahabharat* are the sacred books, which inculcate Hindu political ideas among the people of Nepal. The *Ramayan* teaches the ideal of a king like Rama. The *Mahabharat* idealizes the institution of kingship as the upholder of righteousness. A late medieval treatise called *Sukraniti*, states that by virtue of his deeds in the previous life, the king is the ruler, protector and guardian of the people. Similar doctrinal precepts have been echoed in Kautilya's *Arthasastra* and *Bhagvat Geeta*, the classic Hindu treatises. These treaties provide with the religious and philosophical justification to hereditary monarchy of the Kshettriya lineage as having divine rights and duties.

In the past, the King had been the head of the state and government and exercised absolute power. Each ruling dynasty-Lichhavi,Malla and Shah-traced their origin to some form of divinity and used '*Deva*' at the end of their name to symbolize the divine inheritance. They claimed divine legitimacy to rule. The ruling monarch directly looked after law and order, justice, military affairs and finance.[17] The belief on divine right theory deeply embedded in the minds of kings as well as people received a wide acceptance in the period. Kings were taken to be divine incarnations and the representatives of God on Earth. The different inscriptions of the king represented them as *Indra, Parmeshor, and Narayana Vishnu. Mastya Purna* highlighted this aspect of the 'humanized' divinity when it stated that:

> The king becomes the sun among men when men no longer can gaze at him on account of his luster; he becomes *yama* in his behaviour while properly dealing with his friends and foes at the proper time; He resembles varuna when he punishes the offenders in the way in which they are bound with a noose by that deity; He symbolizes Fire in his mightily dealings with his wicked vassals and he assumes the behaviour of Earth when he supports all creatures and sustains them with affection and care.[18]

These different images as symbols essentially portray divine qualities in context with his different functions he has to perform as a king. This sentimental belief as the core of political culture prevailed during the period. Based on the hereditary principle of the law of primogeniture, the eldest son succeeded the monarch. The kingship was deeply ingrained with divine right theory. Despite the belief in divine right theory, the kings did not rule arbitrarily in an autocratic style but acted as benevolent ruler considering the protection of the life and property of people as his supreme duty. So divinity of king during the period could be justified on the trust and relationship between the king and subject which was high during the period on these grounds:

- There was the general prevalence of the religious belief that wisdom and religious devotion, not force were the qualities of a good monarch.
- A general religious belief that the king working in contradiction to the prevailing rules and customary law based on traditions, socio-cultural values and beliefs would be beset with ill – luck. These considerations discouraged monarch from exercising authority and power arbitrarily
- The divinity inherent in them endowed a consciousness that by striving to improve their own selves, they also improved the possibilities of their fruitful communion with God.
- Faith in the divine inspired them to embrace a certain kind of conduct all through their life stages, which resulted divinity. It is through that individual and collective ethics that social

conflicts were avoided and relationship harmonized between rulers and ruled.

Being highly religious, both king and people in pre-Rana period developed their attitude, behaviour and orientation under the general framework of the Hindu religion. Trust in monarch was a basic cultural belief. "The king can do no wrong," echoed that belief. The depth of that trust was evidenced by the maintenance of close and rapport relation between king and people as father and son. It was within that belief and norms, the culture of conflicts, confusions and crimes were very low. People became more disciplined and feared the curse of gods. In essence, there was an element of truth, justice and morality. It can be assumed that divinity within ruler and ruled had facilitated a better and well-meaning quest for self-realization and self awareness.

The quest for divinity must have got translated into civility in actual social pursuits around the formation of a civil society in the modern sense of the term. They wanted religion to be used for fostering community feeling and promoting service to humanity impartially. But it is because of such deep faith in divinity and religion that the administration was run on the basis of superstition and fatalism though in practice the rulers in general displayed their strong determination and breached their religious pledges to fulfill their political and administrative goals. Reflecting on the state affair in a somewhat fatalistic mood, King Pratap Singh Shah in a letter to his younger brother Bahadur Shah says: "…no one can play a decisive role except the God in the rise and fall of "*Dhungo*" (state) and its expansion and reduction. Everyone should act according to his own fate."[19]

The tradition of religious faith into social life also led to emerge the concept of the superiority of *Brahminism*. So Nepal then had what Sanwal calls "*Brahmanical* Political System" [20] Similarly some of the vital administrative activities– launching attacks on enemies, negotiations with foreign countries were initiated not only in accordance with the administrative and military feasibility and convenience but also in accordance with astrological formula.

***Relation between the Ruler and the Ruled***

Political culture embraces the political orientation of both rulers and ruled. In all polities there are rulers and ruled. The real problem in analyzing a political culture is to explain why one group of people (ruler) gives orders and others (ruled) obey. The inter-play between ruled and ruler helps in shaping the political culture of the period.

The Kirat religious text itself has prescribed that the people have to please the king; otherwise they should be treated just like slaves.[21] The ministers and the king probably made effort to work in a spirit of mutual co-operation and collaboration, thereby facilitating the day to day administration of the country because serious differences of opinion before the king and ministers were considered as unhealthy.[22] During the Licchavi period the relationship between the rulers and the ruled was good. Generally, the rulers had a feeling of public welfare. Amsuvarma's motive of administration was, *Katham Prajame Sukhita Bhavet"* (be the people happy). Similarly, the rulers of the medieval period had the same motive. An example of Mahendra Malla's edict can be cited here. According to which the king used to take his lunch and dinner only after the people had eaten their meals.[23] Likewise, Rama Shah, the Gorkha king used to watch from his palace, whether there was any house from where no smoke came out. If no smoke came out from any house, immediately the king used to send his men to make an enquiry, whether the householders had nothing to cook.[24] The most conspicuous illustration of such rapport and understanding is well reflected in Prithivi Naryan Shah's instruction "*praja mota bhaya durbar baliya rahanecha, rajako bhandar bhaneko raitanharu hoon*" (If the people are wealthy, the court becomes strong. The king's store is his people).[25] The emphasis was laid on the truthfulness and welfare of the inhabitants. These evidences consist of the administrative, moral, economic and social aspect, which give a lot of information about the government based on benevolent and paternal culture during the period. The relationship of that sort between ruling class and general people had consequently given the notion of political culture, which seeks to study and appraise individual and collective orientation to politics and functioning of political system. That made:

- The rulers and ruled, who lived a simple life intoxicated with truth indicate the vision of high ideals of life further contributed to socio-economic development with all possibilities of a healthy social development.
- The cultural, social, historic and psychological gaps between the two communities ruler and ruled were consciously bridged by the ruler and their paternal attitude towards the ruled.
- That could be achieved because the rulers were not self-aggrandizing in their pursuits but represented a transcendence of their personal and subjective motivations and preferences.

The relationship between King and people had always been harmonious in large part because people treated their king as a father who protected the interest of his children. In fact, the King was also often called 'father.' The father connection was an important one derived ultimately from the pervasive paternal dependency that so characterized political culture of the period. This harmonized and collective consciousness was created by common tradition, the growing supremacy of Sanskrit, the social pattern and the epic and *Puran* greatness that followed from the memory of the *Ramayan* and *Mahabharat.* The tenacity of this mentality and the traditional belief in the transcendent dignity and authority of the King had been preserved over the centuries in Nepal's political culture. The psychological roots of this attitude towards the authority lie of course in the religion, socialisation and culture.

***Perception, Participation and Public Opinion***

In medieval Nepal, many institutions like the council of the minister, various types of *Guthis, Praja Panch* and others, played a vital part putting limitations to the ruler's power. The council of ministers always checked the king from evil work that might harm the interest of the state. The ministerial council included members of all the existing social orders. Similarly, General

Assembly reflected an organized representation of the mind and will of the whole community. The net-work of various self-governing communal bodies and different levels of society made the social polity a complex and interactive system of self-determined and self-governing communal bodies. Some high level institutions-*Chumlung* (council of state) of the Kirats, *Antarasen* and *Parmasan* of the Licchavis, General Assembly of the Mallas and Assembly of *Bhardari* of nobles of pre-Rana period did exist during the entire period. *Tharghar* was another high-level institution that originated in the state of Gorkha. Serving as effective institution of decision making on some major national issues, these institutions also worked occasionally as deliberative organs of the state reflecting the views and opinions of the people. The state authority derived its legitimacy to supervise, support, coordinate and maintain the social order based on the value of *dharma.*

The local institutions *Praja Panchas* and *Guthis* had sufficient power to face the high handed orders of the higher authorities even the king. The *Gosthis* of the Licchavis period, (now called *Guthis*) took shape reflecting an element of continuity of social elements. The *guthis* of today demonstrated the resiliency of the *gosthis* of the Licchavi state and resembles the continuity of cultural consciousness and associational life of the Nepalis. It something gives the reflection of democratic culture. By definition, *Guthi* is a group of people in the form of a community founded on extended families, clans and lineage groups for the promotion of their general social, cultural and economic interests. It is sustained voluntarily not only for entertainment but also to stimulate collective consciousness of the people as well as deepen and enrich a person's connection with the society and the state. The Buddhists *suttas* situates individuals in the historical and social context and links their fate to the fate of the community. The people represented by such local bodies like *Praja Panchas* and *Guthis* used to express their opinion freely, which no ruler could even over look. The edicts of the Licchavi Kings "all the people from

Brahmin to the lowest ebb of an area" also give the reflection of a notion of inclusive culture in the modern sense of the term.

Unlike modern seminars conducted in private spheres, hotels and conference halls, restricted to professionals and experts, the discourses then were conducted in public places, opened to all and were autonomous of power considerations. Knowledge and information were public property. Several religious and social cults, founded around temples and monasteries have found a widely known public space for rational contest of ideas and action. Buddhist *bihars* (monasteries) and *Sangha* (mass organization), Hindu temples, *gurukuls* (voluntary schools run by the community) and the *Panchali Pratha* local arbitration system were the fountains of reason, lore, culture and civilization. The discourse was largely attached to the social context, oriented towards the functional needs of society and state was governed by the underlying practices. The disposition of power and knowledge constituted an inextricable harmony in human conduct.

How the political culture of the Malla period gives the reflection on the importance of public opinion and participation is illustrated by a contemporary account. In 1740 King Ranjeet Malla of Bhaktapur, faced a great crisis over the question of succession on account of his illegitimate sons and he was almost overthrown. Father Cassiano, who was then in Bhadgaon gives an eye-witness account of the whole event.

Cassiano writes,

> He (Ranjeet Malla) called a general council of his people on the 26th April, 1742. In the meeting they were to "freely express their feeling and give their opinion". All of them had their faces covered to have their identity and spoke in affected tone not to be recognized. Some scolded the king, even called his names; other threatened him with dire consequence and still a few more tendered what one would like to call a simple advice. [26]

After a long civil war King Sadasiva Malla was overthrown and his illegitimate brother Shiva Singh was enthroned. At the death of King Parthivendra Malla (poisoned to death), the whole peoples *gheroed* the *Hanumandhoka* royal palace and demanded the punishment to the culprit. These evidences prove that the people were quite active in Malla polity where the public opinion and participation were duly considered. If the king did anything wrong, the people and *pramans* (officials) brought that to notice. If the *pramans* (officials) ruled high handedly, both the king and people were to check them. In case the people transgressed the rules it was left to the king and the *pramans* to consider the case. Thus the culture of check and balance was strictly emphasized during Malla period.[27]

The general assembly in medieval period was an assembly of people of all *toles* (localities) of the kingdom in general and their representatives in particular. The participants in such meetings were free to criticize any one including the king in course of their expression of their reaction and opinions on the issues stated in the agenda for discussion. Such general assembly meetings which enabled the government to be acquainted with the public opinion on a particular state issue were in fact the medieval version of the modern referendum.

Civic life in Nepal has grown with the *Vedic* age when *dharma* (institutional duties and role), *Shastras* (moral and legal treaties) and *sastartha* (philosophical discourses) shaped the cognitions and character relationship of the subjects and monarchs, defined the governing norms of the society and polity according to *barnashram dharma* and oriented them towards public welfare. *Dharma* and *Shastras* instilled duties of monarch and subjects towards the promotion of collective good, such as virtuous conduct, promotion of *Sanatan dharma* (eternal moral duty) and culture of loyalty to the state.

Traditional Nepal was not devoid of politics, rather on many occasions it was more alive and more active to promote the culture of people oriented politics and administration. At that time, the state was accountable to the communities and people directly rather than to the bureaucracy, whereas these days, political parties subordinate national interest to their partisan interests contrary to rule of law and civilian supremacy. Although the nature, style, and objective distinguished traditional Nepali political culture from that of present, it had set a kind of standard in all spheres of life, be it the political culture.

## Rana Political Culture (1846-1951 AD)

The chapter deals with the Rana political culture with some positive and negative aspects also. In the previous chapter, it is found that the pre-Rana period political culture ultimately aimed at the good of the people and justified all political action towards that ideal. In that sense it was more modern and democratic as it encouraged genuine discussion and free exchange of the opinion between the ruler and subjects. It developed respect for the rule of law and public opinion through arguments and representations, discussions and demonstrations, deliberations and decisions. It upheld constitutional niceties and democratic norms.

### *Ultra-Machiavellian Framework: A- Moralistic Approach*

The mechanism through which the Ranas ruled Nepal (1846-1951 AD) for more than 104 years and the political and administrative culture which they established had a profound and enduring impact upon the country. In contrast to the pre-Rana period, the political culture of the Rana period could be styled as 'ultra-Machiavellianism'. They viewed the political activity more in ultra-Machiavellian framework or a-moralistic approach in which success needs no justification and power becomes the ultimate goal of politics. The principal actor (*Maharaja*) on the Nepali political stage at the time was generally guided by the essence of Machiavellian teaching than any religion that in politics the end always justifies the means. Whether, an action is good or evil can only be decided in the light of what it is intended to accomplish and, whether it successfully accomplishes it. The fact is that a man who wants to act virtuously in every way comes to grief among so many who are not virtuous. Therefore, if a prince wants to maintain his rule, he must learn how not to be virtuous, and to make use of this or not according to need.[28]

Rana political culture did not refrain from the above principle – the use of unscrupulous methods to secure personnel ends. Apart from the habitual use of deceit and treachery to gain selfish political ends, assassination, conspiracy, poisoning were employed for the purpose. On the whole characterized by extreme form of autocratic regime, Rana rule made king the nominal head of the state and tightly controlled the entire political culture. They treated state revenue as their own private purse. They successfully created an impression among the commoners that they were uncommonly superior to the masses and were born to rule over them and the people to be ruled. That tendency brought the entire socio-cultural life of the people at their own disposal. They not only controlled the entire political administration of the nation but also social values and behaviours of the people. They could change and modify social ways of the life of people at any time to suit their needs and upgrade and degrade the social status of the people. People were treated as the tenants or subjects; not as citizens. The Machiavellian style of ruling class is enough to give a clue of culture of politics of Rana period.

Rana rule for 104 years thrived on the ignorance of the people and selfishness of few families who were henchmen of the Ranas. Common man was not allowed to take any interest in the politics that had little interest in the affairs of the country, stepped in ignorance and poverty as he was.[29] Political culture during the period as manifested that psyche among the people; Rana cleverly took advantage of the situation by keeping the people at a low level of consciousness and based their system on an iron hierarchy whose fundamental political culture was dominated by an utter fear and systematic distrust. Neither people had influence on what government did nor did government activities have direct effect on his day-to-day life. Under such circumstances it was quite natural that political culture too was parochial which varied from class status. The attitude, norms and behaviour of ruler and ruled, therefore did not generally contribute to the growth and maintenance of a people oriented political system.

***Culture of Alienation***

Political participation and particular political activism were rigorously restricted to the Ranas only. Political involvement or action on the part of general public was very few. The most extreme attitude of a ruling culture is its unwillingness to share power with others. That tendency contributed to the growth of the culture of alienation. The subsequent normlessness of ruled alienated themselves from the rulers and vice versa. As a consequence, a big hiatus came to exist between the rulers and ruled. The masses were alienated towards governmental input, output and feedback activities of the system. The sense of alienation of the people automatically resulted into the lack of interest, hope and faith in the political system. There were no institutions to make the government responsive to the public. Instead, the masses were made to realize that they were the *praja* (subjects) only, who had no share in the making and running the governments. Rana oligarchy of Nepal had so much absolute control over life and property that a popular expression of the period runs as follows: "*Jiu Dhan Sarkar Kei*" or in other words "life and property belong to the government". So tight was the instrument of control that one got the feeling that not even leaves of trees dared to shake themselves without the command of the Rana Premiers. People had developed a subservient mentality that the Ranas were born to rule and the subjects were to be ruled, being unable to stand up for their rights. However, the Ranas on occasions acted responsively not because citizens were actively making demands, but because to keep them afar from becoming active. Political activity was rather remote from the main focus of ordinary citizens. Ranas felt that they had much to gain from an official policy of isolation. They believed that a closed society would be a politically stable society. Modernization of the country was anathema to them.

The majority of population had only a latent and marginal sense of their Nepaliness. The Ranas upto the time of Juddha Shamshers (1932-1945 AD) did not call the people as Nepalis. The then government orders referred the peoples as the Pahadis, Madhesiyas and Newars, those residing in mountain region, Terai and the Kathmandu valley. The kingdom was *Gorkharajya* and the people as *Gorkhalis.* The country was also referred as Pahad, Madhesh and Nepal Upatyaka (valley). It was Juddha Shamsher, who developed the sense of Nepalization by referring the state languages as Nepali, the people of whole kingdom of Nepal and the kingdom as Nepal.[30]

The basic thrust of that sort of political process of Rana Nepal embodied the concept of alienated political culture where the energetic and thrilling figure of Rana premier performed his function on his own conscience which was not responsible constitutionally as well as practically to the people. To a large extent, he remained isolated from the real condition and aspirations of his people. It shows that while his existence was generally known throughout the land, he had no meaningful relationship to the lives and aspiration of the average person. Political culture which resulted from such an experience was, of course markedly different from that of the pre-Rana period, where ruler and ruled had a father-son like relation.

### *Patron based Political Culture: Silent Mass outside the Government and Politics*

Rana premiers did not have faith in the efficacy of franchise, which they regarded as the source of great trouble in the country, where the masses were ignorant, credulous, and superstitious. An average man should not meddle with state affairs which were very intricate and technical was the basic principle of the ruling class. All these behavioural patterns of political actors suggest that absolutism which presupposed a centralized autocratic rule with full despotic and arbitrary power was the dominant feature of the Rana political culture. They maintained a rigidly centralized authority backed by steel frame of bureaucratic control for discovering any probable awareness about senselessness of the people's political subjugation. Absolutism not only determined the entire political articulation but also helped to shape the social, economic, intellectual milieu of the period. By adopting the highly authoritarian, absolute, particularistic, assertive and patron based political culture; the ruler had strengthened the process of anti-democratic sentiments. Such behaviours of the rulers give a picture of Rana political culture to be predominately parochial subject political culture with an unusually large obedient, ignorant and silent mass outside the government and politics. The culture of Rana rule engendered compulsory obedience but no effective sense of a right to or even a prospect of positive popular participation in the political system. Government, administration and politics were at the same time their prerogatives. The government functioned as an instrument to carry out the personal wishes and interest of the ruling Rana Prime Minister only. The main domestic pre-occupation was the exploitation of the country's resources in order to enhance the personal wealth of the Rana ruler and his family. As a system accountable neither to the king nor to the people, the Rana regime functioned as an autocratic system, divorced from the need of the people and even from the historical traditions of the country. No peaceful dissent or protest was possible and internal changes within the Rana system could take place only through internal coups and conspiracies. The system continued fundamentally unchanged, so far as its reliance on force and coercion was concerned until its overthrow in 1951. The few changes that occurred during more than hundred years were changes not in their aims and methods, but merely in leadership, the consequence of the endless struggle for power.

### *A Monopolistic Culture*

Ranarchy was characterized by a culture of closed system, patrimonial order, rigid caste system, hierarchy, traditional form of legitimacy, selective justice, a culture of *Chakari* (sycophancy) and the limitation of economic, political and administrative power monopoly within their own families. *Chakari,* not merit, was the path to power and a way to gain favour and reward from the patrons the rulers. The commoner received status by demonstrating their loyalty obedience, submission through *Chakari* (obsequitous attendance) to the rulers. The rulers in turn distributed *Jagir* (jobs), conducted *Pajani* (annual reshuffling of service personnel) and granted *Bakshis* (gift and reward), solely on their own discretion setting a new tradition of institutionalizing the culture of favouritism and nepotism in administration. That made family consideration and important element in the process of recruitment than the capacity of the individual to perform the job. Assertive principles and nepotistic norms together with narrow parochialism had replaced achievement or merit criteria. Blood lineage, family and kinship ties pre dominated the culture of politics during the time. The rulers' character got corrupted in the wake of the heightened inequities of wealth and dominance. That also degenerated the region and made subservient to the widespread inequality, exploitation, oppression and dominance. The monopolistic culture of Rana rule induced a monopolistic pattern to their politics.

During Rana period, the value of hierarchy appeared to be so absolutely fundamental to the political culture that it becomes difficult to conceive of how that system could significantly expand popular participation. Ranas had a markedly suppression and disruptive effect upon political attitudes of the general people. Under the system it was the primary obligation of the common people to support blindly the government which existed for the Rana family rather than for the people, where common man's well-being and social justice had not been promoted. The result was that people were demoralized by submitting to them and ineffective in opposing them. Rana rulers used to be agitated by any innovation that promoted mass culture. Though there was only one state owned newspaper, the *Gorkhapatra,* the radio channel as a media of communication was absent. That sort of absolute and arbitrary nature of the Rana political culture in the first half of the twentieth century prevented the political mobilization within the country. The system of governance based on the exclusion of illiterate mass automatically weakened the power of the public to aggregate, articulate and communicate their interest. That sort of political apathy among the mass was a useful safeguard for liberal political culture too.

## People's Assessment of the Regime

With regard to the positive scenario of the Rana political culture a good argument can be made that the Ranas were remarkably successful in maintaining the broadly defined and respected independence of Nepal, while preserving its cherished cultural and social values against insidious external influences then widely prevalent in India. They systematized full panoply of laws, the *Muluki Ain* (the Civil Code) in 1854, and amended and edited it at different times to regulate the behavior of people and dispense justice on the basis of caste order. They initiated social reforms in the governing institutions (especially the administration and the army), executed social reforms, abolition of the slavery system, the custom of *sati pratha* (widow burning, etc). To quote Rose and Scholz,

> ...the Ranas have usually been denounced as feudalistic, reactionary, and authoritarian by their many critics, but this is not a very fair assessment of their regime. Authoritarian it was, and blatantly exploitative, without any apologies. But the system was not feudalistic, at least in the European or Marxist definition of this term. Nor was it reactionary for its time — the Ranas probably introduced more programme of change, and with greater effect, that any Nepali government before or since. The real complaints, of course, are that the Ranas did not share the spoils with the other elite families on equitable basis and specifically rejected certain forms of economic development — e.g., industrialization — that might have benefited the general public. However, such changes, the Ranas feared, would expose Nepal to massive British and Indian penetration. The determination, with which the Ranas maintained Nepal's isolationist economic policy even at some cost to their familial interests, reflected the regime's extreme sensitivity to external force and influences that it could not easily control.[31]

The quotation suggests that Ranarchy brought enough stability in Nepali politics to sustain national independence and sovereignty. Generally, we have three generations living at the same time. The old generation has seen the Rana rule and feels that there was the existence of law and order in those days. People were more disciplined and feared the curse of gods and goddesses. The rate of crimes was very low and life and property were more secure in those days. As a result, the Rana rule was much better than today. The thinking of older generation clearly shows their attachment to the past notwithstanding the perversion of the Rana period. Although they did not see much the value of freedom, equality and democratic ideal they preferred the dead silence of that period in the name of discipline, obedience and morality. The people from their side always respected an element of truth, tolerance in the name of god. But it is not always true with the educated ones; because some of the educated men belonging even to the Rana family went against that system and worked for the introduction of the democracy. In one of the interviews, Diamond Sumsher Rana, a prominent Nepali Congress worker says that, he had fought against the Rana rule as an army officer at the cost of his life and he does not even regret for what he did even today.[32]

Indeed, it is not relevant to the traditional Nepali political culture in which the governing elite ignored the mass and the organs of the government were used largely for personal gain while the masses were exploited rather than benefited. A very few educated Nepalis in the then civil society formed in Nepal and by the Nepalis in India constituted a mobilized associational arena for the political position of Rana rule and for the creation of a competitive and participatory regime. During the anti-Rana movement, Madhav Raj Joshi founded the *Arya Samaj* (civic society or a society of noble people) in 1890s for the socio-religious enlightenment of the Nepalis from superstition, social prejudice and conservation thinking. It aimed to abolish discrimination against women, child labour, and child marriage and to legitimize widow marriage, initiate social reforms and lead the society on a rational course. Tulsi Mehar

Shrestha, Amar Raj Joshi and Bakpati Raj Joshi, Chakra Bahadur Amatya tried to revive *Samaj* (society) but could not. Sukra Raj Shastri and Ganga Lal Shrestha, Dharmabhakta Mathema and Dasarath Chanda began to arouse public consciousness through the explication of Hindu religious treatises and lift the veil of oppressive silence in the nation. But they all got grilled and later hanged to death. All these activities were carrying forward the demand for a political state in which free citizens would have the right to public office and participation in decision-making on the issues of public importance. The springs of indigenous knowledge thus formed the origins of rebellion. A number of literary societies were formed inside and outside the country for the inspiration of the interest of the citizens in public life and liberation of the oppressed. These societies were based on the approved knowledge of the period and, therefore, constituted an important device to rectify the deviant behaviour of rulers and subjects. In a sense, they tried to vitalize the relationship of the public to *dharma*-mediated knowledge for public awakening and action.

The *Sanskrit Pathasala* (school) students of Kathmandu in the name of *Jayatu Sanskritam* fluttered anti-Rana flags in 1947. The proponents of the movement wanted to modernize the syllabus of Sanskrit teaching by including history, politics, geography and other contemporary subjects, enlarge the scope of learning and animate the spirit of ethical life, political modernization, nationalism and general human welfare. Likewise, in 1947, a workers' strike broke out in Biratnagar with professional demands. As political parties were banned in the nation, they were operating from India, cohering their activities with the Indian nationalist movement to dislodge British rule from the sub-continent and to establish democracy in Nepal.

The incident of the book entitled *Makai ko kheti* (The cultivation of Maize) written by *Subba* Krishna Lal Adhikari is worth mentioning here. The book portrayed in a very ingenious way the nature of the Rana administration through a medium of satire. The policies and the personal life style of *Maharaja* came under bitter criticism. It was the outcome of the conspiratorial attitude of the courtiers in one hand and over suspicious feeling of the Ranas on the other. In the book the writer had written that the street dogs are more useful than the British lap dogs. The insects with the red hats are harmful to the plants. The above account was interpreted in another way. The British lap dogs were identified as the Britishers. Thus it was taken that the writer was opposed to the British. Similarly insects with red hats were also interpreted to refer to Prime Minister Chandra Shamsher who used to put on red cap. *Subba* Krishna Lal was sentenced for six years imprisonment on the charge of seditious writing. All the books except one were brought before the Premier at Singh Durbar and burnt. But since one copy could not be detected, the author was given a further three more years of punishment. Altogether 36 persons were rounded up in connection with the episode, many of them lost their jobs, seven of them were imprisoned from 7-15 days, and others had to pay a fine ranging from fifty to hundred rupees. Krishna Lal passed away before completing his fourth year of imprisonment at a youthful age of 36. A familiar poem *Pijarako Suga* (the bird in a cage) by the poet laureate, Lekh Nath Poudyal narrates the sad plight of a bird in a cage. In fact, the poet had described the condition of monarch and people, who like a bird inside the cage was totally kept in trouble and aloof from the polity and administration of the country. These evidences are enough to give the clue of the nature of Rana political culture.

The family reign depended essentially on a depoliticized genital population, the traditional army and external support. The greater demands for political freedom brought the downfall of more than a century old rule of Rana oligarchy in 1951 and multi-party polity was established in Nepal with the restoration of King's power. The political openness was allowed in 1951 with the abolition of hereditary premiership of the Ranas, who could never think that power divorced from morality is sure road to disaster instead of their orientation towards the realization of the eternal principles of justice and morality.

## Post-Democracy Period (1951-1961 AD) Political Culture

The attainment of political freedom did not bring any perceptible change in the old pattern of political life. Democracy served hardly anything since the majority of people were still living under a traditional bound feudal set up that prizes hereditary privileges rather than achievement orientation. Nepal had a modern political system defined by the Interim Constitution of Nepal Act 1951 and the Constitution of the Kingdom of Nepal 1959, which promised to make government collectively responsible to the popularly elected parliament.

Beneath the surface many traditional habits of mind and flawed practices continued to influence the culture of Nepali politics. None of the usual indicators of modernization were present in Nepal when the country broke from century old geographical and political insulation in 1951. Of a total population of over 9 million only 2 percent had received some kind of education to be called literate.[33] Industrialization amounted to be no more than handful factories in the Terai under the entrepreneurship of some businessmen. Communication and transport facilities were at a primitive stage of development. There was no increasing mobility of people in social vocational and geographical spheres. Modern versions of associations were virtually non-existent. The subsequent education of people to accept democracy through meaningful participation in their political affairs was minimal. Without wide public awareness and an effective public opinion, the political system gives birth to chaos and anarchy.

Nepalis in general behaved in the post-1950 revolution, what was their psychology, emotion and feeling has thus been supplemented in the lines of Malla:

> The post -1950 decade in Nepal is characterised in the first place, by a sense of release and emancipation of the intellect from a century - old political and priestly yoke, and in the second place, by an unprecedented expansion of intellectual and cultural opportunities. The decade can aptly be called a decade of introversion. For it was a

> decade of explosion of all manner of ideas. It was a decade when the pre-existing narrow stratum of the intelligentsia was fanatically and vocal socially, culturally and most important of all politically.[34]

It thoroughly exposed the socio -political attitudes of people as well as the political immaturities of the Nepali elites. They were critical of the then prevailing order, institutions, traditions and value systems. Malla further states that— "they woke up one fine morning from the sleep of the middle Ages and found themselves exposed to the neon lights of an electronic age."[35] These lines suggest that the system of socialization, outlook, and trend for centuries laid the foundation of political culture still unaffected by all waves of change in the Nepali mind.

The theory of political culture asserts that a sudden jump from one system to another does not necessarily make people to give up their past behaviour and attitude especially in a closed society like Nepal. It is so much imprinted in their psyche from centuries that even if they want to give it up, it is not that easy. Political culture which resulted from such an experience was of course limited, parochial dominated by century-old political socialization. Politics in the 1950 was marked by the dubious distinction of democracy and authoritarian, despite occasional rhetorical statements made for democratic rule. Political culture of the period was neither an evolution from the past nor a modification of the traditional political system.[36] Political culture resulting from such phenomenon proved obstructive to the growth of democratic and popular rule in the country. That is because the political culture in the post 1950 period manifested certain cognitive, emotional and behavioural psyche among the general public and elite. The chapter deserves to study people's orientation towards party, leader and system from three levels. They are:

***Cognitive Level***

The cognitive orientation implies the knowledge of political beliefs and objects towards the system. Education affects the level of democratic cognition. The more educated persons are, the more likely they will have the cognitive ability to understand what democracy means, to be aware of the political changes around them and their role in such changes. But at the cognitive level, there was wide spread of confusion among the political parties and public as to the meaning of political democracy during the period. The country had been opened, political freedom introduced and parliamentary democracy announced. But what did that mean in practical term? Who are we? What is our social ideal? What are we expecting with a population and political leaders with no prior experience? These questions hardly got any proper responses from the public and elites considered them to be serious threat to the new system. Rose and Joshi in this context give a picture of the period, which helps us to get the reflection of the level of the cognition of the period.

> ...there was a high degree of reutilization in Nepali social life and the transitional politics also easily acquired similar ritualistic aspects. The Nepali view of the world traditionally had been marked by an absence of causality, rationality and predictability, especially as it referred to the political and physical world. As corollaries to such a belief system elaborate rituals had role of astrologers as the most important technicians in the country had been institutionalised. ...[37]

In theory, however the political elites had accepted the concept of an egalitarian society which would breakdown artificial barriers of status, caste and other social inequalities and would emphasize personal achievements rather than connections as the basis for advancement. But the forces of tradition, individual's obligation, assertive consideration, ancestry and the connection of kingship dominated the culture of politics of that time. In the 1950s the modernization of Nepal had hardly begun. It was the revamping of a medieval, disease- ridden, illiterate poor and backward society. Political modernization in such a context meant a revolutionary change in the form and function of the government, directed towards the creation of a subject- participant culture.

In such a situation the very limited minority could not signify the growth of an effective agency to import political education to the masses. In the absence of such a class inter- communication among various groups, castes and communities, on the basis of new occupational pursuits had not yet taken place. The resulting phenomenon was that the organized social and cultural activities, which serve as means of introducing new ideas, remained largely unknown to the people.

Owing to the absence of a large-scale participation of the people in political movements and failure to reconstruct the country's basic economy on new lines, the traditional basis of Nepali society remained unchanged. The basic pattern of life remained more or less the same as in the past. The impact of new ideas was felt only by a handful of intelligentsia and middle class civil servant groups at Kathmandu, who hoped that they could build a new society from the top by achieving political power. The political culture resulting from such consideration could hardly get the status of a participant culture. The Brahmins and the priestly class who had been enjoying a higher social status began to fear that with the progressive flow of democratic consciousness they would lose their traditional social status. They were careful to hide their real intentions under the cover of religion and sacred customs. As a result, slogans of religion and caste entered politics.[38] During the election caste and religion became important factors to govern the patterns of success and failure of many candidates.

The pathetically limited education of the public and their simple peasant way of life prevented people from seeing and understanding the harsh reality of politics. The political propensities associated with education primarily cognitive in character including information, communication, confidence in understanding politics in one's ability was also virtually nil in the post democratic period. That sort of cognitive gap prevented them from knowing and understanding as a conscious citizen of their civil society.

### *Emotional Level*

At the emotional level, there was mounting frustration caused by the increasing awareness that the new political system was not the panacea that it had been claimed to be. The main task confronted Nepal's new rulers was to instill in the minds of the people an interest and willingness to accept the changes they had proposed to carry at the time of the movement. The democratic forces working in Nepal after the fall of Rana were too weak to bring any substantial change in the attitude and behaviour of the people. The traditions of autocracy and the control over the country's economy by the old ruling classes still remained hurdles in the way to the political system. As politics was rooted less on the grassroots and more on the clan of party personalities confined only to certain groups of people, the average citizen had neither the capacity nor the interest to steer the society in desirable direction. Their function in politics was limited to the mere selection of a ruling political class — the people remaining to be a mute audience unable to create their stake in the governance. From February 1951 to March 1955, King Tribhuvan and the political elites experimented with various governments- in the hope that the new political system would somehow be acculturated to Nepali conditions. But the governments formed during 1951-1959 AD were so enmeshed in interpersonal rivalries and preoccupied with problems relating to their survival that they ignored their national task orientation almost completely and registered their failure.

The atmosphere of frustration and cynicism ruled out the possibility of any rational, predictable and stable party politics which made the nature of transitional politics more personality centered than ever before. The crisis in Nepal's identity precipitated by such a revolutionary upheaval continues to affect deeply the individuals and social lives of the small band of Nepali elites. The period of transitional politics was thus a period of profound anxiety, uncertainty and tension in Nepal's public life. As a result, people in general failed to grasp the value of popular rule or democracy which the politicians professed to build.

***Behavioural Level***

At the behavioural level, according to Rose and Joshi, there was a bedlam of confusion resulting from the free-wheeling enactment of roles imported from abroad and imprecisely defined for the Nepali environment. Between 1951-1959 AD, there were too many parties. So there was an extensive subdivision and fragmentation of public life. Parties were not based on programme and policies but were of a personal nature. Owing to their selfish and individualistic outlook, they were divided among themselves and fragmented into innumerable political parties. As a result, ideological, attitudinal and behavioural confusion was that Nepali political elites became preoccupied with self-expression rather than with problem solving. The leaders fluctuated uneasily between feelings of omnipotence and impotence. They refused to bow to the discipline of facts and were more concerned with striking the appropriate pose than with carrying out a particular course of action. Every time there was a cabinet crisis, which made the political system operate in an irrational and unpredictable manner producing uncertainties in the process. The establishment of K.I. Singh's government in July 1957 and its dissolution three month later was the most striking evidence. The unhealthy culture of competition, in cooperation, low trust, suspicion among the political parties for power created a culture of intolerance and began looking upon the palace for political favours instead of going to the people. Thus the political culture was built upon low trust, confusion, and suspicion. Such political culture is always supposed to reflect a parochial sentiment.

Countries encounter undemocratic experiences in their transitions. During such period, the old system of working having been as strongly entranced as before and the new one not having taken its roots firmly, because of inexperience or unwillingness or lack of drive, the two systems- the old and the new are always in clash against each other. The political culture in the post 1950 period manifested that cognitive, emotional and behavioural psyche among the general people and elite. The political process, which was experimented in the post- movement period lacked deep political commitment of Nepali political elites. Second, the traditional political culture that always glorified authority was strong among political participants. The prevailing norm of the aspirants was to seek royal patronage rather than strive for a mass following. As a result, the ascendance of royal power with the steady decline of political parties as a countervailing force to the King changed the political balance. Now the King "embodies complete and awesome power" reminiscent of the state personified.[39] So preoccupied with both the process of consolidation of power and the popular demands for holding general election, King Mahendra awarded the constitution in his own terms. Consequently in 1959 political parties contested the first ever held parliamentary election on the basis of universal adult franchise. After 18 months, the parliamentary process had terminated by its own creator - the King- on the ground of its incompatibility with traditional ethos of Nepali society.

Dealing with the feeling, attitude and interest in political activities and participation of the general people, Shaha recounts the atmosphere of the post-democratic period in this way:

> ...it was certainly difficult to lay foundation of a democratic political system in Nepal. In a society which believed for centuries in the adage that none can defy royal commands and will of providence, it was not an easy task to establish in practical terms the supremacy of the popular will and rule of law within a period of eighteen months or even ten years. In a country where parents warned their children not to talk of politics and told that their tongues might be pulled out if they did so, it was certainly going to take a long time to inculcate in every person an interest in political matters. In an atmosphere in which every order given by the father is or any senior member of the family was habitually carried out blindly, it would have taken some time to make people assert their individual freedom and common sense. In a society ridden with fatalism as well as social and religious taboos, time was certainly needed to convince the people that a man can build his destiny and that of society through his own efforts. ...[40]

The above paraphrase acknowledges the fact that politics was not a matter of public concern that time. But it is not only the family atmosphere to be blamed for not making people psychologically and mentally prepared for political activities as Shaha says. Even the political behaviour of the political leaders was more responsible for the stagnancy in the society. All the leaders were of the idea "do what I say; do not do what I do." Owing to that patrimonial character, the leadership remained weak in developing democratic citizenship and civic culture. As such the general people were not psychologically and mentally prepared for it. The middle class, the great proponent of democracy was in embryo. For many of the ordinary people of Nepal, the institution of monarchy was easier to understand and was a much more comfortable form of Government that time. With regard to the political culture in the post-revolution period, Baral has remarked that-...elite orientations to representative democracy were at best spurious, and at worst negative. Such an abrupt change in 1951, without having a sustained mass movement, could end the family rule of the Ranas but not the deep rooted authoritarian culture of the past.[41]

What transpired in 1950, according to Rose and Scholz: "...was not a revolution but the beginning of a long gradual and continuing search for viable institutions and processes that met national requirements, while preserving the basic political culture that had evolved over centuries?"[42] It is observed that although a parliamentary constitution had been introduced in February 1959 replacing the constitution of 1951, still a constitutional culture which could hold and claim the deep allegiance and faith of people in democratic culture could not evolve.

**Panchayat Political Culture (1961-1990 AD)**

King Mahendra Bir Bikram Shah assumed emergency powers and dismissed the Nepali Congress government elected with a substantial majority only eighteen months earlier. Arguing that parliamentary democracy was alien to Nepali tradition and fundamentally unsuited for the development of the country, King Mahendra abrogated the parliamentary system and banned all political parties. A monocratic Panchayat system was innovated under the Constitution of 1962 in which sovereignty was vested in the king and powers of state were also enjoyed by the King. King Mahendra's proclamation, promulgating the Constitution of Nepal clears that the purported failure of parliamentary democracy was evaluated in terms of the crisis of nation-building, crisis that only Panchayat democracy could resolve.

> ...whereas, the parliamentary system could not prove suitable on account of the lack of education, and political consciousness to the desired extent and on account of its being out of step with the history and traditions of the country and wishes of the people, whereas, even the installation of the government elected by the people could not impart to the people a sense of participation in the administration.
>
> ...whereas, the country has experienced that the fulfillment of our aim, namely to conduct the administration of the country on the basis of popular consent and to achieve the real objective of democracy by associating the people to the maximum extent possible with the administrative systems, which is possible only through the medium of the Panchyat system which has its roots in the social of our country and is capable of growth and development is the climate prevailing in the country. ...[43]

The system supporters agreed with King Mahendra that the people of Nepal in the 1960s had not reached the level, where they were able to cope with a multiparty democracy. On the other hand, the 1962 Constitution had clearly modern intentions in its aim not to restore but to create by legal means a Nepalese Political Culture.[44] Although there had been many writers to claim the Panchayat system as a polity having its seeds rooted deep in the Nepali soil, a study of Nepali history does not prove this fact so clearly. In the words of Shaha... it is well high impossible to define the Panchayats in precise historical or political terms. Traditionally, after all, the Panchayat had been a council of elders drawn from a particular caste matters. Even if the Panchayat fulfilled certain political and administrative functions at particular times, they were never known to operate as regular units of village or local self-government.[45]

In the same way with regard to the little substantial evidence to corroborate Mahendra's claim Huntington's remarks deserves mention: "the charges that multiparty– politics had promoted conflict and economic instability were spurious. Such criticism of multi party system is really based on the impractical nature of democracy but is based on the failings of weak parties."[46] So, it is obvious that Panchayat system was the product of king Mahendra's own brain. While promulgating the Constitution of that polity, the king embarked upon erecting such a constitutional structure of which he could remain pivot. He put forward a vigorous plea that his democratic Panchayat system with its roots in the soil of the country was better suited to the socio-psychological climate of Nepal than parliamentary democracy, which was alien to its tradition and genius. Shaha makes it more clear that the real rational of the Panchayat system is politically personal rather than ideological or tradition. It is based on tutelary and teleological concept of democracy, which simply assumes that the Nepali people are not prepared to practice self-government. The source of all political authority, the king, has the role and ultimate responsibility to decide what is best for his subjects, politically and otherwise. [47]

With regard to this contradictory opinion towards the Panchayat system, Baral has commented that… the Panchayat political process is characterized by the configuration of elements either inherited from traditional and history or adopted as change and modernity. Nonetheless, the great impact of indigenous Nepali political culture which is predominantly 'subject' and authoritarian' is embedded in the Nepali political tradition.[48] Speaking on the constraints of history and tradition on Panchayat political process, Baral further comments that the post 1950 period popularly known as "democratic era" tried to inject a new political culture by innovating popular institutions of history and tradition. Consequently, the political culture of Nepal today manifests this trend. In the process, however, conflict between old and new values in also discerned despite the pervading subject culture.[49]

The political culture of Panchayat polity was permeated by product of a bureaucratic authoritarian political culture, which subsumed an ensemble of several features: relatively closed system, active monarch, dominants of bureaucrats, paternalistic planning, and controlled media, political exclusion of extra-constitutional forces, protective economy and depoliticization of citizen. This will be studied mainly on these headings.

***Orientation to Authority***

Agrawal has critically examined that "the 1962 Constitution concretized the political philosophy of king Mahendra, the innovator of the system who was itching since 1955 to introduce a political system, which could allow him to wield absolute power and enable him to consolidate his personal rule.[50] The words of Chaturbedi are similar with Agrawal that "the 1962 Constitution which stalled the process of parliamentary democracy and ushered in a Panchayat democracy system making the king the real and authoritarian ruler of the kingdom was the brain child of the king himself." [51] The words mentioned in the Constitution in this regard are... the sovereignty of Nepal is vested in His Majesty and all power-executive, legislative and judicial emanate from him. These powers are exercised by His Majesty through the organs established by or under this constitution and other laws for the time being in force keeping in view the interest and wishes of His Majesty's subjects according to the highest traditions of the Shah dynasty.[52] The Constitution of 1962 in this sense laid down the theoretical foundation of the palace authority under constitutional grab. It sought to vest in the king every set of political power that could be obtainable in a despotic order. The gift Constitution occupied only a secondary role before the power of the king. A study of provision No. 81. (1) and Provision No. 82 (5) of the Constitution is sure to enlighten it. The words mentioned in these provisions are: Provision No. 81 (1) if His Majesty is of the opinion that a grave emergency exists, whereby the security of the whole of Nepal or any part thereof is threatened by war, external aggression or internal disturbances,

His Majesty may by proclamation- suspend, except this Article, all or any of the Articles of this Constitution or any provision of such Articles: and assume to himself all or any of the powers vested in or exercisable by the National Panchayat or any other governmental body or authority."[53]

"Provision No. 82 (5)" Any amendment made by His Majesty by a proclamation under this Article shall form an integral part of this constitution.[54] The Constitution incorporated within its framework not merely encouraged the authoritarian rule of the palace but also curtailed the right of political associations which had been guaranteed by the Constitution of 1959 under fundamental rights. It also withdrew the provision for the establishment of a cabinet system of government making the chairman of council of ministers directly responsible to the palace rather than to the national legislature– the National Panchayat. The king's will was supreme and unchallenged under the Panchayat system. If a minister happened to be out of step with the royal will, he is dropped into political oblivion with little fuss or bothers since he no longer has a political party which serves as an independent source of political support able to take his care to the people. The evident shows that in the Panchayat period the culture of rationality of the polity was rooted into an ethics of personal authority of leaders and officials rather than the institutional culture, duties and roles. The habit of excessive obsession with authority spawned an inflexible attitude towards the citizens and citizen gave rise to atrophy as well as well-known imperfection in the system.

### Durbar *(Palace): Focal Point of Policy and Decisions*

If on one hand, this royal patronage and indulgence have provided stability to the Panchayat system containing the continued *panchas* infighting over the decades, on the other, the domination of a strong ruler over weak institutions and people developed a tendency to look upon the *Durbar* (palace) as the focal point of all policy decisions. The political participants too avoided any risk for taking major decision because as individuals they had a narrow popular base. In such context, the government existed for the King, Palace and elite rather than for the people or the masses. The organs of the government were used largely for personal gain and the masses were exploited rather than benefited. In the absence of an adequate level of social consciousness and opportunity for popular participation, the bureaucratic administrations, consisting entirely of the socially privileged elite cannot be trusted to discharge their duties with a sense of public accountability. So, the political culture of Panchayat polity appeared to be low on trust. Distrust was combined with a strong particularistic loyalty to produce a fragmented and hostile competitive political culture. The political culture of that nature caused people to become alienated from or hostile toward the primordial attachments that gave vitality to their parochial associations. An equal obstacle to development was the wide spread existence of an uncritical and children like trust in the ruler and in all forms of higher authority.

In circumstances of that sort where the king in Nepal performed his functions on his own conscience ascribed to him by religious, traditional and ritual practices, not responsible constitutionally and practically to the people as other elected heads of the government, can that be expected for a democratic culture with a participant nature? The centralized authority centered in the palace which exercised massive influence within the society dominated by absolute monarchy shows that Panchayat Nepal did not have a party less culture but something akin to a culture of one party system. The one party was that of the king.

### *Public Life: Reflection of Political Culture*

A glance at the public life gives a reflection of political culture of the Panchayat period. One of the most remarkable aspects of Panchayat culture was the role of the state in serving the public. In general cases, it is commonplace in the sociological literature to maintain that the modern state claims a monopoly in the legitimate use of force but in Nepal the state also claimed a monopoly in the legitimate expression of public service. The view is best illustrated in the lines of Burghart,

> Hardly, a day would go by without some member of the royal family or some cabinet minister being depicted in the government press opening a bridge, dam, school, hospital, seminar on national development etc. For example, the student union at one of the campuses of Tribhuvan University would organize a clean-up of the town. The students would meet inside the campus and go on procession throughout the town cleaning up rubbish from the roadside. The local police would then be in a quandary. Should they arrest the students, in which case they would say that the government is so opposed to public health that when a group of students decide to clean up the town they are arrested. Or should they not arrest the students, in which case the students would then say that the government is so negligent in its responsibility to maintain public health that honest citizens like themselves have to do the work instead. Interestingly, in such cases the police invariably arrested the students. The state preserved its privilege to serve the public. This service was carried out by the king, or persons acting in the name or with the authority of the king.[55]

As for other private institutions, literary societies, businessmen's clubs and so on, they were allowed to enter public space only with the prior authorization of the state. Every local meeting, publication and procession that was not sponsored by a state organization required government approval. The censorship was often severe but it must be stressed that state repression aimed not at the control of private minds but at the public expression of the private. During periods of social unrest, democratic activities were rarely arrested by local police so long as they remained in their homes; rather they were arrested as soon as they entered the public space of the market. Apart from these channels, the central authority had relatively little access to information about current relations. The king, though in a position of supreme power had thus been at the mercy of those who controlled the communication channels to him. To a large extent, he remained isolate from the real condition and aspirations of his people.

> The purpose of founding a government is to serve the people. To serve the people it is necessary to know the desires and ideas of the people. ...To know the thoughts of the people it is necessary to give them freedom of thought, freedom of speech, and freedom of press. A people oppressed by spying and police are a slave; one may not truly call it a people. If the oppression becomes excessive, an explosion is inevitable. It is necessary for the people to have the power with which to control the government and the services they desire, and the opportunity to define the conditions of administration. Freedom of thought, speech and press provide the means of gaining the opportunity.[56]

Such experiences were frequently practiced during Panchayat period. It was usually criticized on account of the limits it imposed on Nepali society. Personal and political freedom was, in fact, substantially restricted. The newspapers were considered by the government as private because they entered public space they were subject to censorship. By contrast, the public newspapers *Gorkhapatra* and the *Rising Nepal* merely announced the sort of information that was appropriate for a state which defined public order in terms of unity. They were read primarily for announcement of jobs, government tender and the like. For news, the intelligentsia read one or more private newspapers.[57] Since there was a risk of life if one were to involve in opposition politics during the Panchayat regime, it was understood that the family generally discouraged them for joining politics. It is, therefore interesting to note why the people generally prefer to keep their sons and daughters away from politics.

Yet, the developmental process involved a process of depoliticization of the masses, disqualification of indigenous knowledge and institutions and professionalization of those development practices possessing their own indicators of coherence identity and sense. That legacy still resonates today. The administration structure was built on hierarchical principles making administrator and managers accountable not to the people but to the system. The political capacity of the state rested on the concentration of resources at the disposal of the government and the central offices of the state administration. Political freedoms were restricted to such an extent that silence, the absence of political discourse was all too familiar and unswerving.

A very little space was left for associational life, the heart of democracy. Democratic communities require a public space–space unfettered by the state and market institutions– to forge solidarity with each other and work for social justices. Without that space, people's ability to overcome the problems of collective action remains unrealized. The Panchayat elites, bureaucracy, police were deeply suspicious of freedom of speech and organization outside their control that included just about any independent civic group.

Because Panchayat bureaucratic and political circles were pervaded by devotion to hierarchy, the traditional unquestioning submission to superiors, a product of the Hindu culture largely dominated the life of public as magnified by the legacy of the Rana period. The culture of that sort enervated the political system and bureaucracy subordinated looked to a *thulo manchhe,* literally a 'big man' for guidance and decision–making. Consequently, lower levels of the administration and the political system were sapped of initiative, as any item of substance was sent *maathi,* or upstairs', for the attention of a superior who, in turn sent in *maathi.* The practical result of constant referral to superiors was that the most senior levels of the bureaucracy were saturated with trivialities. It was absolutely essential to have the backing of a *thulo manche* in order to obtain a government appointment. Promotion was not a product of merit but connections which is why many levels of the state bureaucracy were staffed by a proportion of individuals whose qualifications for the job clearly did not include competence. *Chakari* was an essential element in that political culture and was associated with the cult of the *thulo manche.* The traditional Nepali Hindu institution *chakari* was important because it was the basic mechanism through which clientelism and patronage networks operated. It was through the culture of patronage networks that Nepal was governed.

Each individual, however lowly, sought a patron who because of their relatively higher status and position of authority would help the supplicant at some future unspecified date, perhaps by getting a relative a job or by intervening with the authorities over some official matter. In return for these favours the supplicant became the *thulo manche's* follower. The symbol of their relationship was *chakari* which is sometimes translated as fawning sycophancy but which is more accurately interpreted as a form of homage. Each day the *chakariwallah* pledged his loyalty to his patron by paying court to him. He always flattered his patron; sometimes he provided him with information and occasionally, in a symbolic demonstration of his dependency, he offered the *thulo manche* a gift. The political culture of *chakari* enforced a system of accountability upwards to higher bodies rather than to the people and constrained the secular acclimatization of public policies.

Conflict and factionalism were built into the very core of Nepal's political culture. The ties of *chakari* divided Nepali society into a complex hierarchy of patronage networks as each *thulo manche* had a *thulo manche* of his own. Moreover, as the status of a *thulo manche* was determined by the patronage at his disposal, it was in the interests of the *chakariwallah* to enhance the power and image of their own patron at the expense of his rivals. The lack of opportunity to acquire wealth and status outside the political system meant that corruption was unavoidable. Corruption became an emotive subject during the Panchayat years, especially amongst foreign observers who looked at the problems from a western perspective. In this context Louise makes clear that:

> In Nepal as in many Asian societies, a fine line was drawn between the truly corrupt and those who were perceived to be fulfilling personal obligations to family and friends. Nepotism and favouritism, which were inseparable from the system of *Chakari* were acceptable according to traditional political codes, because they operated as welfare mechanism. The important official who did not provide employment for his family, friends and supporters would not only have been unusual, he would have been considered socially

irresponsible. He had a moral duty to help provide for others, irrespective of their individual merits.[58]

He further remarks:

> Opportunities to indulge in corruption were seen as a perk of the job. To siphon off funds and materials from the bureaucracy and from aid projects was important for minor functionaries whose salaries were especially low. For those higher in the system it was part of acquisition and maintenance of power. It helped to underline the political and social status. It consolidated the elite's power because it gave them the ability to disburse patronage in a manner whose supporters for past allegiance and encouraged new ones in the attraction of rewards.[59]

What foreigners considered to be corruption was in the Nepali context deemed a practical way of making the system work. For example, in order to conduct official business and to deal with the labyrinthine administration, it was necessary to have an inside contact who would speed up lengthy procedures. That was known as having 'source force'. Cultivation of a relationship with officials in the administration was, therefore, not only useful but vital. Forward-thinking families involved in commerce or industry would even ensure that one of their male relatives pursued a career in the bureaucracy in order to provide the family with a fast track into the heart of the administration. Thus, the Panchayat culture was associated with an increased large-scale corruption. There emerges from this situation in which the mass political culture of Panchayat was dominated by hierarchy, by *chakari* and by corruption in a variety of guises.

The political culture of the Panchayat regime gave rise a situation in which the mass political culture of Panchayat was characterized by attitudes of habitual obedience and subjugation to duly constituted authority compounded with the sentiment that government is something that is done to the common people and largely at their expense by their socio political superiors. The result is which might be called a subject political culture. The evidence indicates that Panchayat system did not empower ordinary people or encourage them to play an active role in politics. The system was hostile to any kind of organization outside its control. The culture of popular participation in interest groups and community projects was formally discouraged and independent organizations were squeezed out of existence because they were seen to constitute an alternative source of power and focus of political action. That process had a profoundly detrimental effect upon the development of a democratic culture that is the theory of civic, participatory practice of the people and for the people.

***Attempts to Evoke Public Beliefs and Sentiments***

The Panchayat system, since its inception was taken as a dubious polity because of party less character. The people and political leaders assumed it as an undemocratic polity. They took but little interest in that system. It was natural for them not to prefer the system because they had lost opportunity to experience their own role in the decision making process which they had got under parliamentary system although for a brief period. "As a result the political system was opposed in general by those who thought it to have marred the opportunity of their role in decision -making process."[60] The political leaders who participated in that polity were very few and they too participated in only because of the high positions offered to them by the king. But when they found themselves thrown out from the power center, they too blamed the polity as most defective and prorogated for restoring political parties. To quote verma... the Panchayat system showed cracks quite early. Ironically, the eminent founding members of the system, when out of power, complained of the lack of enthusiasm of the people in the working of the government. The architects' of the system blamed it on its undemocratic ...[61] Being aware of all the weakness from the very beginning, he tried to evoke public sentiments towards the Panchayat by undertaking various measures.

The Panchayat system was based on different tires — the Village and Town Panchayats as the lowest, the district, *Rastriya Panchayat* (national Panchayat) at the highest. Elections to all of these tiers were indirectly held, but in Town and Village Panchayats the procedure was direct. Subsequently, however, local elections were held on the basis of adult franchisee making them livelier than others held for upper tiers. If members of District Panchayat were indirectly elected by the representatives of Village Panchayats within a district, the *Anchal Sabha* (Zone Assembly) that was formed by all executive members of district falling in a zone, constituted the Electoral College to elect members from various districts of the zone to the *Rastriya Panchayat* (RP). There were altogether 125 RP members representing the Panchayats (90), class Organization (15) graduates constituency (4), the royal nominees (16).

All Nepali with Bachelor degrees could participate in the Graduates' constituency elections. Being direct and representative in character, the conscious segment of Nepali society could articulate their grievances through these elections. Elections from Graduates constituency had almost invariably been characterized by anti-panchayat overtones and ideological encounters. Consequently, this constituency became an arena for openly raising basic issues affecting the 'Party less' system in 1975, the second amendment to the constitution of Nepal changed the election procedures abolishing the Graduate representation to the *Rastriya Panchayat*.

Institutions of public opinion were maintained but their powers were limited in scope, thus maintaining the institutional framework of political democracy. The power of initiating vested almost completely with the king. The RP had some constitutional functions e.g. the recommendation of Prime Minister and the making of laws but the king could veto the RP's decision. The contradiction lies here that the cabinet executed the royal directions and the centrally formulated policies but the cabinet could not take bold political initiatives without informing the king. All *panchas* had unquestionably accepted such an overriding role of the king which had shown a uniform political behaviour regarding their faith in the active royal leadership and "party less" nature of the system.[62]

The legislator was thoroughly deprived of any meaningful legislative authority. Opposition was outlawed. Free and fair elections were not held. Political parties were banned. Channels of communications were censored. In the absence of political parties, the bureaucratic class had a natural coalition with the *panchs*. It also monopolized the decision making process, although professional class organizations those dedicated to youth, women, peasants, ex–soldiers and workers groups were created. But it hardly encouraged people's participation in development. These organizations were not autonomous of the state power capable of free collective bargaining and negotiation. Quite contrary to that they were based on class co-ordination and were socialized and mobilized with a statist ideological orientation.

Characteristically, these organizations formed an intrinsic part of the Panchayat political culture what seemed to emerge in practice was thus an optical class society lacking sufficient dynamism and creativity. Although they were created to denounce the concept of class conflict in favour of class coordination, they were not representative but were client-oriented, the client being the government in the words of Shaha. He further remarked that…the members of the class organizations were not active at all and had not been able to develop ever the subject — participant orientation which characterizes the political culture of states, where a single party dominates the system. …[63] … despite the public claims advanced by these groups their motivations were deemed by the government to be founded in self — interest. Hence they remained as state private interest groups. …[64]

To inspire greater support for the system and to propagate its ideals, King Mahendra launched his 'Back to the Village National Campaign' (BVNC) programme in 1967. More accurately, the BVNC was designed to popularize the Panchayat order and to increase the authority of the monarchy. It no longer retained its capacity for system mobilization. So, the campaign was more ritual than device for system mobilization. Although it got the constitutional status after the second amendment in 1975, the achievements of the Panchayat system during king Mahendra's period was no doubt the political stability and growth of national sentiments. In spite of these achievements, the system could not march ahead towards the goal. The people did not find any miracle within their sight. National sentiments though aroused to a large extent, proved insufficient when realities of hard life were reasoned out. In 1979 responding to the two-month long student agitation and demands of the outlawed parties, king Birendra who himself called the agitation a "storm" put the entire political system on trial by ordering a national referendum in the country. The king gave two options to the people — continuation of the Panchayt system with reforms or multiparty system. Such a decision was interpreted as yet another move for defusing the immediate political crisis heightened by the student movement. Despite such contentious interpretations, the royal proclamation of May 24, 1979 and the freedom granted to the Nepalis afterwards were indeed of far-reaching consequences to the structure and function of the system. King Birendra declared:

> ... with the objective of clearly ascertaining what type of changes our countrymen desire in the context of the situation prevailing in the country today, and taking appropriate steps thereafter we hereby proclaim that arrangements will be made to hold a referendum by secret ballot of the entire Nepali people throughout the Kingdom of Nepal on the basis of adult franchise. Such a national referendum will be held on two basic questions: Should the existing Panchayat system be retained and gradually reform or should it be replaced by a multiparty system of government. ...[65]

The referendum result went in favour of the Panchayat system with reform by a narrow margin of 10 percent i.e. the Panchayat side got 55.3 percent as against 44.7 for the multiparty side but most political groups supporting multiparty during the referendum rejected the verdict, though the Nepali Congress leader, B.P. Koirala, who was all along championing such an exercise said that, he would accept the verdict however "unexpected" and "inexplicable" it might be. He added...the fundamental rights of the people are inalienable and cannot be taken away on any excuse, referendum or otherwise. The vote's case for the multi-party sides are votes committed to democracy. We will have to build our democratic strategy in the days on the basis of this committed support. ....[66]

Following referendum results, the King proclaimed third amendment in the Constitution. The amendment brought forth certain minor changes so that the Panchayat system may appear like a democratic system representing parliamentary democracy. After the third amendment, the general election was held in Nepal once more on the basis of adult franchise. The political parties already being banned, there were no organised political platforms, programmes and campaigns. The result was that the general election too could not generate enthusiasm and zeal among the people. In order to display their negative attitude towards the system, the people in the heart of the capital cast their sweeping vote in favour of an ignorant and illiterate woman, Nani Maiya Dahal. They sent her as their representative to the national legislature. It was the expression of deep dissatisfaction of the educated voters about the Panchayat system from the capital. The order given by the governing leaders to elect Mrs. Kamal Rana was ignored even by the soldiers in the barracks (where the polling booths were arranged).

During those days, the political situation was deteriorating. The corruption rampant within the Panchayat system caused the people to become deeply illusion with the then political system. A number of professional associations often collaborated with intelligence agencies of the government and went the anti-system against the system. The Panchayat's command over educational and media institutions, however, remained relationally relaxed and, therefore, they provided the critical breeding ground for political parties. The global wave of democratization helped the Nepalis to confront the realities of power and organizational control in 1990. And the success of the people's movement in 1990 helped to establish multi party democracy.

**People's Movements (Jan Andolan 1, 1990 and Jan Andolan 11, 2006)**

The transformation of party less politics to a multiparty system was the most striking phenomenon of 1990, which fundamentally changed the feature of Nepali political culture in three important ways:

- The power of the king was reduced to symbolism by limiting the monarchy to a figurehead and transferring the real power of the king to the people.
- Political parties were legally recognized to assume a political role in mobilizing electorate towards party programmes and policies and the elections would be competitively contested on the basis of adult franchise.
- The democratic rights of the people were guaranteed by the Constitutions-all being the source for the emergence of a modern legal rational state. The new democratic order which has emerged as a result of those major shifts calls for a change in the political behaviour of the citizenry.

Nepali politics was in a state of transitional stage. The initial transition phase backed by the spirit of the 1990 popular movements and restoration of multi-party system in April 1990, promulgation of a new constitution in November 1990, general election 1991 and local election 1992, was smooth in demolishing party less Panchayat structures and setting up democratic institutions. The stability of the obtaining democratic structure was ensured by the constitution providing for popular sovereignty, constitutional monarchy, multi-party parliamentary system, and fundamental rights of citizens. The avowed commitment to the fundamental principles of the constitution both by the rightist Rastriya Prajatantra Party (RPP) and several leftist splinter groups showed how the first phase of transition was successful in setting up democratic structure and in assimilating major ideological and political forces into the mainstream of parliamentary process. Unfortunately, the first phase of transition came to an abrupt end with the defeat of the ruling Nepali Congress (NC) in the 1994 mid-term election

Nepali politics had entered into the second phase of transition towards consolidating democracy. But contrary to expectations democracy in its functional attributes, overwhelmed by power centric intra-party and inter-party conflicts was widely eroding. It had manifested in the instability of the government since the emergence of a hung parliament after the 1994 mid-term election. In the last five years (November 1994-May 1999), Nepal had experienced 8 governments of different types and nature, chronologically: 1) Communist Party of Nepal, Unified Marxist-Leninist (UML)'s minority government (November 1994-September 1995), 2) NC led Centre-Right coalition government with RPP and Nepal Sadbhavana Party (NSP) (September 1995/March 1997), 3) RPP led Right-Left government with UML and NSP (March 1997-October 1997), 4) RPP led Right-Center government with NC and NSP (October 1997-April 1998), 5) NC's minority government (April-August 1998), 6) NC led Center-Left government with Communist Party of Nepal, Marxist-Leninist (ML), a new splinter party out of the UML, and NSP (August-December 1998), 7) NC's minority government (December 1998) and 8) NC led Centre-Left government with UML and NSP (December 1998-May 1999).

The frequent changes in the government proved the degenerating nature of Nepali politics transforming itself into nothing but a naked power struggle. Basically, the political culture after the restoration of democracy 1990 was directed towards the power centric intra-party conflicts, erosion in leadership quality, unhealthy inter-party competition, and instability of the government, pervasive corruption, mismanagement, irresponsibility and unaccountability in the public sphere. Deeply affected by the complex factors of political corruption, leadership crisis, excessive use of aberrant means in the game of government making and unmaking, de-professionalization, the whole state and governmental machinery had suffered from the culture of indiscipline, disorder, aberration and anarchy. In such a situation it is not, therefore, unnatural for the anti-systemic elements to mount challenges against the government that has flaunted democracy. In fact, the Maoists[67] problem in Nepal arises due to the sheer inefficiency and negligence both on the part of the political parties as well as the governments formed within the decade of democracy.

For the general public in Nepal, the Maoist was quite unknown entity until they burst into the scene in 1996. Among the problems facing Nepal in its democratic transition since over a decade after the success of the Jan Andolan in 1990, the Maoist insurgency started on February 13, 1996 from six districts- Rukum, Rolpa, Jajarkot, Salyan and Gorkha in western Nepal and Sindhuli in the east had spread in all 75 districts. Baburam Bhattarai (the leader of Maoist movement) presented the Nepali Congress-led coalition government of Sher Bahadur Deuba with a list of 40 demands related to "nationalism, democracy and livelihood."[68] Since then involving violence had become the most troubling one for the people and government in Nepal. The Maoists had defied the parliamentary democratic system by openly declaring that they were against the system. Their participation in the political process after the restoration of democracy in 1990 was limited only to the extent of exposing the parliamentary system. Indeed, they were the champions of the republican state for the realization of which they could go underground and launch violent revolution.

Political parties were never serious to face the challenges posed by the Maoists. The governments representing one or several political parties were immobilized by the burden of their own intra-party factionalism. It had happened even under the majority Nepali Congress government formed after the May 1999 elections to the parliament. The question how to deal with the Maoists had remained inconclusive in the parliament, parliamentary committees and the Home Ministry as the latter was responsible to impart the sense of public safety. Ironically, the government was still wrestling with the question whether the problems created by the Maoists were of terrorist nature or political one. Though the government had formed an Advisory Committee under the leadership of the Prime Minister

Sher Bahadur Deuba to study the nature of the problem. Instead, Deuba had asked Prime Minister Koirala to provide him with the required governmental mandate to negotiate with the Maoists with whom he was said to be in touch. Although the government had finally authorized Deuba to negotiate with the Maoists, the squabbles between Prime Minister Koirala and Deuba on the issue had glaringly revealed the inner party rivalries of the Nepali Congress. The result was that people killed in the Maoists insurgency had been increasing every month. Between February 1996 and September 2000, some 1,312 people had been killed.[69] The Maoist insurgency pushed the country into the vortex of civil war causing the huge loss of innocent lives and challenging seriously the very survival of nation-hood. The Maoists were taking full advantage of the prevailing confusion. The governmental failure in every aspect of public life simultaneously increased the distrust of the people. The Maoists were, therefore, counting every loss on the part of the government as their gain. The government insists that the security forces are making major gains. The truth is that at the rate of one thousand Nepalis killed every month, the only losers and the ones truly bereaved are the Nepali people. Violence, war revolution all may provoke changes in political values and beliefs with subsequent strains on the political system.

The question simply is: who dares own the Nepali people? Under such a precarious situation, the common mass was at predicament and was further bewildered with the ineffective retaliatory action on the part of the government. Will they create the trust for a peaceful resolution to the present crisis and pave the way for negotiating a future for Nepal in which they will be partners? An extension or re-imposition of the emergency could strengthen the hands of the forces of retrogression and status-quo. The six months long emergency had clearly shown that it was neither conducive nor desirable to a political resolution of the crisis. A democracy under sustained emergency can seal its own fate. Thus the normal democratic exercise was hampered and the country was bogged down in the vortex of violent conflict. This had enormous difficulties for the people, deepening uncertainty provoking outside interference, aggravating social and political contradictions in the society and economically damaging the country.

The 1990 Jan Andolan brought out one crucial dimension in the political culture of Nepal, i.e. palace versus people. Although the Constitution of the Kingdom of Nepal 1990 limited the role of the king as constitutional monarch in contrast to his active and assertive role as sovereign ruler in the past, some statements of support for the monarchy during the period could be cited -support for the monarchy had been a key plank in the Congress party programme: even the party's conference in February 1990, which was the prelude to the Jan Andolan, Ganesh Man Singh (Supreme Leader of Nepali Congress, Commander of the 1990 mass movement) had declared that "abolition of the monarchy is tantamount to the end of democracy in Nepal."[70] An event of Gorkha district may be cited here in this connection. On 31st October, 1998, The Rastravadi Samuha, Gorkha (National Group of Gorkha), organised a public meeting at Gorkha Bazar. In the meeting, the *Samuha* (group of people) emphasised for an active role of the king expressing like: After the introduction of democracy, the people are being forced to suffer from price-rise, corruption, oppression, terrorism and other problems. Leaders and ministers are utilising democracy as a means of accumulating black money. As such, the active leadership of the king has become indispensable. [71] Similarly, processions were organised at Nepalgunj and Birgunj asking the king to come to the forefront for saving the nation.

The Nepali people in lieu of expressing resentment for such a move kept themselves mum. Thus, they expressed their displeasure towards the political leaders and the multi-party democracy too, because of their failure to launch programmes for delivering them from day to day trifles.[72] The UML General Secretary, Madhav Kr. Nepal had also expressed that- "The king who is the protector of the interest of the whole Nepalese people, rather than of any particular group or country, is never involved in any controversy.

... Everybody should make effort to enhance the glory of the constitutional monarchy."[73] In the same way Nepali Congress President and former Prime Minister Girija Prasad Koirala quoted in the *Kathmandu Post*, "If the present politicians realised that monarchy is deeply rooted in Nepali society they could perhaps make some progress themselves. Those who oppose the monarchy will be opposed by the soil."[74]

These statements of support for the monarchy were, of course, put forward for tactical reasons rather than out of conviction. A peep into above mentioned supports revealed how the king although transformed into a constitutional monarchy had been praised for accepting the role of constitutional monarch with such good humour. The queues of supplicants waiting outside the palace gates to be given *tikka* by the king had begun to grow again. The pictures of king Birendra and Queen Aishwarya were once again garlanded with flowers and silk scarves, which after the Jan Andolan they had either been removed or were turned to face the walls. The newspapers once again carried reverential stories about the royal family and even ostensibly progressive journals produced supplements on the auspicious birthdays of the king and queen. All the evidences indicated that king Birendra had abided by the democratic constitution most sincerely. The monarch played a part in the creation and maintenance of moral consensus as the successive polls had demonstrated that the public not only reacted positively to the monarch but still considered as the man of integrity and symbol of unity.

### *Jan Andolan II (2006): State Transformation*

The death of entire family of King Birendra and his heir - apparent, Dipendra, on the fateful night of June 1, 2001 shoot-out mark the tragic end of an era of direct succession of kingship established by the founder of Modern Nepal, King Prithivi Narayan Shah in the beginning of the $18^{th}$ century. King Gyanendra who had succeeded to the throne after the Royal massacre dismissed the elected Prime minister, and subsequently took over the state power on February 1, 2005. He declared a state of emergency and imprisoned political leaders. The King's action once again resulted in setting back the democratic process. There had been no parliament at least for five years and no local political bodies since their five year term expired in June 2002.In the absence of representative institutions, democracy and development activities remained in limbo. The Royal actions contributed to the culture of polarization of the political forces pushing the parliamentary parties and the Maoists in one side against the King. Following three and half years of derailed democracy, a new government of the Seven Party Alliance (SPA) was placed and parliament was reinstated through a popular movement jointly launched by the parliamentary political forces and the Maoists, after they signed a 12- point agreements in Delhi in November 2005.[75] In 1990, the Nepali people launched a movement against the established ethos of absolute monarchical rule. The consequences of the movement were a mixture of the old and new. The old values prevailed for some time when political parties once again failed to give democracy a fair trial by taking the steps towards institutionalized democracy. Again monarch became ambitious for almost discarding the multi party system in 2005 but to which the Nepali people opposed by making yet another decisive movement for finishing off monarchy itself.

That no fundamental change had been effected after the success of the first People's Movement, time was ripe for the second Jan Andolan that finally saw the monarchy making way for the people's sway. It might also be euphoric to recall the people's participation for making the April revolution successful beyond all dreams. Yet, even when the monarchy was ousted, the vestiges have still remained in many spheres of life the obvious reason for this to be evident is the apparent failure of the political leaders to take to heart the sacrifices of the people in the unprecedented circumstances. The leaders seemingly felt that they were the heroes and so had to reap the benefits in the form of perks and positions of power, and not what has to do with the interests of the people, particularly the conclusion of the peace process and completing all tasks to have the new constitution promulgated.

The success of the historic Jan Andolan II (People's Movement) in April 6, 2006 set the pace for this new transition. The 19-day long people's movement unprecedentedly shook the roots of the 240 years old Shah monarchy thus compelling the King to renounce his power by a declaration on 24 April 2006. In his declaration, the King recognized the people as the source of the state power and accepted the road map of the agitating Seven Party Alliance. He also made a call for sustainable peace, progress full democracy and national unity in the country.[76] So the transfer to a republic from that of monarchial system despite many speculations was accomplished peacefully. The movement led the people to believe that their aspirations would be fulfilled soon thereafter. Political parties that had lost credibility due to their dismal performances in the past also started getting support from all sections of population. The participation of people was unprecedented both in size and intensity.It spread across the country with the same popular support bringing about a radical change.

The national movements made the people politically aware. The people now are increasing their political participation and the political culture exhibits the participant type of political culture. During the movement, the people had explicitly expressed three major things to achieve: the end of monarchy and the dawn of republican democratic era, the end of Maoist people's war and return to peace and redefining the people- state relationship by restructuring the state. Consequently, the peace process began in 2006 and election to Constituent Assembly was successfully held on April 10, 2008.

Nepal has chosen CA as the most apt method and the most democratic, transparent and accountable procedures in constitution making which is set through numerous negotiations and changes. With the election of the Constituent Assembly, Nepal entered into a new phase of discourse on the kind of polity it aspires to have. But the success of Jan Andolan II had clearly signaled the end of monarchy and the beginning of a republican era in Nepal. The monarchy was denied any right to rule and president to head the republic as head of the state. The functions relating to governance are vested with the Prime Minister. However, it had to go through some processes to make the republican transition smooth and legitimate. Confronted as they are by the problems of rising aspirations and rising frustrations of peoples it has been acknowledged that Nepali politicians were under pressure to accommodate the maximum number of people belonging to various ethnic and religious groups. Numerically, such an approach seems to correct the past imbalances but has not made any substantive difference in actual wielding of power and prestige. Grievances were raised by the concerned sections that political parties working under the 1990 constitution were insensitive to the demands of the deprived or marginalized people. The 2006 movement that came against the background of Maoist insurgency and pressures being inserted by various ethnic groups, Madhesi, Dalits, women and others could change the representative scenario in CA election.

The Interim Constitution 2007 adopted a mixed electoral system –first-past –the –post (direct) and proportional electing 240 members directly and 335 on the basis of proportional representation (PR) system. In a house of 601, the representative character has undergone a sea change. There has been a phenomenal increase of Dalit (48), women (197 or 33 percent ), Muslim 18 hill Janjati*s* 159 (26 percent ). It has boosted the morale of these deprived people. In the past the House of representatives (lower House) was composed of 205 and the national Council Upper House) had 60. Many people ask and for valid reasons what was the purpose of increasing the size of the CA which also works as today's parliament for drafting a new constitution?

Following the Comprehensive Peace Accord of 21 November 2006 concluded between the Government of Nepal and the UCPN (M) the Interim Constitution 2007 (IC) was adopted, which opened the door for the Maoists to join the transitional political process. They were brought into the interim parliament and also into the interim government as a force to be reckoned with. It covered the major aspects of the peace and constitution making process, conflict management, management of arms and armies, normalization of the situation, human rights and dispute settlement. This accord was followed by an Agreement on Monitoring of the Management of Arms and Armies on 8 December 2006. This Agreement addressed the pivotal issue related to the practical matters of monitoring of the management of the Maoist combatants in particular and the Nepal Army in General. Notwithstanding, different political parties and groups spearheaded agitation in the different parts of the country and the Southern plain of Nepal remarkably became restive putting several demands including the demand of the federal system in the country. All these accords and agreements paved the way for the election of the CA in April10, 2008. The UCPN (M) emerged as the largest party in the CA election, but without majority, in the legislature-parliament and the major political parties opted a competitive mode rather following the cooperative mode of politics adopted before the election of the CA. As a result the major political parties entered into a new agreement on July 7, 2008 paving the way for constitutional amendment thus to go for a competitive politics in the legislature parliament. Consequently, both the president and the prime minister were elected on the basis of party alliances.

The Nepali Congress bagged the seat of the President, the UCPN (M) acquired the post of the Prime Minister and the CPN (UML) got the post of the Chairperson of the CA. Thus a kind of political balance was established among the three major parties of the country. However, despite the remarkable work in constitution making and the peace process, the political parties neither could complete ongoing peace process nor promulgate the new constitution in a stipulated period of time. Making and unmaking of the government and apparent competition for power dominated whole scenario of the politics since the election of the CA. The Maoist combatants are still in the cantonments despite several agreements and understandings among the parties and within the

Special Committee (SC), which is constitutionally mandated to decide regarding the Maoist combatants.[77] Similarly, the exercise of regrouping of the Maoist combatants in the cantonments and decision of the SC regarding integration, voluntary retirement and rehabilitation is not implemented so far. It has again created stumbling blocks in the road of conflict management and conflict transformation thus casting the shadow of violence in the country.

The peace and constitution making process is also stalled due to the internal bickering and dilemma in the UCPN (M) and crisis of confidence among the major political parties. The Maoist party and the Maoist-led government seemed much haunted by the psyche of the Maoist violent struggle and raised slogans during that period of time. Several agreements and understandings, including the much talked 7-point understanding signed on November 31, 2011, have not brought desired results so far. Rounds of talks between the parties are seemed exercises in futility if judged by substantial results needed to the country and the people. Resolution of the issues like the integration and rehabilitation of the Maoist combatants, restructuring of the state, form of governance, independence of judiciary and the election system might concretely contribute to conflict transformation bringing the phase of Maoist violence to an end. It may have positive impact to calm down other types of violence done by non-state actors and to strengthen state authority and functioning at the given context as well.

***State Restructuring: Agenda of New Nepal***

Nepal today deals entirely with new political values and cultures such as secularism, devolution, inclusion, republicanism and federalism. Nepal at this transitional stage struggles with the legacy of ten years of conflict in which around 15,000 died and 1,350 disappeared while countless were dispossessed, displaced, bereaved and traumatized. Worse still, the underlying causes of the conflict have not yet been resolved. Nor have most of the results of the conflict been addressed. Despite pivotal roles played by Nepali political parties in the modernization of state and society, the main challenges they encounter in the democratization process are: gaps between the ideology and policy, incoherence between constitution and constitutional behaviour, weak-enforcement of party laws, unstructured political participation of citizens moving beyond party, parliament and constitutional system, exclusionary political culture sustained by politics of negation, lack of balance between individual, groups and human rights, absence of mechanism of inter and intra-party conflict resolution and a tradition of centralized leadership facing tension with the social groups demanding regional, social, gender and intergenerational representation.

Nepal at the moment is passing through the most crucial phase of history ever since its foundation in the late 18th century. Following the success of the historic Jan Andolan II in April 2006 and the Madhes revolt in January-February 2007, Nepal has decided to transform the present unitary state into a federal one. The Constituent Assembly was a result of political negotiations at the height of political conflict in the country. Although political parties are the primary actors, the CA was the only mechanism through which decisions regarding the future political course of the country within the parameters of democratic norms were to be decided. The CA was overwhelmingly mandated to frame the constitution along federal republican lines. The Interim Constitution of Nepal (2007) has already recognized cultural pluralism of Nepali society and declares Nepal to be a federal democratic republic and has left it to the CA to decide on the modality of the federal states. And the government is expected to chalk out the course of transition from unitary to federal state. In that course, the country has undergone multiple transactions from:

- Monarchy to republic;
- Authoritarianism to democracy and human rights
- Hegemonic to a participatory system of governance;
- State wholly pervaded by one religion to secularism;
- Heavily centralized unitary system to one characterized by decentralization and autonomy at the regional levels.

Over the years, the country did make some progress in some sectors and areas. The Nepali state is being transformed because of new popular demands for inclusiveness, empowerment, distribution of power and resources through the redesigned state structure. However, many uncertainties continue to prevail which cast doubts on smooth constitutional transition. In its process of transformation, Nepal has discarded number of factors of the past- single official language, a national anthem and a national code of dress. Nonetheless, all its citizens have common fights and obligations that can eventually contribute sense of national identity and cohesion in tandem with the preservation of cultural diversity. Although restructuring of army, police, bureaucracy and political parties are also the main agenda of restructuring of state, state restructuring, especially the agenda of federalism is one of the controversial issues. Because of the changed context of ethnicization and regionalization articulation of federalism has drawn more attention. Each ethnic group wants to create autonomous states with the right to self determination in their respective names. The Limbus of the Eastern Hills, for example, want to make Limbuwan, the Rais want Kirat Pradesh, and the Sherpas, the Gurungs, the Magars, Tharus all follow such patterns. Only the caste group-Brahmin, Chhetria, Dalits and Muslims-and a few others have no such identity, although the Maoists proposal for carving out 14 regions include two regions based on castes.

The "one Madhesh Pradesh" demanded by the Madheses includes the territory of plane-stretching from the eastern to western border The demand, however lacks consensus as the Tharus, the Muslims and the Dalits of the Terai do not want such one single Terai as a unit. Nor do the other hill communities like the Limbus accept it on the grounds that their demand of Limbuwan also includes some parts of the Terai. The Maoist leadership too never delved into federalism and its value. Rather it used ethnicity for the purpose of expanding and consolidating the insurgency. Its version of autonomy did not have democratic content, but a party-controlled command structure which hardly corroborates with federal values. Other political parties such as NC and UML never thought about federal Nepal. They are dragged by the exigencies.[78] Political parties in Nepal operate in a highly centralized structure and the political culture lacks federal republican contents. Each of them has winners take all tendencies. Within both NC and UML anti-federal opinion is still prevalent.

The establishment of the state restructuring commission as per the provision of Interim Constitution only in November, 2011 is evident from unwillingness and reluctance of all the major political parties. There was serious time constraint before CA. Its schedule had already been changed several times which had raised suspicion among the people already that the constitution would not meet deadline. However, the parties could not reach an understanding and could not frame the constitution on stipulated date. So the CA was dissolved. In this regard, the political parties, particularly the three major ones have to strike a deal if the derailed peace process and the constitution making are to be given the proper passage. Of special interest is the peace process which is particularly focused on the integration and rehabilitation of the Maoist combatants. But it seems Maoists are not giving any serious thoughts to it, because at the moment they have control over those in the cantonments. Once they come under the control of the special committee concerned, the Maoists fear it will be their significant strategic loss. The conflicting situation in the process of drafting a new constitution created extreme difficulties and the process is derailed as of the moment. Any way the exit of the United Mission in Nepal (UNMIN) opened the door for the handover of the Maoist combatants to the government and Army Integration Special Committee (AISC) with effect from January 22, 2011.

However, the peace and the constitution making process have yet to be accomplished. This augurs well in that it has created a new setting for the issue to be resolved as it befits the national interest. The issue is still sensitive and, thus calls for the sustained and sincere efforts of the political parties to arrive at the modalities. It is an oft-heard line these days that Nepali society has become polarized into federalists and anti-federalists. The recent decision of various associations of indigenous communities to open a new political party seems to corroborate the idea that the fresh elections to the CA will be a show-down between the two camps. But a debate about, whether Nepal should transfer into federal path or not is a gone issue. The dominant question is: what type of federalism suits to Nepal? Questions have been raised over the viability and desirability of federal units based on ethnic divisions. Republic, federalism, and secularism are the other pillars of the New Nepal according to which the restructuring of state needs to be designed.

Since the new regions to be created are likely to be asymmetrical in size and resources, the foundation of state structuring should not based on ethnicity alone, however, identity and capacity/natural resources/historical legacy/integrity of the nation should also be taken into consideration. Then only a federal Nepal would be a good way of addressing the common aspirations and wishes of nearly two- thirds of the total population of the country, who are seeking social identity, political representation and economic development. A federal culture is required to make the federal system sustainable and successful. According to Koller a federal culture calls for mutual trust, a readiness for mutual dialogue between diverse but equal partners, loyalty towards the federal government, and a consensus that diversity is an enrichment of the federal state rather than a threat to the state's integrity.[79] Now it is the time for the leaders to evaluate and judge themselves how far they have been prepared to go with the federal norms and values. The whole politics of the country has swept by a federalist wave either for populist purpose or with some genuine reasons. But deeper in the mainstream politics due to too much ethnicization of the issues has caused concerns and crisis of confidence even among those leaders who proclaimed to be the federalist. In such a situation what type of federal democrats are we going to be?

### *Democratic Constitution: People's Expectations*

In the name of constitution and regime change, people have suffered a lot. The success of the 2006 Jan Andolan, the subsequent peace process and the Madhesi Andolan raised hopes that new leaders would emerge to carry the country forward and improve levels of security, development and stability across Nepal. Public expectations increased again after the constitutional assembly election, some put their faith in the UCPN (Maoist), and others in the Madheshi parties to provide new leadership that would be accountable and effective. Over all, many are disappointed with the willingness of all parties to make promises that they have subsequently proven unable to implement. Through the 12-point understanding, the Maoist directly agreed to transform themselves into a political agency for competitive multi-party politics. Amid the violence of the insurgency, they have also contributed much towards raising the awareness of the socially deprived and voiceless section of the population about their right to autonomy, dignity and livelihood. This made people hope that this positive side of the people's war and eventuality of the Maoists' joining the competitive political process would induce a change also in the SPA towards a people-oriented political culture with justice and equitable economic and social programmes. This step of the Maoists also made every Nepali aware that the absence of such culture and public policies in the past led to the corruption and eventual interruption of the democratic process and the rise of conflicts and insurrection in the country. But the Maoists appear unable and unwilling to reconcile the ideology and the political culture and methods of people's war with the responsibilities they have assumed under various agreements and understandings with the SPA.

Many times their conversations and conduct, especially at the cadre and militia levels show that they may not even be aware of the fact that they are now a part of the state, which admittedly is a novel experience for them. On the other hand it is quite likely that various elements in the SPA and the forces of status quo in general do not wish to see the Maoists making any positive impact on the lives of the people. Perhaps they would rather have the Maoists behave in an irresponsible manner and de-legitimize themselves politically than see them winning the hearts and mind of the people through progressive economic and cultural initiatives. When the people welcomed the 12-point understanding between the Maoists and SPA in November 2005, they were also energized by the possibilities of epochal change at the societal level that would be realized with the new constitution drafted by a popularly elected Constituent Assembly (CA) and the restructuring of the state and society that it would allow.

With the reluctance of the political forces in power to move politically and collectively in this direction, the country is now in the grip of a new round of conflict. It has arisen from the assertion of political, social and cultural rights by the indigenous, ethnic and other historically and socially oppressed groups of citizens including women and also the "third gender". They had participated and contributed to the success of the movement with the hope of restructuring the state in their favour. The new conflict is a part of tension any society goes through when it tries to transform itself from the "old" to the "new".[80] The political parties could have avoided much of the current strife culture by showing some sagacity and political maturity and by being faithful to the mandate of the movement when they finalized the interim constitution. The people's movement was about harnessing the awareness of the diverse people about their rights and for the correction of the oppressive and unequal system dominant in the state, society and the economy.

The post-2006 politics has not improved the conditions necessary for developing political system. The future of institutionalized democracy is still unclear. Huntington in his article *Political Development and Political Decay* and later in his book *Political Order in Changing Societies* stated clearly that political development without institutionalization is political decay".[81] Democracy without being institutionalized tends to be a passing phenomenon as has happened in Nepal after 1951. As it has been said "a stable regime is one that is deeply institutionalized and consolidated, making it likely, therefore to enjoy a high level of popular legitimacy.'[82] It is a proven fact that restoration of democracy in intervals do not also make it work for long. Although the April revolution of 2006 has underlined the spirit of the future political system, it has not spelt the type of a democratic system. CA so far could not come out with any conclusion on the crucial areas such as restructuring of state with a focus on federalization, system type and electoral system.

Structurally, Nepal has now a republican system but from normative point of view, most of its features are characterized by trends ubiquitous in other traditional system. No governments regardless of parties and ideologies could be identified as distinct from one another so much so all did not even depart from the style and patterns of the party less regime. The thirty years party less exercise plus the antecedents of Nepali history and political culture has powerful impacts on elite orientation in the post-1990 democracy in the country. The ethos of the past regimes- Shah and Rana have had been replicated in the present pattern of governance. It was not only during Rana and Shah Rules, but also during the decade of renewed democratic period, the personalized system of governance has become a regular feature of political culture. During the Shah and Rana systems, the exercise of authority was characterized as rule by *Hukum* or peremptory command. Contrasted with the past system, today's governance process is, nevertheless, more transparent but not necessarily accountable because of the failures of both political parties and civil society for effectively articulating and aggregating the agendas of efficient and accountable governance culture. As a result, whichever parties come to power they are only casually alluding to peoples' cause resulting in perpetuating the trends of old regime. Thus the clash of old and new values are embedded in the new democratic system. But the old traditional values and practices appear to be more powerful and pervasive than the universally acknowledged norms of governance triggering off a series of crises to which both governments and parties pay scant attention to redress them.

The fundamental characteristics of Nepali politics over the centuries have been struggling for sovereign power or executive power leading to the rise and fall of regimes and breeding political instability. Right from its unification as a nation state there had been whole arrays of coups and massacres in Nepal's court to capture sovereign power among the courtiers and Royals.[83] Historian Upreti argues that traditional politics in Nepal consisted of inter-family and intra-family feuds to get hold on sovereign power, characterized by sinister plots and counter plots ghastly murders and massacres with always the same object, the attainment of political supremacy without the involvement of masses.[84]

In short, traditional politics in Nepal was not the mass politics of the twentieth and twenty -first centuries brought into focus with organization of political parties, civil society and mass media that work to mobilize international civil society organizations. It appears that modern day politicians are motivated by the same idea of their predecessors in exercising sovereign power regardless of public purpose. The only difference is that they are using to serve their interests wherein victims are poor people which certainly were not the case in the past. At present a new culture is being seen in Nepal that all the parties national, regional and individual, see the constitution through their respective prisms and interest. If the NC is rigid on the issues of parliamentary system, the UCPN-Maoist appeared to be confused as it wanted to make a fusion of both presidential features with parliamentary control. The CPN-UML is also unclear about the type of government, but wants to ensure political stability by electing a prime minister directly by the people. These are not big problems if parties approach them.

Now the term of the CA has expired with the CA letting the people down without delivering a new constitution as they were mandated to. This would not have been the CA that the people had elected. It created confusion in the minds of the people and the political leaders that the CA would be extended as per the will of the CA indefinitely and perhaps it is the reason that caused the end of the CA without delivering the constitution. After waiting for more than six decades to have a people's constitution, Nepalis have failed again in getting a constitution from the CA duly elected by the people. The CA was initially elected for two years as per the Interim Constitution (IC). However, its tenure was extended four times in the past finally doubling its original tenure.

The issue of extension had engaged the attention of the Supreme Court by way of its judgments delivered on petitions filed before it. Its first verdict had approved the first extension of the tenure of the CA by one year declaring that the CA would last till its prime duty of adopting the new constitution was completed. It was gross violation of the spirit of IC, which permits extension only in case of emergency, that too for six months. An elected CA was the product of an election. An election is a process where a voter transfers or delegates his/her power to his/her representative. The voter deliberately deprives himself of his certain power till his representative utilizes it. Does a voter surrender his right to his representative as per the wishes of the representative? Or how long a representative can represent his elector without his approval? The present government now regarded as care taker one has set the date for fresh poll first in November 22, 2012, but has again extended to April, 2013 (Baisakh 2070). How long do people wait or how many elections do they have to go through to get constitution? The complications are too glaring and an immediate passage is not visible. The whole focus of the people is now on how the constitution is going to be drafted and promulgated. The state has not reached the terminal point; neither has it given the people any promising picture for the future. For the first time in its history the country now stands at the most critical juncture without constitution and legislature. Democracy is in peril, so is the validity of the state. Prolonged transition and polarized uncertain politics may be more alarming. Nepali politics is losing both the purpose and direction of change; no definite picture is yet clear. In the given context where politics is fluid and uncertain, people's expectations for peace, security and stability may not be possible. This would not have been the result Nepali people have expected with their sacrifice and arduous struggle for New Nepal.

What must be borne in mind is that the constitution has to be framed, whether by reviving the dissolved CA if possible or go for an exorbitant election for a new CA .Whatever the means; it has to come from all-party consensus. If the parties distance themselves from any attempts for consensus, the delivery of a new constitution cannot be done. People still do hope that Nepal will be able to overcome many of its daunting problems through the constitutional mechanism. People still pin high hopes on Nepali politicians who are not as much rigid and orthodox as in many other countries. On the contrary, they are perennially engaged in dialogues so as to reach a negotiated settlement to many outstanding problems they face. The only thing left is how political elites develop their own ability to understand the situation keeping in mind the minimum norms and culture of consensus and compromise.

## NOTES

1. G.C. Pandey, *The Meaning and Process of Culture,* (Agra: Shivlal Agrawal and Co. 1972), pp. 102-3.
2. Ashis Nandy, "Culture, State and Rediscovery of Indian Politics," *Economic and Political Weekly,* Vol. XIX, No. 49, (December 8, 1984), p. 2081. Quated in Anam Jaitly, *India's Political Culture- In Search of a Framework,* (Jaipur: Aalekh Publication, 1991), p. 19.
3. *Vedic* scriptures elaborate four different types of human conduct: a) *bad conduct* hurts others and inflicts anguish and pain to them; b) *normal conduct* is meant to regulate and sustain personal and family lives without hurting others; c) *virtuous conduct* is designed to help others by means of promoting voluntary services, such as establishing resting places, inns, schools, hospitals, digging wells constructing water spouts and uplifting the poor and powerless sections of the society; and d) *supreme conduct* is attained by performing *Yagna*, protecting earth, heaven and the cosmos.
4. Baburam Acharya, *Nepalko Sanskritik Parampara,* (Kathmandu: Srikrishna Acharya.1998), pp. 9-23.

5. Rishikesh Shaha, *Ancient and Medieval Nepal,* (New Delhi: Manohar Publication, 1992), p. 7.
6. Rishikesh Shaha, *An Introduction to Nepal,* (Kathmandu: Ratna Pustak Bhandar, 1975), p. 63.
7. Dhanavajra Vajracharya (ed.), *Licchavi Kalka Abhilekha,* (Kathmandu: Nepal Ra Eshiyali Anusandhan Samsthan= INAS, 2030 BS), pp. 124-130.
8. T.R. Vaidya, *Nepal: A Study of Socio-Economic and Political Changes,* (New Delhi: Anmol Publications, 1992), p. 107.
9. *Ibid.*
10 T.R. Vaidya, *Prithivinaraya Shah: The Founder of Modern Nepal,* (New Delhi: Anmol Publication, 1993), p. 169.
11. Vajracharya, *op cit.,* f.n. No. 7, pp. 336-37.
12. *Ibid,* p. 641.
13. Vaidya, *op cit.,* f.n. No. 8, p. 41.
14. *Ibid,* p. 44.
15. Queen mother – Samrajya Laxmi Devi, Subarna Prabha Devi, Tripurasundari and Rajrajeshori ruled as regents. Rajendra Laxmi (mother of minor King Rana Bahadur Shah ascending throne at the age of two years) ruled from 1777, 1785 AD, Bahadur Shah (uncle of the minor King Rana Bahadur Shah) from 1785-1795 AD, queen Samrajya Laxmi and Laxmi Devi from 1837-1846 AD ruled as regents.
16. Finally Bhimsen Thapa emerged as the strongest man of the kingdom and dominated the arena of politics unfettered continuously for 31 years from 1806-1837 AD.
17. Jagdish Chandra Regmi, *Ne* Political Culture of Nepal: A Historical Perspective *203palko Baidhanik Parampara,* 2nd ed., (Kathmandu: Tanneri Publication, 2054 BS), p. 16.
18. *Matsya Purana* (226-3-12) (Sanskrit Series), (Poona: Ananda Ashram, 1967). Quoted in Jaitly, *op cit.,* f.n. No. 2, p. 34.
19. Tulsi Narayan Shrestha, *Nepalese Administration: A Historical Perspective,* (Kathmandu: Rhino Publication, 1989), p. 203.
20. B.D. Sanwal, *Nepal and East India Company*, (Delhi: Asia Publishing House, 1965), p. 54.
21. Shrestha, *op cit.,* f.n. No. 19,

22. *Ibid.*
23. Mahendra Malla's (King of Kantipur 1560-1574 AD) official instruction that his people to take their lunch from 9 to 10 AM and their supper within 10 PM so that all his people had already taken food reflects the concern of the rulers to be closer with their people.
24. Yogi Narahari Nath (ed.), *Gorkha Vamshavali*, (Varanasi: Aryabirassngha Kasi, 2021), p. 7.
25. Yogi Narahari Nath (ed.), *Dibya Upadesh,* (Varanasi: Pracharini Mahasabha, 2016 BS), p. 14.
26. D.R. Regmi, *Medieval Nepal,* (Calcutta: Firma K.L. Mokhupadhyaya, 1966), p. 247.
27. Vaidya, *op cit.,* f.n. No. 10, p. 46.
28. Niccolo Machiavelli, *The Prince,* (London: Penguin, 1973), p. 99. Niccolò Machiavelli (1469-1527), Niccolò Machiavelli was born in Florence in 1469, wrote *The Prince* in 1513, in which he allowed the conclusion that politics has nothing to do with morals, ethics, and religion. Machiavelli has become infamous for this political advice, ensuring that he would be remembered in history as an adjective, "Machiavellian."
29. Nepali authorities generally estimated the population of Nepal 5,200,000 or 5,600,000 in 1856 but according to British source it was less than 1,950,000 and this figure was probably more accurate than the figures given by Nepalis, who tended to exaggerate their numbers for the satisfaction of their self-pride. Nepal's annual revenue was about 7 to 8 million rupees in the mid – 1850s. The literacy rate was below 3 percent (see old-field, London cavenaugh and others).
30. T.R. Vaidya, "Gorkhanization of Nepal," *Nepal: A Study of Social Economic and Political Changes,* (New Delhi: Anmol Publication, 1992), pp. 185-192.
31. Leo E. Rose and John T. Scholz, *Nepal Profile of a Himalayan Kingdom,* (New Delhi: Select Book Syndicate, 1980), p. 30.
32. Rabindra Khanal, *Political Institutionalization and Political Culture in Nepal,* paper submitted to one day National Seminar, organized by Dept. of Political Science, T.U. in corporation with (FES) (November 20, 1998), p. 11.

33. *Census of Population of Nepal 1952/54 AD,* (Kathmandu: Department of Statistics, 1952), pp. 39-41.
34. K.P. Malla, "The Intellectual In Nepalese Society", *Nepal in Perspective,* Pashupati Shamser J.B. Rana and K.P. Malla (eds.), (Kathmandu: CEDA, 1973), p. 277.
35. *Ibid.*
36. Leo E. Rose and Joshi, *Democratic Innovations in Nepal: A Study of Political Acculturation,* (Berkeley: University of California Press, 1966), p. 487.
37. *Ibid,* p. 508.
38. Anirudra Gupta, *Politics in Nepal 1950-1960,* (Delhi: Kalinga Publications, 1993), p. 229.
39. David E. Apter, "System, Process and Politics of Economic Development", *Political Development and Social Change,* Johnson L. Fomlle and Richard W. Gable, (eds.) (New York: John Wiley and Sons, 1968), p. 452.
40. Rishikesh Shaha, *Essays in the Practice of Government in Nepal,* (Delhi: Manohar Publications, 1982), p. 175.
41. Lok Raj Baral, "Political Culture and Political Process in Nepal", *Nepal: Perspective on Continuity and Change,* Kamal P. Malla (ed.), (Kathmandu: Tribhuvan University, CNAS, 1989), p. 319.
42. Rose and Scholz, *op cit.,* f.n. No. 31, p. 34.
43. P. Neupane, *The Constitution and Constitutions of Nepal,* (Kathmandu: Laws, Books Management Committee, 1968 AD), p. XI.
44. Rishikesh Shaha, *Nepali Politics: Retrospect and Prospect,* (Delhi: Oxford University Press, 1978), p. 64.
45. *Ibid.*
46. S.P. Huntington, *Political Order in Changing Societies,* (New Heaven: Yale University Press, 1968), p. 405.
47. Shaha, *op cit.,* f.n. No. 44.
48. Baral, *op cit.,* f.n. No. 41, p. 317.
49. *Ibid.*
50. Hem Narayan Agrawal, *Nepal: A Study in Constitutional Change,* (New Delhi: Oxford and IBM Publishing Co., 1987), p. 56.
51. S.K. Chaturbedi, *Nepal: Internal Politics and Constitution,* (New Delhi: Inter–India Publications, 1993), p. 92.

52. *The Constitution of Nepal,* (Kathmandu: Laws, Books Management Committee, 1968), pp. 8-9.
53. *Ibid,* pp. 44-45.
54. *Ibid,* p. 46.
55. Richard Burghart, "The Political Culture of Panchayat Democracy", Michael Hutt (ed.), *Nepal in the Nineties,* (Oxford: Oxford University Press, 1993), pp. 8-9.
56. Donald N. Levine, "ETHOPIA: Identity, Authority and Realision in Political Culture and Political Development", Lucian W. Pye and Sidney Verba, (eds.) *Political Culture and Political Development,* (USA: Princeton University Press, 1989), p. 278.
57. Burhghart, *op cit.,* f.n. No. 55, p. 9.
58. T. Louise, *The Challenge to Democracy in Nepal: A Political History,* (London: New Fetter Lane, 1996), p. 73.
59. *Ibid,*
60. Indra Deo Mishra, *Understanding a Political System: In Reference to Nepal,* (Varanasi: Vijayashree Enterprises, 1985), p. 35.
61. Yugeshwar P. Verma, *Nepal: Progress and Problems 1972-80,* (Mahottary, Nepal: Prativa Verva, 1981), p. 9.
62. Baral, *op cit.,* f.n. No. 41, p. 318.
63. Shaha, *op cit.,* f.n. No. 44, p. 8.
64. Richard Burghart, "The Political Culture of Panchayat Democracy", *Nepal in the Nineties,* Micheal Hutt (ed.), (Oxford: Oxford University Press, 1993), p. 8.
65. HMG/N, *His Majesty King Birendra Proclamations, Speeches and Messages, 1972-81,* (Kathmandu: Department of Information, 1982), pp. 126-27.
66. Lok Raj Baral, *Nepal's Politics of Referendum: A Study of Groups, Personalities, and Trends,* (New Delhi: Vikash Publishing House Pvt. Ltd., 1983), p. 58.
67. The Maoists are a group of people from the several splintered Communist Party of Nepal who did not join the United Left Front during the Jan Andolan 1990. Instead, they had formed their own Samukta Rastriya Janaandolan (United National People's Movement) who had radicalized the political scene during the period. After the formation of the Interim Government in May 1990, this group had demanded the formation of the Constitutional

Assembly to draft the national democratic Constitution. Consequently, they rejected the November 1990 Constitution promulgated by the King. For detail see in Pancha N. Maharjan, "The Maoist Insurgency and Crisis of Governability in Nepal", *Domestic Conflict And Crisis of Governability In Nepal,* Edited by Dhruba Kumar, (Kirtipur: Centre for Nepal and Asian Studies (CNAS), 2000), pp. 163-187.

68. 40-points demands of Maoists Party included mainly abrogation of both the 1950 and the Mahakali treaties with India (one on "Peace and friendship" and the other on the sharing of the water on the Western frontier river); introducing work permits for foreign (i.e. Indian) workers in Nepal; curtailing all privileges of the royal family; drafting of a new constitution through a constitutional assembly; nationalizing the property of "Comprador and bureaucratic capitalists," declaring Nepal a secular nation; and also details such as providing villages with roads drinking water and electricity.; and complete guarantee of freedom of speech and publication etc.
69. *Himalaya Times*, (Kathmandu: Himal Media Pvt. Ltd., June 16, 2000).
70. Quoted in Hacchethu, "Mass Movement in Nepal", *Contribution to Nepalese Studies*, Vol. 17 No. 2, (Kirtipur: Centre of Nepal and Asian Study (CNAS), T.U., 1990), p. 182
71. *Ghatana ra Vichar*, (Kathmandu: November 6, 1998).
72. *Sandhaya Times*, (Kathmandu: November 3, 1999).
73. *Gorkha Patra*, (Kathmandu: June 27, 1995).
74. *The Kathmandu Post,* (Kathmandu: Tuesday, Dec. 28, 1999).
75. In short the 12-points were:

    (1) establishment of absolute democracy by ending autocratic monarchy; (2) restoration of the Parliament with the force of agitation by forming an all-party government with complete authority, holding election to a CA through dialogue and understanding with the Maoists and transfer of sovereignty and state power to the people; (3) establishment of permanent peace along with the solution to armed conflict by putting the royal army and the Maoist armed force under the supervision of the UN; (4) commitment to competitive multiparty system of governance, civil liberties, human rights, etc.; (5) Maoist commitment to create

an environment, allowing the political activities of other democratic parties displaced during the course of the armed conflict to return to their former localities and live there with dignity, return their home democratic parties displaced during the course of the armed conflict tc return to their former localities and live there with dignity, return their homes, land and property seized in an unjust manner and carry out their activities without hindrance; (6) no repetition of past mistakes by the Maoists; (7) seven political parties also not to repeat the mistakes committed in the past in the Parliament and in government; (8) respect for human rights and press freedom; (9) boycott of municipal and parliamentary elections to be conducted by the royal regime calling upon the people to make it a failure; (10) friendship with all the countries of the world, neighbours, especially China and India, and end of narrow nationalism of the regime; (11) call upon the civil society, professional organizations, various wings of parties, people of all communities and regions, press and intellectuals to actively participate in the peaceful movements lunched for democracy, peace, prosperity, forward–looking social change and the country's independence, sovereignty, and pride; and (12) settlement of any problem that may arise between parties through peaceful dialogue at the concerned level or leadership level.

76. Proclamation to the nation from his Majesty King Gyanendra on 24 April 2006. Agreements and Understandings on peace Negotiation of Nepal, Government of Nepal, Peace Secretariat, Kathmandu Nepal, January, 2007, p. 9.
77. *Nepal ko Antrim Sambidhan 2063,* Article 138, (Kathmandu: Nepal Government, Ministry of Law and Justice, Law Books Management Committee, 2010), p. 67.
78. Krishna P. Khanal, "Democracy and Federalization of the Nepalese State Challenges and Opportunities," *Sangam Journal quarterly*, Vol. 1, (Kathmandu: Sangam Institute for Policy Analysis and Strategic Studies, 2009), pp. 15-16.
79. Arnold Koller, *Federalism in a Changing world –Learning from Each Other,* (Montrealand Kingston: McGill Queen's University Press, 2003), p. 6.

80. Devendra Raj Panday *Looking at Development and Donors; Essays From Nepal*, Seira Tamang (ed.), (Kathmandu: Martin Chautari, 2011), p. 387.
81. Samuel P. Huntington, *Political Order in Changing Societies,* (New Haven: Yale University Press, 1968), p. 40.
82. Lok Raj Baral (ed.), *Constitutional Government and Democracy in South Asia*, (Kathmandu: Nepal Centre for Contemporary Studies (NCCS), 2011), p. 18.
83. Babu Ram Acharya, *Aba Yasto Khailyi Nahos*, (Kathmandu: Offset Printing Press, 2056).
84. Prem R. Upreti, *Political Awaakening in Nepal: The Search for a New Identity*, (New Delhi: Common Wealth Publishers, 1992), p. x.

# 5.

# Emerging Trends in Nepal's Political Culture: Perception and Assessment

Political culture refers to the typical beliefs held by people in a society about their basic political institutions. These institutions comprise the government, parliament, elections, and political parties, courts of justice, and citizens' rights and duties in regard to political participation. Learning about the attitudes of people towards political institutions provides one with insight on the extent to which individuals are informed or satisfied about political institutions and process in the democratic process. As we know, political culture is not only related with what is happening in the world of politics but also concerns how people react with those happenings. Now a number of institutions are involving in politics, many political actors and many political issues. About what aspects of a political system would it be useful to know the basic orientations of the members of the system? The number of subjects to ask such questions about is unlimited. There are, however several criteria that can serve as useful guides for the selection of the significant aspects of cultural orientation. So it would be appropriate to look for aspects that are most relevant in the present context, those aspects of politics about which most people would be expected to have orientations that is to have beliefs, values and feelings about, which after all constitute the political culture of Nepal.

The chapter mainly focuses on people's orientation towards political parties, oppositional politics, leadership role, people's participation, union demonstration, public protest, security and bureaucracy, along with people's overall satisfaction and dissatisfaction. How do Nepali people in general perceive, asses, evaluate and react with those variables in the country constitute the core of political culture of Nepal. The cognitive, affective and evaluative orientations of people towards those phenomena give the glimpse of emerging trends of political culture in Nepal after the Jan Andolans. Learning about the attitudes of voters or responders towards present political institutions provides one with insight on the extent to which individuals are informed about political institutions and process, whether they are satisfied with the efficacy of various institutions and processes in the democratic process. The chapter informs the political parties and leaders about what the people think of the political institutions as evolved after 1990.

In a context where people listening passively to politicians had been the norm, the chapter informs to reverse the roles where people speak out and politicians have to listen. The chapter actually represents the voice of the people. Analysis of data based on survey researches, opinion polls and development reports collectively provides with a reliable snap shot of the Nepali political culture, especially as it relates to democratization and changes in it since 1990. It also provides clues to the nature of political culture pattern; nonetheless, political culture is of such importance in regulating the performance of a political system that it is worth a substantial effort to get reliable information about it.

**People's Perception on Political Parties**

Government in all democratic states is party government. The political parties are the promoters of political culture and values among the people. They bring people into politics, mobilize, activate, train, prepare and socialize them in running the state machinery at different levels according to their respective ideologies. They also perform the role of articulating agents in arousing public sentiments either in support or against one party or the other ruling party. It is the political party that brings the people and mass into the political community.

Nepal has a brief history of political parties, but they are as old as the history of democratic struggle in the country. As the principal agents of democracy, parties have played a crucial role to install democracy and have waged and led at least four political movements. Majority of political parties have come into existence after the People's Movement of 1990 except the NC and Communist parties. It is, therefore the attitudes of political parties are also influenced by their evolution, time and the political culture of that period. As the political parties were freed only after 1990, the study of political parties can be commenced from the introduction of the present constitution and the post 1991 election so far. Though the concept of universal suffrage prevailed in Nepal since 1959 and the constitutional order guaranteed a system where there would be representation in parliament of citizens, the majority of voters were confused about the relative positions of the parties and did not have sufficient amount of perception towards the political parties for their assessment in the first general election, 1959 (2015 BS).

During the period, majority of respondents were only aware of the simple differentiation of political parties based on two polar: democratic or communist. Nepali's have shown their extra-ordinary ingenuity by having participated in many elections held across the 60 years period. Nepal's electoral democracy suffered a setback from 1960 to 1990 when political parties were banned. After the referendum of 1980, efforts were made for the establishment of universal suffrage to permit the manifestation of popular will in representation and in the formulation of public policies. Political parties' credential as change agent was established by people's decisive role only in the 1990 mass movement. After the restoration of multiparty democracy, Nepali citizens have participated in two local elections, in 1993 and 1997 and national elections in 1991, 1994, and 1999 and one Constituent Assembly election in 2008 with most deprived people coming to CA through the mixed election system. The resulting electoral trends suggest the familistic, paternalistic and clientelistic political pattern socialization of parties which demonstrate that the democratization process has been halted by undemocratic behavior of political parties. It seems that all parties-Left and Right-suffer from internal crisis. So political parties have been blamed as the main agents who created democratic deficit and led the successive political crisis in the country.

The number of voters increased substantially from 11.1 million in 1991 to 12.1 million in 1994 and to 13.5 million in 1999. The number of candidates contesting also increased from 1,345 in 1991 to 1, 442 in 1994 to 2,224 in 1999. Does the increase in candidates suggest a higher electoral turnout and a greater democratic role of the people? Results show that electoral participation remained highest in Nepal in 1991 (65.15 percent). The second midterm election began to show a surprising decline (61.86 percent).

What motivates the voters to vote? Survey researches reveal that Nepali voters have multiple motivations to vote: party affiliation, candidate's qualification, ability, talent, political contribution, kith and kin factor, proximity, money, political philosophy, ideological orientations, their confidence and ability to improve existing conditions by voting, etc. Of the different criteria for deciding to vote, according to 1999 General Election Opinion Poll, party principles and manifestos constitute only (38.1percent ) followed by the assurance that the concerned political party or candidate will engage in "development" (33.5 percent), followed in turn by what the household members and others say (9.1 percent). The personality and behaviour of the candidate constitute (7.5 percent), personal acquaintance with the candidate (5.1 percent) and candidate's prospects of winning (4.5percent). Still nearly 1 percent of the sample said they vote for a political party or candidate looking at his or her caste or ethnicity.[1] It is, therefore voters are not interested to put party's doctrine as the basic parameter for the selection of either party or their candidate for election purpose. Going with the poll results, the selection of party based on its doctrine is found to be 38.1 percentages against almost 62 percentages. It indicates that the role of party doctrine has less influence in the selection of a political party in the multi-party system, whereas it is the key parameter in other countries. The result corroborates with the survey result conducted by public political opinion survey in Nepal of 1994.[2] Compared across the multiple from voter, 58 of the respondents said, they vote on the basis of the own person or relative *Aphno Manche* (One's own circle). Caste is mentioned close to 47 percent, promise for development is around 13 percent. Party ideology is mentioned less frequently by voters at just 10 percent.

It can be analyzed that the culture of egocentric attitudes and assertive values continue and the command structure of the party is overwhelmingly influenced by personalities more than party ideology and people based programs. It also proves that ideology does not play a major role in Nepal's political culture because Nepalis are preoccupied with their own inner world. Dependent relationship (patron-client) determines the extent of a leaders' power rather than the ideology. The political loyalty of the followers is governed more by a sense of identification with a concrete group-communal, ethnic or sectarian rather than with the policy or ideology of the party. The followers expect that the leaders seek to maximize communal, ethnic, and sectarian interests rather than the ideological interests of the party. The personalized nature of power provides the party and government leaders with a high degree of freedom in determining the matters of strategy and tactics. It, in turn, determines the nature of the political loyalty of the followers. Institutions are used to formalize the decisions made by a particular clique in some leader's living rooms. The culture of personalized power structure has led to an emphasis on the principle of proximity. In Nepal, there is a fierce drive to be near those who are at the top of political decision — making.

Nepal's political culture has been dominated by the personalized power structure which lays emphasis on the principle of proximity. No one has noticed any change in the culture of patronage politics even after the restoration of democracy. So the relationship of politics to public life stood essentially manipulative and propagandistic where the public played no role in it except to exercise their power of electoral choice. Considering that electoral manipulation and malpractices are rampant, even voting is not carried out with policy and principle in mind. Votes cast either because one belongs to a party or because the charisma of some particular leader is appealing. Hence, individual voters do not consider themselves as a part of the nation, but as a member of a particular party and carry out their entire public life inside that sub-culture. As a result, the consciousness regarding national culture twists from torment to pain.[3]

Exclusives of people's interest and internal factionalism remain the dominant trends of the party political culture in Nepal. It seems that all parties-left and right-suffer from lack of commitment, vision, policy and programmes which are essential to expedite their declared objectives, i.e. good governance, political stability and economic development. These stated goals have been sidelined since parties' leaders and the workers are highly indulged in self-aggrandizement by all possible means. They are, therefore more interested in the game of government making and unmaking. Majority of respondents who are dissatisfied with the working of political parties are found from the educated background. More than 50 percent of the total populations think that parties do not respond to the people's real problem. In other words they fail to articulate and represent their interest which has made the ordinary people say, "they are all alike."[4] They think that the large number of parties is an impediment to the party system. They are confused by many parties that exist and their tendency to merge split or disappear.

The crises of performance of political parties based on public political opinion survey in Nepal can be said to be caused by the culture of lack of ideological clarity, orientation towards power rather than the people, a dearth of institutional culture, hereditary elements in leadership, politicization of social life and insidiously consumerist behaviour among the politicians. These factors are quite responsible for a negative perception of the people towards the working pattern of political party in the country. The same thing is evidenced in the survey conducted for the understanding of political parties and parliamentary system of Nepal which states similar reality. The majority of respondents of all parties have shown their dissatisfaction in the party's way of functioning; NeWPP occupies the top position in this regard (96.1percent) followed by NSP (95.6 percent), UPFN (82.5 percent), RPP-C (78.1percent), CPN-UML (69.7 percent) NC (64.8percent), RPP-T (61.2 percent) and CPN-U (50 percent). The intensity of dissatisfaction in the way of party functioning is greater in the CPN-U. Nearly half its members have vented their displeasure. Dissatisfaction also figures in RPP-T (37.6 percent), NC (33.9 percent), CPN-UML (28.3percent) and RPP-C (21.9 percent).[5] It shows a larger number of respondents are still dissatisfied with the way party function.

The respondents in 1990's movement probably had high expectation for the newly born party system. Now they have come to realize that the parties have failed to respond to their needs. The inability of the parties to take root in the electorate is an inhibiting factor of the progress of democracy. This is why when a common man or woman express dissatisfaction with the state of public affairs today, they tend to attribute it to the party and its leadership. In a democratic political culture, certain political skills and techniques should be present both among the population as a whole and among the political leaders. This is the motivation that inspires both leaders and followers. On the contrary, neither people nor the party leaders in the country are motivated to go further by creating and maintaining a civic political culture that is essential for democratic order.

Out of the 74 political parties in Nepal, 54 contested the CA elections while 25 are represented in the CA reflecting various size, ideologies, interest and identities. The outward appearance and agendas of Nepali political party is largely democratic but they are criticized for not practicing internal democracy within their own organizations. They have failed to evolve a set of rules, a common code of conduct, governing inter-party and intra-party relations, or to establish norms of behavior and political ethics in democracy, or inject public life with a sense of political morality. Wining of elections for them is more crucial than how it is won, actually. It is observed that Nepali political culture for the last two decades has been overwhelmed by intra-party fighting, making and breaking of inter-party conflict and coalition. In such a culture of power centric politics, the need and interest of the people has been grossly ignored.

The dirty business image of party politics extends to the way in which the struggle for political power and survival is carried out, often including the manipulation and instrumentalization of political institutions. Contrary to all parties' display of people-oriented electoral campaigns rhetoric, there is a growing tendency of political parties being less and less able to take the lead in actually formulating and debating reform-oriented policies, which determine and reflect people's aspirations and the societal mood. Though the party is conceived as a linkage institution between the state and society, parties have largely failed to observe their basic duty of linking citizens' preference with public policy. One obvious reason why parties are moving closer to becoming a part of state rather than consolidating themselves as people organization is found in the parties' rank and file's preference to accumulate property and pursue a luxurious life by all means, particularly through the manipulation of state machinery and resources. Besides, as a consequence of their failure to deliver public goods to the masses, their mindset is preoccupied with a new way of party building, through granting selective incentive (power, status, money, job, and other material rewards) to party clients. The idea has led the political parties to revolve around the circle of the vested interest groups.

The UML during its minority government tended to propel the party as an active and powerful state organization through party-run clientelism under the purview of the party's State Affairs Department. The splinter group, the ML had carried out this scheme, while becoming a junior partner of the NC led coalition government believing that it could expedite organizational building activities by being in power and thereby being able to mobilize state resources and machinery. But it soon broke coalition with the NC since it differed with Prime Minister Koirala's plan for early election to parliament. The UML and NSP joined the government in response to Koirala's call for an all-party government to conduct the 1999 general election. Other parties like the NC and RPP are not exceptions in using their position, while they were/are in power, for party building through granting patronage to the persons of their choice and their own party fellows in executive posts of state apparatus at all levels. Although Unified CPN- Maoist has joined the political mainstream by abandoning (principally) arms but it has developed its strong cadres called the Young Communist League (YCL), seen less willing to relinquish militant posturing. Other political parties have also constituted militant youth forces that are now in the open confrontation in the streets taking law and order in hands. The transition is thus getting perennially dogged by these problems.

The lack of vision to reorient parties in the changed context could be found among the parties in their pursuit of party reformation. Though each major parties- UCPN-M, NC and CPN-UML have developed and diversified organizational structures, the responsibility of most of the party structures and sub-structures have exclusively been confined to the parties' internal affairs or to look after the business of elected wing of the party. They lack that culture which would be directly responsible for public policy formulation functions. Such an inward looking approach of party reformation also reflects on the much vociferous demands for the norms and value based politics in each party's internal affairs.

The obvious target of the demand is to overcome the problems of in-fighting, division and indiscipline against the increasing tendency of individualism, selfishness and opportunistic characters of the party. Such inward looking approach of party reform could be said as renovation rather than innovation. Nepali political parties hardly appear moving towards new way of party building. So, the nation and democracy governed by parties, which lack clear principle, vision, goals, policies and programmes have suffered from the culture of directionless drift.

Democratic political culture cultivates the habit of public communication, compromise and collective action, not deadlock causing a crisis to the public life and public policy. But the deficit of democratic political culture across political parties and non availability of mechanism to resolve inter and intra party conflicts through dialogue are considered as the main causes of political deadlocks in the country. For years, Nepal's failure to develop was linked to the geographical constraint of being a land-locked nation. Now, despite immense potentials to raise the living standards of the people through socio-economic development, the state is locked in political battles and has been unable to give adequate attention to economic growth and good governance.

These days it is seen in the political culture of Nepal that politics of closure provided incentives for the rise of regional and ethnicity based political parties, such as Sadhavana party, Madeshi Jana Adhikar forum (MJAF) and Tarai-Madhesh Loktantrik Party. Political parties also have tendency to combine class with caste, ethnicity and territoriality in their social and national programs. Due to ethnic and regional politics i.e. what is being called the identity politics has become a serious threat for national security and integrity ahead. In Nepal, identity politics symbolizes an expression of unsatisfied social needs. Whenever, political parties move into power they are habitual to capture both political system and the state mechanism. This practice has developed neo-patrimonial culture which sees personal relations more important than interest-based solidarities. Political parties select members in the central committees not on the basis of seniority, meritocracy, and popularity but on the basis of personal relationship with few decision making leaders. They do not share political agendas to resolve political crisis in the country. Likewise, there is no social representation of political power, which is causing perpetual political tension-factionalism, split and reunions. The continued trend of internal fictionalization and split of political parties of Nepal has become a normal phenomenon.

The split of Madeshi Janadhikar Forum (MJF) into Madeshi Janadhikar Forum-Democratic (MJF-D) and the split of Tarai-Madhes Democratic Party (TMDP), led by Mahantha Thakur, which had 20 seats in the CA had come into existence just a few months prior to the CA election in early 2008 split in two with nine of its lawmakers led by Minister for Industry Mahendra Prasad Yadav announcing a new outfit Tarai-Madhes Democratic Party-Nepal.[6] The defection of 13 lawmakers from the Madheshi Janadhikar Forum-Nepal and subsequent formation of MJF-Republican has come as a rude shock to the leaders of parent party.[7] In the same way, the radical faction of UCPN-Maoist, which had established a separate structure within the party, finally announced the Communist Party of Nepal– Maoist, led by Mohan Baidya Kiran, a vertical split after years of ideological infighting.[8] These evidences show that politics in Nepal is largely based on personality rather than institutions. As a result, leadership roles within the government, the parties, and public institutions are personalized without any sense of accountability to the general people. When clash of interest occurs within a party, aspiring leaders have a quick tendency to create new parties rather than seek a resolution to the conflict.

Political parties of Nepal have also introduced the culture of clientele politics that has highly politicized Nepali society under partisan lines.[9] The emergence of successive political crisis during 1990s largely owes to this culture. It appears that Loktantrik government is also fascinated by the same culture. This has also been manifested in the result of the CA election which has brought family members of political leaders, their close associates and business partners into politics. All the political parties are dominated by the traditional elites that secure votes more on the basis of their family history and social standing than their service to the communities they claim to represent.

The appointments of members of planning commission, university[10] officials, ambassadors, secretaries at the ministries, members of various commissions, among others including the chairman and the executive director of Nepal Airlines are other examples of clientalism.[11] Security agencies such as army, police and armed police have not kept themselves away from partisan politics. Compared to police and armed police, army is less politically polluted. Recently, it had been reported that even army officers scrambled for getting favour from the concerned politicians to whom the army Headquarter responded with a warning that no such campaigns would be tolerated as it may create bad precedent for the neutrality of army.

Police is the worst affected security agency as politicians always try to use it for various individual and partisan interests. Since the government powers are vested in the leaders of political parties, people identify themselves with one or the other party deriving some basic values and goals from them. It is difficult to find a Nepali who is not identified with a political party, regardless of whether or not he/she is visibly engaged in politics. It has become a compulsory culture to be associated with political parties, in one-way or the other, because one cannot have things done if he/ she are not the member of political parties or without the backing of political leaders.

During the Panchayat time aspirants for governmental resources used to spend their time in *Chakari* (obsequious attendance) around the homes of Royal Palace Secretaries. Now they have moved to the courtyards of the party leaders and ministers. Once the *Chakariwal* gets a feeling that the person he is doing *Chakari* is no longer a powerful personality, he/she quickly withdraws from his regular ritual of *Chakari* to that person and moves on to another person whom he considers to be powerful. So the popular psychology is that those who possess power have to command more influence and accomplish more things than ordinary citizens. People want to be followers of a strong personality who can provide them with security as well as with prestige. The political bickering, too much politicization of daily life for either protection or benefit has also rendered independent thoughts to be paralyzed. Professionals are also bound to be associated with one or other political party, for either patronage or survival or to seek protection from physical threats posed to them.

The survey conducted by the US-based United States Institute of Peace among 8,000 members of the general public and well over 4,000 respondents (various stakeholders), including NP, Civil society and political parties has come up with the findings that nepotism, favouritism and corruption even in the transfer and promotion processes-have been rampant in the Nepal Police. Many police officers believe that they personally have been denied professional opportunities because they did not pay bribe or lacked family or friend connection.[12] Within Nepal there is no point in arguing that one set of *Afnomanchhe* is better or worse than another. The only accountable quality in an individual is the need for membership of the circle in question. Attributes like academic qualification, training, background, working discipline, integrity of character are not as important or helpful as the sense of belonging to a particular circle. The repercussions of this culture are anchored through public frustration and declining efficiency of governance to connect citizens to nationality. The way things stand at the moment, political parties do not feel the need for making any fundamental change in their style of party running, nor in the manner of their functioning. Their leadership does not seem to read the popular mood craving for change in the leadership and in the organizational structure of their parties, nor is it willing to take the least pressure from any quarters to respond to these urges.[13]

The anti-intellectual culture runs very high across political parties. There are no provisions of consultation with experts within the parties. The technical matters are being manipulated by party interest. Even if the consultation takes place; it is not on the basis of expertise and meritocracy but on the basis of ideology, kinship and patronage. The major parties–particularly the UCPN-M, NC, CPN (UML), and Terai Madheshi parties are peculiarly characterized by a culture of personalized groupism, often at the cost of their credibility and popularity. Political parties from the

Terai Madheshi parties have the potentials of being divisive due to personal rather than ideological reasons. Since Nepal Sadbhawana Party is the product of Madheshi movement (2007) principally launched by the Madheshi Janadhikar Forum for establishing a distinct identity in Nepali politics, fragile coalition did not help consolidate them as a unified force for achieving their declared objectives. Although all of these Madheshi parties have same types of pretentious Madheshi agendas, their weakened position is not likely to get them fulfilled.

The advent of democracy has in its wake brought into focus a number of pervasive socio-economic problems of the country in different forms and shape, i.e., gender issues, minority problems, grievances of the disadvantaged groups, unemployment, corruption etc. But political parties appear largely not sincere in addressing such emerging social and economic problems and give realistic and pragmatic policy incentives. Power seems to be the single most important target of all parties. The culture that political parties understand is that democracy is about winning elections and for winning an election, a party or a leader can stoop as low as necessary and collect the wherewithal for personal and party uses. In the name of policies, they violate the law; they are expected to enforce in pursuit of their peripheral and parochial interests. The party in power, whichever that may be tends to justify their position with the recurring rhetoric of political instability and democracy in danger. So democracy in Nepal has been a free ride without obligation. The weak and undemocratic party system is one of the most important reasons for our undemocratic political culture and unstable democracy. Since people are losing confidence in the parties and the leaders, one cannot deny the fact that the people's euphoria and enthusiasm awakened by the successful mass movements in 1990 and 2006 has turned into the culture of indifference, frustration and disillusionment towards the political parties, the political leaders and the government in general.

There is a huge gap between rhetoric and action. The parties have not been able to contribute much to provide relief to the people and society. There has been no tangible progress in the socio-economic condition of the country in the last seven years, nor has the progress in the peace process and constitution drafting been satisfactory.[14] The failure of CA is an example of this. Had the political parties been able to protect the procedures and democratic decision-making processes, they would have been able to deliver a new constitution in time.Political parties in Nepal are intent on just making claims that they represent the people while actually working against people's interest in running of the state and political parties. When it comes to delivering the fruits of democracy to people, the author herself has observed two major problems. One the parties ignore constitutional processes and mechanism for individual and partisan interests. Secondly, they do not have good knowledge, political skills and culture in running a state. These aspects indicate that the conventional political parties in Nepal will continue to be unsuccessful in the future in addressing peoples' concern. As the gap between political parties and people widens, there is real danger that a new popular force may emerge in the empty space.

The gap can also give space for extra-constitutional forces that can claim to work for the people at a time when conventional political parties have failed to carry out that function. Political scientists have made a distinction between the representative function of democracy and procedural function of democracy. While the concept of constitutional democracy emphasizes proper functioning of the checks and balances as well as mechanisms enshrined in the democratic constitutions, the concept of popular democracy emphasizes the process of people's participation and element of by the people. Unless we are not able to strengthen the checks and balances as well as ensure that the parties in government follow proper democratic procedures in running of the state, the people are going to suffer the worst.

Political parties in Nepal although are unable to represent the interest of the people, we cannot imagine the Nepali state without political parties. Now it is time for the parties to think about the Nepali people instead of trying to fool them by using outdated jargon and rhetoric. It is an accepted phenomenon that one can fool all sometime, one can again fool some all time but one cannot fool all, all the times. Keeping all these contradictions in mind it is strongly advised that political parties should be structured in line with democratic norms and values. Democracy flourishes when there is complimentarily of interest among political forces, their sister organizations and civil society. It is important that democratic forces communicate with each other regularly at the various layers of party rank and file (horizontally and vertically) and also with civil society members to disseminate message to the people and serve their interests. The approach of party reformation should also have outward looking content relating to general people's concern. Unless political parties do not rise above their personal and partisan interests they cannot contribute towards democratization process.

National political parties should act as the new equivalent of a centripetal force, drawing people from social diversity, aggregate their interest, articulate them into public sphere and engage them into collective action. Only a state founded on an understanding and awareness of a given historical unity could provide the necessary grounds for realizing these objectives. An inclusive democracy presumes an inclusive political party in its construct, reflected in its party hierarchy. Parties should have a broad and inclusive recruitment policy for its primary, secondary and tertiary workers, and an equally inclusive composition of its party r ınkings both in the districts and central organizations. Parties should spend their efforts in debating new and emergent ideas on the issues of governance and safeguarding of individual freedom and human rights.

Political parties must work at developing a political culture in which each gives public recognition to others' good work. The changing time and situation demand that the party should advance with new perspectives, new vision, and new outlook setting new objectives. The formulation of realistic and effective policies and programmes rather than ideological rhetoric and leadership cult could be a new source of strength for the parties in Loktantrik Nepal.

## Opposition Culture: Imbalance between Co-operation and Competition

Politics rests upon collective actions which in turn depend upon a basic spirit of trust and a capacity for co-operation. At the same time politics involves conflict and competition too. Myron writes that "one of the most disruptive crises in modern times has been caused by the efforts of that not in power to gain access to power or to influence decisions made by governing elites."[15] The capacity of political culture to manage this problem usually depends on how the basic socialization process handles the problems of mutual trust and distrust in personality development. It has been suggested that in the United States the basic socialization process emphasizes to peculiarly high degree basic trust in human relations. American political culture stresses the need to distrust institutions, to check power and to demand strict accountability of all public officials.[16] But the case is reverse in many transitional societies where the socialization process instills deep distrust of human relations, while at the same time, people are asked to have complete and uncritical faith in their public institutions. Two cultural values emerge as critical for stable democracy. The first is tolerance, particularly a willingness to accept the articulation of opposing views. Tolerance must include a readiness to participate in adversarial relationship without allowing feelings of aggressions to take over. The second cultural value is trust. The ability to trust other is crucial not only as a foundation for building civic associations but also for reinforcing people's sense of political efficacy. If the people do not have a sense of political efficacy, the belief that their participation is worthwhile– democracy cannot be stable. Putnam labels trust as a "feature of social organization that can improve the efficiency of society by facilitating co-ordained action." [17]

The problem is that in some societies, the primary process of socialization tends to provide people with a strong optimistic view of life and a deep sense of basic trust in human relations, while the later stages of political socialization emphasizes cynicism and suspicion of political actors. As a result, the political culture is characterized by a critical and contemptuous view of existing political practices and is also coloured by a strong utopian faith that reform can ultimately remedy the existing situation. Don't that dynamics seem to be at practice in Nepal's political culture? Because in Nepali society, distrust of contemporary political institutions and personage is preceded by an earlier socialization process which instills a sense of fundamental distrust and suspicion, with the result that people have little faith in reformist solutions and feel that political improvement requires cataclysmic changes. Doesn't Nepal provide an example with that culture? The lack of respect for the opposition which is antithetical to civic and democratic culture persists in Nepal. One of the requirements for democratic stability is tolerance of difference of opinion. Schumpeter points out that democratic government will work to full advantage only if all the interests that matter are practically unanimous not only in their allegiance to the country but also in their allegiance to the structure principles of the existing society.[18]

It shows that opposition is a civic-culture tradition for democratic stability. A democratic political culture presupposes elimination of the use of violence responsiveness of leaders, especially the elected ones and correct relationship between the government and opposition. It is argued that the intensity of political competition should not undermine a sense of social, economic and political purpose set by the state and polarize the voters in opposite direction. Almond and Verba recount the fact that the political orientations that make up the civic culture are closely related to general society and interpersonal relations. …[19] The relationship is so close, in fact, that co operations and social trust are called a component of the civic culture. …[20] Although this does not however, eliminate the possibility of collective action, a co-operative strategy is regarded as the most effective means for achieving collective benefit. Generally, a political party in the West does not criticize other parties in its manifesto. It describes its vision, issues, objectives, means and options for achieving them.

Nepalis lack the propensity to work with other. They lack the civic cooperation which is important in the functioning of democratic system as it helps to determine the amount of pressure an individual or group can exert and the probability of success. The survey studies have consistently encountered low levels of interpersonal trust guided by low level of civic cooperation in Nepal. The tenacity of this mentality has a very tendency to demean others. Party leaders are seen to instrumentalize and prepare their cadres and voters to see opposition as an enemy which is very dangerous for democratic culture. This is because they have suffered from the wrong socialization by the political leaders and party schools. Such attitude has implications on the integration of both society and state.

Trust in fellow citizens is a basic cultural belief. But mistrust and suspicion have long been regarded as important elements of Nepali political culture. A feeling of suspicion about human relations tend to prevail among us, because interaction with others, outside the narrow circles of family and friends is viewed as risky and dangerous in the society, which has been a major theme in the Nepali attitude and behaviour. So, collective action becomes difficult. Most Nepalis remain suspicious, uncooperative, rigid and insistent upon certain formalities of government in order to protect their own positions and personalities. As a general rule, trust arises when individuals share a set of moral and familial values in such a way as to generate mutual expectations of honest behaviour. In this context Dahal says:

> How is democratization possible when there are fundamental flaws in our political make up? We do not have independent schooling system where people can learn about democracy. Each party prepares its manifesto on the basis of its ideological imperatives. Cadres are socialized on the basis of manifesto which claims that, that party is the best and all others are the worst. When people are socialized in a sort of cacophony, democratic values cannot be stabilized because of the extent of diversity and the political cultures of the principal parties which too are diverse. Educational content of political parties creates a sort of combative situation which makes them fundamentalist rather a tolerant one.[21]

The reason is that students, young workers and cadres are socialized only in a confrontational, agitation politics, not in the skill and sensitivity that is really needed for democratic competition. How the opposition parties are non cooperative and myopic in their roles and how the prime minister, ministers and party functionaries seem to be more casual and often contradictory on important policies, both domestic and external can be best illustrated by the myopic roles of the CPN (UML) for influencing the World Bank to delay the funding of Arun III Hydropower project. The UML General Secretary had a written letter to the World Bank urging it to postpone its decision until the verdict of the mid-term elections in November 1994. It was also argued that such big dam project was not conducive for the overall interest of Nepal. In a number of cases such as the Tanakpur Treaty, Labour Act, work permit for Non-Nepali etc., arbitrary decision of the government had crossed over bounds of constitutional democracy, debates raged on even after the political blunders were corrected by the verdict of the Supreme Court deeming them unconstitutional. Had proper civic education been provided to party workers, they might have corrected such behavior.

It shows how the ruling parties and the opposition do not agree even in the most important national cause giving importance to the short term interest of their respective parties. They are out to destroy one another even at the cost of the system. They are jealous, arrogant, and selfish and power hunger and would do anything to go to the power which has already demonstrated in making and unmaking different political coalitions. Lack of patience and the authoritarian feudal mentality handed down from generation to generation hardly permit one to listen to another. There is always a tendency to impose one's own opinion on the other. That is why within minutes of the start of a debate, hot exchange of words ensues and the meeting ends up with personal vilification and at times it even ends up with fist-fights. On the question of relationship between the NC and opposition parties, 49 percent in the district and 46.6 percent at the national level respond to the question as bad, while 41.1 percent and 43.9 percent respectively consider it to be fair and 7.2 percent in the district and 4.3 percent at the national level see it as good. [22] It shows that although the manifestos of the parties provide the framework under which relationship between the parties can operate, a clear pattern in the interaction between the ruling party and the opposition is still lacking. This is how in the absence of co-operation and the culture of tolerance, opposing goals in the polity are causing a lot of crises and deadlock in the lives of innocent people and political process.

How Anand P. Shrestha characterizes the political culture of the country in an interview taken by *The Telegraph* is worth mentioning here to show how the political culture of violence and confrontation evolved through the stages and history and has its impact on the state:

> The country right from the time of Bhimsen Thapa right down to the present times failed to develop the culture of the politics of development. Throughout history the politics of revenge and vendetta has been rise in our body politic. In the old day it was Thapa's vs the Pandey's infighting among the Rana, Jung Bahadur family vs the 17 brothers, then A class Rana vs B and C class Ranas. M.P. Koiralla vs B.P. Koirala, B.P. Vs. King Mahendra, G.P. Koirala Vs Ganeshman, Ganeshman vs K.P. Bhattarai, Deuba vs Shailaja Acharya, R.C. Poudel vs Madhav Nepal vs Bam Dev, K.P. Oli, S.B. Thapa, vs Chand. The list is endless. In the existing political scenario it is somewhat difficult to foresee development politics emerge.[23]

Legacy and political culture of conspiracy and violence have influenced generations. *Kot Massacre, Alau Parba, Makai Parba*, etc. are glaring examples. If one goes deeply into Nepal's history, one finds how the ubiquitous influence of the political culture of revenge and conspiracy has served as a motive force of history, change in power equation, revenge and even elimination of elites. State building process in Nepal is a continuing phenomenon often hastened by conflicts and contradictions in the society. In that process, Nepal has witnessed various forms of conflict and violence, some time low and some time high intensity and in the form of rivalry and competition in different phases of its history.

It is seen that several critical elements of civic culture, such as the culture of tolerance, accommodation and consensus building are often missing. Unnatural political polarization is widespread. The dearth of far sightedness, tolerance and harmony among the prominent leaders cast a dark shadow over Nepal's political culture. In Nepal, as democracy is yet to transform the political culture, which is largely based on the use of coercion– to one based on the culture of consensus, mutual co-operation, trust and confidence cultural tolerance between the various political parties is required. So legitimate questions of the nation need to be discussed within the parliament where there is a better scope for the opposition's concern. This is the only way to discourage the emerging tendency to resort to extra- parliamentary, extra-constitutional and anti-system opposition.

**Leadership Crisis: A Culture of No Win Situation**

Leadership devoid of a sense of group power and enough authority to bring recalcitrant party leaders to book defies the expectations of people and their own party manifestoes. It is this condition that has forced the executive leaders into suffers from the credibility gap between promise and performance.

Generally, leadership is an outstanding quality i.e. superiority intelligence, character skill, power, and standard setters to the social values.[24] In broader term, a leader is he/ she who stands at the surface of realities. [25] Leadership role can be broadly explained in two types: transactional and transformatory. Transforming group having a vision of society sets about doing something to implement that vision. The transactional leaders, on the contrary, merely operate trade-offs or exchanges one advantage for another. Among the variables that determine democratic consolidation through system building, the leadership role has become crucial for Nepal. Unless democratic system becomes fully institutionalized or routinized committed leaders matter much for building the democratic process. Here I must present the positive and negative picture of Nepali leaders who by comparison although do not stand up to the level of committed and ideal leaders, but who are no less crucial for dynamic evolution of Nepali democracy and society. Although all parties' leaders come from the same middle or lower middle class background of a hierarchical society, they are also flexible to adopt change. The holding of periodic elections and the systemic capacity to respond to challenges have had been possible due to the strong democratic orientations of leaders. Leaders are also credited with their pragmatism and sense of time. In the changed context of the second phase of transition towards democratic consolidation, the party and the leaders were supposed to prove their worth by their ability to lead and govern the nation effectively. But instead of that all political leaders have invariably failed to make the general people feel the essence of democratic change, despite their long struggle for achieving democracy with equitable social justice. Even the leaders elected overwhelmingly by representatives of parties' conventions became ineffective in running the parties and government.

The UCPN-(Maoist) and CPN-UML which are supposed to be well knot organizations befitting the communist norm are undergoing organizational strains. The UCPN-Maoist leaders speak in contradictory voices reflecting both ideological and strategic divergences in their approaches. How are the people to believe them when they speak of a break through within a few days? The three core leaders of party–Prachanda, Mohan Baidya, and Baburam- do not share a common agenda of party building or democracy's development on the basis of the agreements signed with other parties. Interpretations vary creating a climate of political uncertainty. Such idiosyncratic behaviours of Maoist leaders have emboldened people to point out their fingers at the former as if they are the villains' fall stalling the transition to constitutional order. So there has been a serious trust deficit not only within the Maoist camps but also between the Maoist and other party leaders. Another party, the CPN-UML because of poor organizational disciplne and leadership role, all the apex leaders are at war with each other trying to put a check on the ambition of the other. Opposing to the hilt, one section of party led by the Chairman, Jhal Nath Khanal, didn't tolerate Madhav Kumar Nepal as Prime minister. Later Madhav Nepal and Khadga Oli team has adopted a similar strategy to pull down the Khanal-led coalition government supported by the Maoist party. So no Prime Minister despite being the leader of the party can function with confidence and determination. NC leaders do suffer from similar malaise. With the death of G.P. Koirala, NC is said to have been run by a collective leadership or'triumvirate" of Sushil Koirala, Sher Bahadur Deuba and Ram Chandra Poudel. Surprisingly, however the NC leaders have not come out with any socio-economic agenda except crying foul of the Maoists for being irresponsible and anti-democratic. Baral remarks that in the changed political landscape, NC's politics of reaction may not be able to mobilize the people: nor will its past democratic credential alone help the party.[26]

Still the Nepali leaders are credited with their pragmatism and sense of time. Baral further remarks that the leaders of the major parties have not only survived monarchical absolutism and the vagaries of multiparty parliamentary politics of the 1990s and early 21st century, they have also not failed to be as much dynamic and flexible as circumstances and context demanded. If the Maoists have accepted the multiparty system and other core values of democracy, Baral expects that the NC, a diehard constitutional monarchical party could transform into a republican one. On many other issues such as federalism, inclusiveness and secularism all the parties are together.[27] But people's only worry is to see them play much more positive role for making a smooth transition to democracy.

In the Nepali context, today most political parties' leaders owing to personal interest for power and position are transactional in view of their over indulgence in short-terms gains. Presenting themselves as mere power-seekers most political parties' leaders in the post movement period are generally perceived by the people as having been driven by a strong desire for power. Lack of minimum level of organizational solidarity, both inter-party and intra-party transactions are more or less confined to such games that could seldom be used for larger interest of the people. As a result polarized emotions and conflicts overtake the culture of rational argument.

Transformatory leaders, on the other hand, bring about a qualitative change through the instrumentality of movement and actions. They would transform the conditions under which economic and social policy making would take place in the country.[28] Three general elections have already been held and all political parties had a chance to be in power. Yet, how far the underlined spirit of the movement has had been adhered to by the leaders and parties? The manner with which the political leaders of various parties seem to be haunted by their complex and lack of confidence in carrying out radical socio-economic policies for transforming the status quo, they cannot be called transformatory leaders.

The other typology of leadership in Nepal is related to charisma as a phenomenon. Charisma is understood as the leaders having been graduated into leadership roles due to family background (*khandan* or *Kul Gharan) or* through some ascribed social positions like former *Zamindars* and local *Thalus*. Such links are often employed as a pass- partout for any role. [29] Social and family ties are prominent where this type of political culture is found. For them party is a tool for realizing their selfish, personal interests, which they maneuver cunningly with the help of their chosen coterie and members of the family. It has given rise to a cult culture that has tempted party workers and followers hang around to 'cult leaders' to grab the public space. The personality cult prevails in all political parties which dominates "decisions and development" across political parties. This often means that some families run the government and others have little to say about it. This reflects an older attitude that embraces a hierarchical society. Government is seen as an actor with a positive role in the community, but the role is largely limited to securing the maintenance of the existing social order which is viewed as best because that is all which is required to meet the needs of those in power. Political leaders socialized in this background play largely a conservative and custodial role rather than being innovative.

The most dramatic change that is observed in Nepali political culture after 1990 is the sharp decline in public trust and confidence in political leaders and institutions as recorded in many public opinion polls. The stability of democratic regime depends on the ability of the political elites and party leaders to work together to deal with the problems confronting their society and to refrain from exploiting those problems for their own immediate material or political advantage.[30] The serious impediment to democratization is the absence or weakness of real commitment to democratic values among political leaders in Asia, Africa, and the Middle East. In those regions, however, elected leaders themselves were also responsible for ending democracy: Siangtan Rhee and Park Chung Hee in Korea, Ferdinand Marcos in Philippines, Lee Kwan Yew in Singapore, and Sukarno in Indonesia. These leaders won power through the electoral system and then used their power to undermine that system.

The democratic development history in Nepal also shows that political parties continued struggling for democracy when in opposition but failed to build institution while they were and are power. After they became successful and occupied power and other positions, they soon forgot their mission. Most political leaders generally exhibit contradictory tendencies. They fight for democracy, suffer for it and corrupt it by their behaviour after coming to power.[31] Theories on leadership explain that leadership devoid of a sense of group power and enough authority to bring recalcitrant party leaders to book defies the expectations of people and their own party manifestoes. It is this condition that has forced the executive leaders into suffers from the credibility gap between promise and performance. What I need to stress here is that movements alone do not sustain democracy; political forces involved in such movements should have minimum culture that can be manifested in institutions. It is ironic that democratic culture which ensures institutional behavior is still a distant thing in Nepal. Neither procedural nor substantive aspects of democracy– building project are underway.

Nepali politics is closely intertwined with personalist leaders vying for power, prestige and privileges, making a zero-sum system with little scope for optimism to build a peaceful and healthy competitive society. Political leaders out of office have good reasons to advocate democracy. The test of their democratic commitment comes when they are in office. The leadership of Prime Minister, the highest post in the parliamentary system is weak and circumscribed by the politics of hung parliament and power equation within the ruling party/parties. The personality of the post-1994 prime ministers was overshadowed either by a system of a high command of coalition parties (constituted outside the purview of the state apparatus but working as steering committee taking all important decisions of the government) or by dominant personality of the second man in the cabinet: deputy prime ministers Madhav Nepal and Bam Dev Gautam during the governments formally led by Prime Minister late Man Mohan Adhikari and Lokendra Bahadur Chand for instance.

All governments under hung parliament were/are obsessed with survival crisis and the priority of all Prime ministers was/is to retain the post as long as possible rather than consolidation of one's own leadership position through providing effective and strong government. The directionless drift or transitional period may also be seen as a byproduct of the leadership crisis in Nepal. The image of the leaders of Nepali political parties except those of RPP has been built on the ground of their long struggle and sacrifice for the cause and principle. Their contribution in the early phase of democratic transition- notably in the restoration of multi-party system and transformation of sovereign power from the palace to the people- was highly appreciable. So, the popularity of some parties' leaders particularly, NC's top leaders late Ganesh Man Singh (commander of the 1990 mass movement) and Krishna P. Bhattarai

(PM of Interim government), and also UML's late General Secretary Madan Bhandari attained a peak.

For any country or institution to restructure and transform, it is necessary that new thoughts come to the forefront and replace what existed. But our leaders never seem to let go what they have in their hands. Entrenched traditional values and the failure of parties and leaders to orient themselves in the new changed context on one hand and a growing popular disenchantment with the behaviours and performances of parties and leaders on the other has dimmed the scope of sustainable democratic evolution.[32] It is observed that the highest number of voters falls between 18-35 years of age group but there are few leaders to represent this age-group across political parties. Non-stake holding of youth in politics has caused their alienation, cynicism, migration and militancy. The democratic world outside has seen several generations of change in the leadership structure of their parties. In Nepal, the same ageing leaders are continuing in their leadership positions from the 1990s, and some even from the 1950s. This may be because party leaders who are in leadership positions just by virtue of their age and seniority in party ranks rather than on account of their energy, drive and commitment to the politics demanded by the public.

In all political parties there is a tendency to remain in the power at any cost as long as they can. For this reason, the mainstream parties have become stagnant with the same leaders, voices, programmes and propaganda. Their leadership patterns don't allow the fresh recruitment of leaders from new social classes. Political parties in Nepal are top-heavy with no middle layer of political leadership that can connect them with the masses. Only the younger generation of the traditional elites is allowed to replace them. For example, two major political parties — Nepali Congress and the CPN-UML have same people holding highest and key party position for more than two decades. Nepal's political culture still reflects not only a contradictory mix of deference for senior leaders due to their age, a wish for their idolization but also distrust of their authority and a culture of confrontation rather than compromise.

It is being observed in Nepal that youth are capable of bringing unprecedented changes on all fronts of socio–economic structures. Studies also reveal that the tolerance of the youth to change is greater than the older generation. Since youth constitutes a significant percent of Nepal's population, it is undoubtedly crucial that they are represented at all levels, as clearly reflected in the constituent assembly (CA) where the older generations were convincingly sidelined by the younger generation of leaders . The explanation given in the power distance index (PDI) of Geert Hofstede,[33] a Dutch psychologist, is very relevant in Nepal's context. The indicator measures the extent to which the less powerful members of organizations and institutions accept and expect power to be distributed unequally. Structurally, Nepal has greater PDI difference in almost all spheres of life, family, office and politics. Interestingly, in his explanation, Hofstede says," the acceptance of the followers' matters as much as that of a leader."[34] If the same analysis dimension is brought to the Nepali structure, younger generation has lesser decision influencing power as compared to elders. But if it is radically believed that the younger generation is the only answer to improving the country's political situation, it can also be supposed that it would be no different than choosing different parties to vote.

The sudden domination of the UCPN (Maoist) in constitutional assembly, right after their commitment to peaceful mainstream politics, is one such example where the Nepali voters wanted change. However, the outcome was far removed from their expectations. Just like the population of Nepal has tested the political parties and leaders, the young generation leadership will be ultimately tested in the long run. Has it really brought about stipulated change? While youth definitely have the capacity to bring change, are we not expecting too much from youth leadership? What we often ignore is that youth too are bound by the same societal norms and psychology as the older generation. They too are the result of the same social structure as the older generation. So it is time to have a discussion on how they should be socialized, trained and prepared and their voices should be heard in the political process.

The outstanding quality of the leaders both older and younger is not reflected in their performance- in management of intra-party affairs as well as in administration of state and government machinery. Rather the increasing tendency to seek the price of their past struggle and sacrifice in terms of power and position has tended to constrain a healthy development of the party system and democracy. The present leadership seems to be harping on the glory of the past rather than thinking for the future. Apathy and hollow promises are what the leaders have the expertise in rather than working for providing relief to the people. Do not these situations make it high time that the Nepalis also learn from the Egyptian case and groom a new leadership? These are questions that are repeated by the new generation.

How long do we go with the same politicians in the name of democracy or people's verdict and keep the country in a zero-sum game? Consequently, most of the parties have turned into conflict ridden organization overwhelmed by power and culture of ego centric tussles among their respective party leaders which would ultimately lead them towards the culture of disintegration. So, what the leadership power appears to be used more for destructive purpose than for constructive one gives the clue of political culture in the present context of Nepal. The erosion in leadership quality has become responsible for the spillover effects of intra-party conflicts, instability of government, degeneration of political morale and ethics, lack of rule of law, compromise of democratic norms and values followed up by economic recession and stagnation of national development leaving the situation a no-win situation for every player. So people's enthusiasm for democracy and participation in electoral politics has all declined significantly.

The leadership also lacks any sound vision of federal Nepal and its commitment is motivated by short-sighted political expediency. The Maoist leadership too never delved into federalism and its value. Rather it used ethnicity for the purpose of expanding and consolidating the insurgency. Its version of autonomy does not have democratic content, but has a party-controlled command structure which hardly corroborates with federal values. Other political parties such as NC and UML never thought about federal Nepal. They are dragged by the exigencies.[35] Political parties in Nepal operate in a highly centralized structure and the political culture lacks federal republican contents. Each of them has winners take all tendencies. Within both NC and UML anti-federal opinion is still prevalent. The reluctance of all the major political parties is evident from their unwillingness to form the state restructuring commission as per the provision of Interim Constitution, which came to establish only in November 2011. As a result, the CA committee which was supposed to recommend constitutional provision related to federal structure did not have even minimum information and options that would provide inputs to the parties.

After the signing of 12-point agreement, joint efforts by the political parties to stand against the then King had given hope to most of the Nepalis that the nation was changing and the leaders had learnt lessons from their past mistakes. The Constituent Assembly (CA) election was held and people accepted the results. Despite the mandate for two years, the parties extended the life of CA for an additional year and people gave the nod to bring the country out of the stalemate. With the 5-point agreement among the UCPN (M), Nepali Congress (NC) and the CPN (UML), the tenure of the CA was again extended for many times for going ahead with the peace process and constitution–drafting point[36] that has raised suspicion among the people that the constitution will never meet deadline. One does not have to travel far in the time zone to observe the fallacy of the leader's commitments. So many commitments and promises, yet fulfilling them is only an iota.

People had thought that the leaders would come to a broader understanding concerning national interest and people's aspiration. But they have realized that both the old parties and a new party with its revolutionary background (as they interpret) are successful enough to be national leaders, but interested in only consolidating their power with alliance that emerges from the dark room at the last hour either to prevent its competing leaders getting broader consensus, or letting some other parties into power. This is how incompetent leaders have made CA election for power struggle than to draft a constitution that would, in broader terms, reflect Nepalis aspirations of secular democratic republic. In the absence of these credentials, leaders are subject to heavy criticism. Only the leaders are enjoying democracy without any responsibility. They fail even to rationalize their quest for power through appropriate policy, commitment and implementation. People want to see their leaders innovative, dynamic, clean, and visionary and bold who can take right decisions and implement them. The burden of discussion on party restructuring should surely lie in cleaning the party stable first that democratic process can become more accountable, predictable and transparent.[37]

Now political leaders are under tremendous pressure to be democratic and progressive at the same time because of the upsurge of ethnic–nationalism, regionalism and demand for a just society and polity. The context has dramatically changed picture due to greater emphasis on inclusiveness and empowerment. Their upbringing, socialization and orientations are not only diverse but also hostile to one another. But to their credit, the leaders of various parties have found a common ground to steer the course of New Nepal. They are republican, secular, democratic and progressive. All agree that Nepali democracy cannot survive unless it is inclusive, secular, and egalitarian with social justice. Now, the crucial test of leaders has come; how far the political leadership would be able to manage the turbulent transition to stable democracy. So the problem is with the leader's behavior and parties and not problems with democracy.

The lesson to be learnt at the end is that when the tensile strength of tolerance crosses its threshold, it has to break. The crisis of today's Nepal is about the failure of leaders to make democratic governance more effective and qualitative. The system output suggests that the stability of the government and system may be in doubt, if the level of output becomes less satisfactory. At this critical juncture, more accountability, sincerity and political honesty have to be forthcoming from the political leaders in fulfilling the aspirations of the people and also redeem their image. This is also necessary for a result oriented move forward. Now, innovative young leaders have to think about taking the country in the logical path than remain in the state of zero-sum game.

## Participation: Union Demonstration and Protest Culture

True democracy means effective citizen, control over policy, responsible government, honesty and openness in politics, informed and rational deliberation, equal participation and power followed up by various civic virtues. Democracy involves the two dimensions –contestation and participation. It also implies the existence of those civil and political freedoms to speak, publish, assemble, and organize that are necessary to political debate and the conduct of electoral campaigns. Governments produced by elections may be inefficient, corrupt, shortsighted, irresponsible, dominated by special interests, and incapable of adopting policies demanded by the public good. Tolerance to dissent and legitimate opposition in the parliament are essential preconditions for the control of government's power for maintaining public scrutiny and transparency. For it people's representation and participation are necessary.

Participation is defined as the involvement of people in economic, social, cultural and political activities that affect their lives. Citizens can either participate directly or through their representatives or organizations. In the political processes, citizens participate through their legislative representatives or through politically oriented organizations established under a country's laws. However, representation alone cannot fulfill citizen interests unless their representatives participate effectively in the making of policies and laws that benefit the groups they represent, especially groups of the excluded.

People participate in various ways, chiefly through union activities, public discussions, citizen initiatives, petition-signing, and participation in public protests. As democracy is often described as rule of mob, they are aroused over trifles in the name of case, community, religion and riots. Demonstrations are organized, protests staged and riots engineered in the name of language, caste, religion to build up vote banks for the interested political parties and their leaders. Passions are set aflame over trivial matters and peace endangered frequently in various parts of the country.

The inclination to protest is something inherent to the very nature of society and right to peaceful protest is a vital part of democracy. A protest is an expression of objection by words or actions against particular events, policies and situations. It has a long history but unfortunately disruptions and violence have been a prominent culture of protests in Nepal these days. Nepal is no exception to such protest, the only outcome being public hardship and huge losses by way of damaging to public property which eventually haunts the common person in the form of affected services.

It is seen that opposition parties often use civil disobedience as a means of strengthening their own political position by eliciting mass support. Large numbers of people often support such movements when other channels for influencing public policy are closed. The response by government to most of these movements is to treat them as threats to its authority. The most usual methods have been the *bandhas* (the Nepali term for a strike) i.e., unauthorized marches, blocking of vehicles, *chakkajams* etc. None of these activities represent an absolute novelty. Episodes of bombing, assaults, kidnapping, burning of cars, effigy burning, damaging public and private transportation and infrastructures, destruction of public and private property are frequently seen in the last few years in Nepal, while the frequency of these untold behaviours were rare and isolated in the past. All these have given birth to a new culture of protest in the country.

As such, participation has largely taken the forms of union demonstrations and public protests. Generally, trade unions, student unions, and other politically affiliated organizations and their community counterparts call for *bandha.* They are no different from sister wings of political parties. Parties use them and they use parties for mutual gains. Similar is the situation of academic institutions, teachers union and student's union. It takes various forms, including *bandha* of markets or road/transports systems, educational institutions. The spate of *bandha* which is on an increasing mode has become so common that it is now a norm and an established culture of Nepali society.

The United Nations Office for the Coordination of Humanitarian Affairs in Nepal recorded 755 major events in 2008 alone. Every day of February 2009 was marked by *bandha*; indeed, the *bandha* was called for by two to five organizations during a day of the month, excluding the single day of the 15th.. Despite their popularity, b*andha* involves significant economic losses and thereby impact livelihoods, especially those of the poor and day laborers not only in terms of wages, but of higher prices for food, and other daily necessities. A day of no work or business means having to incur tremendous losses. A *bandha* is hard on the people as the day to day affairs come to a halt. It is especially harsh on daily wage earners for whom it means hungry stomachs. It is quite difficult for people who have difficulty in meeting their ends meet. The success of any protest is measured by the extent of disruptions it caused to daily lives by way of *bandha.*

The federation of Nepali Chambers of Commerce and Industries has estimated a loss of NRs. 28.7 billion during a 20-day long Terai *bandha* in 2007.[38] Frequent strikes, road blockades and insecurity in the day broad light are the reasons for a poor economic growth in recent years. The country's current economic growth rate is 3.5 percent while neighboring India and china are clocking 9 and 10 percent respectively.[39] The political sphere is marked by a phenomenal rise of protest movements that weaken both public confidence in the country's investment climate and the government's authority. Active participation of citizens and low institutionalization of political parties including inner- party democracies and civil society has increasingly made civic engagement progressively anomic and extra- constitutional. The radicalization of public sphere is eroding the social base of traditional parliamentarian political parties giving birth to partial associations, lineage groups, regional associations and several revolutionary groups. These are the reflections of pre-democratic politics rather than a civic culture.[40]

People's participation in *bandha* and other protests is organized with little consideration of the population as a whole; ambulances carrying patient, hospital, and media are targeted and vandalized. Very often, they damage the interests of the general public. They involve little public discussion and are sometimes violent. Violent is the negative side of conflict which if not addressed properly, may escalate. They originate not only among party-affiliated organizations and groups, but are also triggered among the parties themselves. Political culture dominated by such negative behaviour is an obstacle for the consolidation of democracy in Nepal. Studies shows that this sort of protest political culture in Nepal gives the reflection of unhealthy and destructive opposition rather than compromise, consensus and co-operation. A particularly obvious example was the continuous 59 day suspension of parliamentary work in 2008 by the Madhesi-based regional parties in their monopoly of the rostrum to voice their demands. This was followed up by a 15-day rupture in April 2009. John Galtung's, interview by *Nepal Times* with regard to Nepalis perception towards demonstration and violence is worth mentioning here. In answer to a question of how does he assess the Nepali people's potential for peace, he says that, "Nepalis have a capacity for negative peace. The 10-year long conflict was a testament to their potential for excessive violence, while during the 18 days of Jan Andolon II in 2006; they toppled a 240 year-old monarchy without resorting to violence." He further adds that, "Nepalis are especially good at negative forms of non-violence like civil disobedience, demonstrations, and non-cooperation, but they struggle when it comes to positive non-violence like nation-building and constructive actions towards peace."[41]

According to *www.nepalbandha.com,* a single–day *bandha* is estimated to result in a loss of NRs. 1.98 billon to the country. The industrial sector alone suffers a loss of NRs. 386 million from a single day closure. The hourly loss due to *bandhas* comes to approximately NRs. 83 million. In the last eight months (Jan. 2011-Aug. 2011), it is recorded that the most number of *bandha* is due to extension of time to draft the constitution.[42] However, there were lots of *bandhas* called but the constitution was not drafted which shows how futile *bandha* has in achieving their objectives. *Bandhas* have repercussions on the entire economy which directly hits the Gross Domestic Product (GDP) and other indicators that measure poverty. The main reasons for the violent protests are:

- Lack of public confidence in constructive and peaceful means of change, and
- Perceived delayed governmental response to public demands.

Indeed, the government often takes no action unless a protest becomes violent. However, it should also be noted that public protests have become so frequent that the state cannot deal with all the stated demands without neglecting other vital governmental functions. The *bandha,* where rule of law is violated and security of life is vulnerable are generally politically motivated. Avoiding these protests lie in consensus among the political parties. Otherwise, this negative culture of participation will not only wreak economic damage, but undermine public confidence in democracy. In a revolutionary move to make political parties of Nepal responsible, transparent and inclusive, a bill was moved in the Interim Parliament of Nepal in March 2007. One of the provisions of the Bill was to make illegal for political parties to declare *bandha* and prohibit them from calling strikes that would impact national economy. However, the Bill was not passed.

It shows that democracy has a reverse direction in transitional Nepal. It is far from the people; it is off the people; it buys the people instead of for the people, of the people and by the people. All should keep in mind that a forced closure is the wrong way to address the issue. *Bandha* as illegal as per the Interim Constitution of Nepal and the reason for many closures is not the solution for a problem, regardless of the reasons it is called for. There are 198 other methods of non-violent forms of protest, where exercising the personal freedom will not violate other's freedom. The majority of the *bandhas* being called these days have very less to do with the issues of national priority.

The opposition has the duty to oppose. But opposition in Nepal is not conceived as necessary adjunct to a democratic polity. Casting them in the enemy image creates a reactive propensity on the part of the opposition. Lack of respect for opposition in Nepal has, however inspired extra-parliamentary, extra-constitutional and anti-systemic opposition seriously weakening the ability of political system to maintain democratic balance. As soon as a political party is seated into power, the opposition starts engineering devices to oust it and its entire energies are consumed in maintaining a confrontational posture through agitation and vituperative politics, intrigues and machinations. The government- in- power on the other hand, mobilizes all efforts, for somehow holding on to power. There are thus hardly any movements towards achievement of national goals and objectives. The enormous national potential remains hostage to politician's self-seeking propensity and in that process they rob the sanctity of parliament, which constitutes the quintessential value of a democratic polity. Power assimilation on the part of the head of the government to sustain the myth of invincibility is what transforms democracy into an aberration and a contradiction in terms –"democratic monarchy."[43]

Personality cult and democratic polity are antithetical to each other. Abraham Lincoln said: "I would not be a slave, so I would not be a master". Our politicians are a different breed. To them being a master is the essence of power- in fact a super master. The opposition finding it difficult to deal with the overly centralized power structure deems it too expedient to join hands even with those with whom it had adversarial relations and possibly worst ideological antagonism to agree on one point agenda–remove the government. George Bernard Shaw once remarked: 'the chief defect of democracy is that only the political party out of office knows how to run the government." No political government has had an opportunity to claim that it remained into office for the full tenure, as provided in the constitution. What is seen in Nepali political culture today is that no governing elite is capable of looking at the drawbacks, so long as he is in power, and close to the seat of sovereignty, but the moment they have fallen from grace, they start a hateful tirade against the organization and government.

Only elections alone do not make democracy viable. Even reasonably free elections, by themselves amount to votocracy rather than democracy if it cannot give security, law and order, voice, civic participation, service delivery, non-violent resolution of multi-polar and multi-layered conflicts. Enthusiasm and public's confidence in the ability of democracy, participation in electoral politics have all declined significantly. Human security means protecting people from critical threats and situations that menace their well-being. It means fostering processes that build on people's strengths and aspirations. It means creating political, social, environmental, economic, military and cultural systems that together give people the building blocks for survival, livelihoods and dignity. But this is not what we see in Nepal. We can judge the security situation in Nepal where never a single day goes by without any violence, killings, kidnapping, shut-downs and explosions. A total of 107 armed outfits, especially ethnic based are operating in Nepal.[44]

A stable democracy results from the presence of the civic culture. Political culture in a positive sense is civic culture. But the evidences show that although Nepal may remain rich in culture, she is poor in civic culture, i.e. political culture. Nepal is now exercising democracy under federal democratic republic state rarely with democratic culture. In the transition from a feudal and unitary political culture to a democratic federal structure, it would certainly be senseless and in the end be only an excuse to refuse democracy if one first wanted to wait for the complete development of a democratic political culture before democratic institutions are established. The phrase 'people are not ready for democracy' is always an excuse by the elite to refuse democracy to the people. Although establishing democratic institutions governed by rule of law is the best prerequisite for developing a democratic culture, it is nevertheless no guarantee for democracy. In addition to the establishment of democratic institutions themselves, the best prerequisite for developing and gradually stabilizing a democratic political culture is the visibly friendly democratic behaviour of leading political class of the country, people and public officials. If these factors go together and their development is promoted, the emergence of democratic culture is probable. Political culture denotes the entire knowledge actually available in the society, instinctive attitudes, and moral and ethic values in relation to politics.

A democratic political culture brings the actions of society and the political elite in line with the laws and rules of democracy. Whenever the majority principle is misused as a lever to inconsiderately establish the personal interest of the present majority against the rest of society, mistrust grows and the state is regarded only as prey by more and more participants so that they can establish advantage for their own groups at the cost of all others. This is what is happening in Nepal in the context of constitution making, peace process and government making. This has drained away even minimum level of value consensus in politics and consequently, politics has been defined in a highly confrontational term. Social pluralism and different level of development of society have made adversarial elite politics easy, thus posing a crisis of governability. Erosion of ideology and fictionalized party politics thus continue to polarize the institution of governance. This has boosted the scope of aspiration politics in Nepal consequently affecting the politics of rational management, a cornerstone for civic political culture.

We should not forget that Nepali society is endowed with rich potential to promote political culture conducive to democracy if the subcultures thriving on regionalism, sectarianism, and money barons, who misuse the system for amassing wealth, are rendered weak and relatively ineffective. It has been argued by Lipset long ago in *Political Man,* that democracy becomes truly stable only when people come to value it widely not solely for its economic and social performance but intrinsically for its political attributes.

The bitter conflict between the opposition UCPN (Maoist) and the ruling coalition for power sharing and different approaches to state restructuring along federal lines, form of governance, integration and rehabilitation of Maoist combatants, democracy, structural reforms, autonomy of judiciary, political pluralism, election, citizenship criteria, etc is framed in a utilitarian zero-sum way. The persistence of deadlock is caused by a lack of habit change and formulation of correct strategy for compromise. Nepali political culture at present is nothing but a prescription for total national disintegration. Despite its transformation from party less to party system and monarchical to republican there is evidence of a corresponding societal decay and rise of factionalism. Along with the extension of the CA tenure again and again political parties have also lingered the transition process because of which all development activities have been halted while the law and order situation has not been maintained. Such orientations have made politics more difficult to inculcate democratic culture.

Political culture cannot itself come in full bloom, unless the attitudinal pre-requisites, values and beliefs sustain its growth and nurturance. As Lary Diamond maintains: "prominent theories of democracy, both classical and modern have asserted that democracy requires a distinctive set of political values and orientations from its citizens: moderation, tolerance, civility, and efficacy, knowledge, participation."[45] This view corroborates with Huntington that "a democratic regime is installed not by trends but by people and democracies are created not by causes but by causers. Political leaders and publics have to act.[46] These statements are enough to clear that it is the people who make the change happen and solve the problem not the institutions. Nepali political model is devoid of all these in varying degrees. What is, therefore, imperative that value orientations must change through institutional anchor.

There is a desperate need for a change in the ways we protest. We have to develop new ideas to make government more responsive while causing minimum disruption and maintaining non-violence. Each demand and allegation should be backed by relevant laws and rules. Publications, posters and pamphlets can be used to spread awareness on an issue and garner larger mass support. Public figures and the media should, therefore raise awareness of the undesirable effects of *bandha*, including its violation of the rights of others. Mass support can be used to put pressure on concerned authority to get demands fulfilled. Organizing seminars, workshops and social audits on an issue and inviting officials, ministers and political leaders to speak on the issue and make public commitments can also be useful to ignite intelligent revolutions, i.e. protesting the right way.

**Politics: Business Enterprise and Politicized Bureaucracy**

One of the senior judges of neighbouring country has remarked that,

> The politics seems to have become the best profitable business of the day wherein the individual enjoys the fruits of political power and becomes holder of several new accounts in the Indian and foreign banks and these accounts fatten day in and day out. ... Politics today is treated like a business which requires no installation of factories, no toiling of day and nights and earning fabulous amounts without being answerable to any law enforcement agency.[47]

Democracy is best understood as government of the people, for the people and by the people. Democracy demands rationality and institutional norms and values. It needs a system in which all institutions function on the basis of accepted culture and rules. The happiest thing that can be said about democracy is that it is one of the few systems that have even been willing to risk for the sake of giving man a chance to grow in mind and responsibility. But democracy in Nepal is not about people; it is about access to state power and pelf. Entrance into the political arena is driven by a desire for personal gain not by a genuine commitment to serving the people, where heredity, family and dynastic connections, rather than ability and character determine success in politics. It has indeed become a business and of course, a 'lucrative business.' Political culture has been influenced by professional activity where the sons, daughter or close relations of the ruling class have been inducted into a sizable numbers to make money in the present context. Most Nepalis remain suspicious, uncooperative, rigid and insistent upon certain formalities of government in order to protect their own positions and personalities. This kind of behavior often results from the extremely short-sighted maxim. It is seen that how in congruent personal and parochial values have intruded themselves into the more modern political processes to give Nepal a political culture which is unique.

Politicians are expected not to profit from political activity. But the leaders and political elites in general have approached politics as a profession, an earning source which in turn becomes a resource for winning elections and perpetuating positions of power. It has thus created a nexus between the politicians and illegitimate source of income. Money power brings along with it the muscle power for furthering the prospects of electoral gains. Political parties' leaders are increasingly becoming hostages to the providers of funds mobilized from a variety of sources. The parties when they are in government make maximum use of governmental channels for resource mobilization. And those who allegedly provide part of such earnings to the party leaders continue to be in government contrary to their public image. All political appointees and members of parliament and others who earn by virtue of being the role incumbents are required to pay part of such earning to the party. Many of the leaders make politics as an exclusive profession. They are apparently motivated by a psyche of getting rich quick for both livelihoods as well as for continuing in the electoral politics which is increasingly becoming expensive and competitive.

The induction of the element of new-heredity is a unique feature of Nepal's political culture, unrivalled elsewhere in modern democracies. Since politics is a business and not service, that alone can be a reasonable explanation to explain the rise of neo-heredity in Nepali political field. The unique culture of politics as a profitable business enterprise without any investment distinguishes the present political culture from that the one which stands for collective good and service where the leaders sacrifice their life for the people and country. Politics is not a means of livelihood; but a calling, a mission. National heroes and leaders of the past gave specific importance to the moral aspect of politics, to the purity of means towards the attainment of ends, to the principle of national development. They conducted politics honorifically, that is by independent means. That was a culture of moral persuasion and self-discipline. That was a culture anchored in moral values that stood for the sake of people and nation based on reason and reasonableness. In this culture type society is held to be more important than the individual. Individualism is not submerged in any way, but the group recognizes the need of individuals to assign value to the group. But a new process of individualization has begun in working style, life, culture and politics which is less characterized by the traditional notion of public and political life. Shaha has remarked that,

> in traditional Nepali society, the individual at least thought beyond his own self-interest in terms of the family, the tribe on the clan. Now the social ties between individual and family, tribe or clan are fast disappearing under the impact of rapid social change, and at the same time the elites have not been able to forge new social ties in the shape of increased awareness of their responsibility towards the nation.[48]

The moral political culture emphasizes the common wealth conception as the basis for democratic government. Serving the community is the core of the political relationship even at the expense of individual loyalties and political friendships. In contrast, the present political culture lacks public spiritedness and civic conscience where all the values of political culture have been diluted. It does not have any direct concern with questions of good society. Dirty politics tends to be accepted as a fact. The key to understanding this culture is that people accept dirty politics as the way things are and should be. The intra-rivalry attitude existing among different political parties has added extra impetus to the deteriorating trend. Not a single political leader and party is found there to save the country from such anomalies or deteriorating culture. Their decency in public life has quickly faded from the memory of ruling class. This trend has to do with the still moribund or again deteriorating state of popular accountability and transparency of democratic representation and elected representatives.

An alliance of business and politics is not unknown to history. But what is new is that politics itself is being transformed into a business enterprise. Everybody knows who gets, what, when and how but names do not surface easily. Political culture is repleted with a false sense of ego, the lack of adherence to ideals and ideologies, the decline of cosmopolitan and a rise of parochial elements in power politics and political process. The expenditure by the ruling class on tours and telephones, on *bhashans* and *udhaghatan* on palatial residences and holiday resorts, on security guards and household services and on medical treatment abroad is beyond the capacity of an ordinary citizen to imagine. Such an extravagant expenditure is in terrible contrast to the wretched existence of under absolute poverty and growing unemployment where the younger generations are living in dark. The extravagate and unproductive expenditure by the governing elites, theoretically in the name of development, but in practice to strengthen their vote banks is one of the major aspects of Nepal's political culture these days. Commissions, pay offs and kickbacks are paid in deftly contrived international or native deals. The whole affair of creaming off commission purchase is a conspiracy against the nation. The transformation of politics into commerce of the coarsest kind and the adoption of the hole and corner method is a peculiar feature of the political culture of Nepal's ruling class. With regard to the deteriorating culture, Dr. Sunder Mani Dikshit in an interview taken by *Janadesh Weekly* expresses:

> … the so-called leader who could not afford even for a slipper yesterday are riding on Pajeros and making huge bungalows by inflicting taxes upon the people. They are the only people who got fostered in this multi-party system. Nothing is being done for the poor people. Today family rule is being practiced in the name of democracy. The concept of people's welfare is being thwarted. This multiparty system is not suited for the country. Those who enjoy life by looting can not think of its alternatives. … [49]

Leaders' responsibilities and performances are always subject to public scrutiny. Leaders represent the nation, which indirectly put them in interactive roles with the international community as well. But in Nepal, it is being felt that members of parliament are perceived as rulers, not as representatives of the poor people of Nepal. Lack of proper judgment in allowing MPs to import luxurious tax free triggering off widespread condemnation and denunciation from the public in general(nicknaming it a *Pajero* Culture) was a serious miscalculation of most leaders irrespective of parties. All, except a few members and leaders, transcending parties were unanimous in purchasing such vehicles.

Elections have become costly affairs leading political parties and candidates to look for ways to raise donations and funds by every means available. Party and leaders are thus lured towards business persons and wealthy individuals for contributions. There is an emerging consensus among the elites of politics, the economy and administration which is adjusted to the functional requirements of their privileges rather than the polity and people. Sources of party funding have made political parties dependent on big houses, non-governmental organizations, extortion, smuggling and other criminal ways of amassing wealth. So any party that comes to government wants to take such portfolios that can generate wealth for individual minister as well as for his party. Corruption has, therefore become rampant and politicians are involved in one way or the other turning government's institutions as fund raising agencies.

Holding the polls while in power had been the prime target of all major political parties in the country. It means that the party in power will have advantage to use/misuse the state resources for election purposes. An election is used for expanding the organizational base of their parties. So far, political representation in Nepal seems to have taken an irrational twist as the parliament has failed to respond to popular interest, and parliamentary elections appear to have been driven more to select government leaders rather than composing a system of good governance. Representation has suffered as the elected representatives have not yet been able to stand above their family and other dominant interest groups to appraise their duties and opportunities. Can public opinion then really lead to process of providing public choice through election in Nepal?

The role of the parliament is to redress public grievances. But the Nepali parliament has itself become a focus of public grievance and unable to address them. To more and more voters the parliament seems arcane and ineffective. The local election of 1997 can be cited as an extreme example that one of the ruling partners of that time, the UML was accused of its excessive manipulation of the state machinery for its landslide victory in the election. It beat all previous records of manipulating state mechanism for election purpose. All parliamentary parties, big or small, desirous of being in power at the time of election obviously means that they wanted to manipulate state power and resources to bring the election result in their favour. The 1999 general election held by the NC led coalition government with UML and

NSP was not an exception. But the more the party relies on state machinery and resources for party building the more the party is driven away from the masses.[50]

Bureaucracy is an important part of the state which is responsible in carrying out the day to day functions of the state, including management, laws, rules and regulation and its implementation with a major hand in the development works of the state. On the other hand, politics is a larger part of sate, responsible in forming a government, discussing the plans and policies, passing bills and overall representation in a democracy. These two important parts of state–politics and bureaucracy– are connected when it comes to transferring the plans and policies into action. But for this to happen, the two should proceed with minimal interference from one another. When such interferences are made through discretion, the repercussions are what we are seeing right now. Corruption gets institutionalized and bureaucracy becomes inefficient and ineffective.

Legitimacy and capacity are two pillars of modern political system. For achieving them regulatory and policy making are also significant. Regulatory powers are exercised by the government through mechanisms such as bureaucracy and security agencies. Bureaucracy is considered as an "important independent variable that greatly influences any kind of transformations in the developing countries, be it social, political or economic", writes Joseph La Palombra.[51] However, how the political actors make use of bureaucracy depend upon a variety of factors. Social environment, historical backdrops and orientation of political leaders determine bureaucratic functioning. It must, however be admitted that authoritarian and parochial cultures continue to overwhelm Nepali bureaucracy. The Nepali bureaucracy, an agenda of reform remains a mixture of the old and the new political culture. Old culture is embedded in *Chakari, Bhansun* or source and force for either getting promotion or to be in lucrative places. A lack of responsive political culture can be the basic cause of a legitimacy crisis. As a result, the legislative, the executive and a number of constitutional bodies remain unaccountable to the rule and law and discretionary authority has become a norm in Nepali bureaucracy.

The culture of excessive partisan interference defying all established practices and standards have marred bureaucracy. Thus bureaucrats are increasingly becoming insecure and ineffective. Politicians have priority for putting in place their own cadres or camp followers or turn coats sacrificing quality and standards. Bureaucrats are required to follow *mansaya* (desire) of their superiors to take decisions on any issues that come before them. Such a practice has been handed from the past, but the new political actors of Nepal too seem to be embedded in the same Nepali political and administrative culture. A marked discrepancy has also been marked between the exposures that the Nepali bureaucrats get abroad, theories they read about the modern bureaucratic system, and overall socio-political and economic environment in the country. They try to emulate the universalized norms and standards but such norms and principles can hardly satisfy the politicians' desires. As a result, conflict and trust deficit are soon generated thus creating negative impacts on making the system inefficient and corrupt. Despite much credit given to the political leaders for their transformatory roles, they lack the art of governance in accord with the spirit of democratic culture.

The uncultivated approach to politics has thus led to the growth of deformed culture in the shape of mass upheavals. The exploitative culture of the old political system has remained unchanged at present. Those in government who continue to practice the same old style of politics tend to become corrupt with the result that the people are demoralized by submitting to them and ineffective in opposing them. The result is that although the masses still remain submissive, they are increasingly discontented. Because the system of rewards and punishments within administration does not encourage a shift in attitude and behaviour, in spite of exhortations found in official studies that lower level bureaucrats must learn to accept greater responsibilities. The lower bureaucrats know that punishment is almost never given for inaction, and that praise is not given to individuals who by pass or reinterpret rules so as to bring about the prompt solution of problem. The political culture of the ruling class has either politicized bureaucracy or demoralized them to such an extent that bureaucracy is no longer a potential modernizing agent. Most of the bureaucrats are at the beck and call of the ruling class. Able and honest bureaucrats are either shunted out or sidelined.

After the restoration of democracy successive governments of Nepal have introduced the spoilt-system in administration which has made the bureaucracy accountable to the party and not to the people. It has broken the chain of command, discipline and increasingly politicized them. Even after the restoration of democracy, i.e. Jan Andolan I and II, hardly any concrete measure has been made in creating a democratic culture.

The frequent shuffling of bureaucrats with a view to putting their own favorites in important places is the routine of any new government. Discarding meritocracy in bureaucracy, leaders of parties have continued the old system of *pajani, chakari* and other forms of personalized behavior for encouraging their favorites. The bureaucracy in post-2006, Nepal as other organs of the government, has suffered from over partisan spirit. The culture of inherent tension and tussles that have gone wrong especially after the 2006 April revolution, between secretaries and ministers, i.e. between political leadership and bureaucracy are a common place.[52] Ministries headed by respective parties have their own sets of bureaucrats and political appointees for working as middle persons for striking various deals. It makes the government both corrupt and ineffective as it has to cater to the interest of various groups and individuals. The prime minister, who heads a government composed of heterogeneous parties and whose bureaucratic machinery is demoralized and is preoccupied with its own survival, can hardly become effective. Even when he tries to project his image by issuing *nirdesan* (direction) to carry out the decisions of the government speedily and effectively, they go deaf ears of his ministers and administrative staffs.

The crisis of governance, therefore boils down to the gradual loss of respect and authority of political leaders since they have not been able to free themselves from the grip of old and feudal political cultures. The system of *pajani* (reshuffling) continues in different garbs and the language the politicians use is not at variance with the culture found during the royal regime. At a time when Nepal's transition to a new political set up is causing a lot of pain, these incidents have generated further dissonance.

How can people expect bureaucracy to work for public welfare when minister pressure secretaries to work to fulfill their partisan and personnel interests that too going against the rule of law. Whereas, Max Weber, a German sociologist, in the 1930s, wrote a rationale that described the bureaucratic culture as being the ideal way of organizing government agencies which has a consistency orientation for a stable environment where rights and privileges protect individuals from organizational injustice–and equity prevails regardless of "who you are". Bista, an anthropologist of Nepal gives a contradict situation in Nepal that the most important asset for anyone is not "what you know, but who you know". A member of one's own circle is naturally preferred, even without a particular capacity to perform in some organization role."[53] In such atmosphere, the public atmosphere cannot become competent. Rather it frustrates people. Development however requires just the opposite- i.e. competent civil and public administration.

During the transition phase, it is up to the bureaucracy to provide stability and good governance. However, bureaucracy has been subject to the whims of political forces, which continue to undermine the capability of stats institutions. After the restoration of multi party system, people had great expectations that all the corrupt people would be punished. But, those who should have worked to ensure that the corrupt were punished became corrupt themselves. This has institutionalized the culture of *chakari* and *chaplusi*. The low level of motivation in the performance of work and the inflexibilities often present in administration have given rise to a widespread system of bribery and corrupt practices in dealing with government officials. Most officials deliberatively behave in that fashion hoping that the customer will try to respect him and please him with gifts.

The culture of payment or *bakshish*, in Nepali term which is highly stable has made among the businessmen and politicians a feeling that anyone with money, gifts and good contacts can get action and things done. If one goes by the perception of any person, Nepalis or foreigner, who frequently or otherwise interacts with government employees in ministries or government departments or public sector organizations, the average general feeling is not positive, if not bad. This impression and the performance indicators of the bureaucrats have created a total dismal image of all the governments in the past decades. Coordination, cooperation, interdependence, and win-win attitudes are rare commodities in all those dealings. Although the people are mostly aware of this deceptive attitude of government officials, they are not only helpless, but also afraid that they may be penalized further if they challenge this procrastinating behaviour. How can people expect bureaucracy to work for public welfare when the average citizen finding the clerk behind the counter tending to his own paper work before turning to the customer or the local administrator more oriented towards serving superiors than serving the public on the other?

Nepali bureaucracy cannot be divorced from the reality of inter and intra-party competition of power and remain isolated from growing public expectation of service responsiveness. The constant reshuffling of civil servants after every change in government has eroded institutional autonomy, performance and responsiveness.

The Global Corruption Barometer (GCB) of Transparency International (TI) showed bribery to be common in public institutions in countries including Nepal- which stands at the second most corrupt country after Afghanistan in the region as per the 2011 Corruption Perception Index (CPI).[54] People are sick of paying bribes just to get on with their daily lives and they are sick of sleaze and under influence of public servants. According to the Civil service act 2049 (1993) the Ministry of General Administration (MOGA) has the power to make transfers. The Act also states that the MOGA shall transfer civil employees of one ministry or department to another ministry or department provided there is a proper ground for it. In case of the transfer of the secretary of MOGA the Secretary at the office of Prime Minister and council of Ministers make a transfer through a meeting. The Act also states that the concerned authority must make transfers generally once in a year.

The transfer and promotion of the civil employees happens all over the world, with different countries implementing their own laws and Acts. According to the Department of Civil Service, New York, "Civil employee can only be transferred, promoted or suspend by the approval of the department of civil service." The Civil Employee act of Nepal and New York are similar regarding basic guiding principle, but the problem lies in execution and implementation. The list of laws and Acts clearly indicates that a civil employee could only be transferred by the MOGA and that too only in a year's time. But from the past experience, we have frequently seen that every time the Government or a minister changes, the officials are transferred based on political guidance. Without developing contacts, paying obeisance to leaders of political parties and their brokers no good assignment is possible. Political parties' functionaries from top to bottom are allegedly involved in such deals. It has been admitted by the police officials and other bureaucrats that they require to spend huge amount of money (bribery) for getting promoted or posted in good places. The Civil Service Act itself needs to be implemented properly in the first place because it is seen that the ministers have the upper hand in the transfers and promotions. The transfers and promotions based on the evaluation and performance of the civil employees would be much more effective than those manipulated by politics.

The interference of politics in bureaucracy would eventually make the civil employees more focused on pleasing the politicians rather than carrying out their designated work which is a malpractice and could eventually disrupt the whole bureaucratic process. The government, ruling party and the ministers change so frequently in Nepal, but bureaucracy is here to stay and carry out the necessary function of the state. The involvement of politics will have short as well as long-term effects on the bureaucracy. Separating politics form bureaucracy could be the stepping stone for the agenda of good governance and zero tolerance towards corruption.

Another important issue with the unpredictability of the government and its consequent effect on the bureaucracy imposed through such discretionary transfers, the development works as a whole is affected-directly and indirectly with frequent transfers. Development work initiated by one bureaucrat is left incomplete and most likely to be discontinued. This leads to the tendency of the government officials to focus more on instant gratification than the primary objectives. Another problem that needs to be addressed is that of output, credibility and accountability. The sudden transfer highly affects the bureaucrats and hence, their credibility among the general public decreases. Also when reward and punishment is set on political decisions of the incoming ministers, the incentive system encourages bureaucrats to be more accountable to the politicians than the general public. From the several examples of transfer and promotion that we have come across, we know that the politicians are bending the rules for their self-interest and benefits. As such, bureaucracy has fallen into a decline.

Democracy is not a *Hukumi sashan* run by peremptory and preemptory command personified in an individual. It needs a system in which all institutions function on the basis of accepted norms and rules. Nepal's new rulers have learned the art of launching movements while in opposition, but lack the knowledge of developing institutions. As a result all-round institutional decay and collapse are being observed. Unless leaders who come to power realize the spirit of institutionalized bureaucracy, no efficient and dignified government and bureaucracy are possible.

Bureaucracy being the backbone of the state especially designed to carry out the day to day function of the state should not be politicized as heavily as we are experiencing now. In the politics controlled bureaucracy, transfers and promotions by ministers distort the idea of creating an incentive system that can keep the state mechanisms running in favour of the public.

## Public Security vs. Culture of Impunity: Criminalization of Politics

Nepal is in the midst of a complex process as it formulates a new constitution, and many neglected and unexplored issues are now emerging demanding to be addressed. Removing impunity, promoting the culture of accountability, guaranteeing human rights and security and strengthening the rule of law are the major challenges. The zero- tolerance to impunity is necessary, so that democratic political culture can be institutionalized based on the rule of law. But the prevalence of widespread impunity that has tremendously grown since the 1990s, ultimately hindering the promotion of human right and peaceful conciliation in Nepal has challenged the public's conscience, human tolerance and human rights culture. Perpetrators are not punished, and the victims do not get proper justice because impunity has not been addressed properly through the constitution and domestic laws. Institutionalized corruption, criminalization in politics, and the nexus of the culprits with the power centers, have bolstered the culture of impunity. Political protection of the criminals which includes hiding crimes withdrawing legal charges, escaping legal punishment or giving undefined state pardon to the criminals is a major challenge in the fight against impunity.

Theoretically, impunity, meaning "exemption from punishment," is an anti-human right approach. In the international human rights instruments, the term refers to a failure to bring perpetrators of human rights violations to justice. So impunity constitutes denial of the victims' right to justice and redress. Wide spread impunity in Nepal is a manifestation of a combination of social and cultural factors– such as the illiteracy of over 13 of 22 million people and a feudal past and non-existence of basic human rights still exists. The "Culture of Impunity" or lack of fear of punishment has not only weakened the concept of the rule of law, but also is the cause of people's erosion of faith in the system with the result that the people are demoralized and increasingly discontented. The lack of fear is a manifestation of the unwillingness or inability of the government to punish.

The Informal Sector Service Center's "Kathmandu Declaration on Human Rights 1996" says that impunity in Nepal has been a part of tradition. Not only are criminals not punished, they are even rewarded. Those that violated human rights during the Jan Andolan uprising for the restoration of democracy and human rights 1990 have not been punished but have been taken to respectable positions.[55] Due to such culture of impunity, the political environment has been corrupted to such an extent that it is difficult to find instances of the abuse of law where some parties or individuals that identify with certain parties have not been involved.

Abuse of authority by public officials, misuse of public resources by party leaders, workers and sympathizers and corruption by all and sundry to such an extent that the concept of the rule of law is now virtually only on paper. The infamous "Red Passport"[56] scandal in which parliament members have been accused of misusing diplomatic privileges is a case, where society has failed to punish both to responsible officials and other allegedly involved in the violation. A government committee was formed to "look into recommend ways to prevent the same in the future. Even though an inquiry was done, it came with built—impunity. However, the reports of those investigations have not been and are not expected to be made public, because of the possible involvement of powerful people from all major political parties."[57]

Independent constitutional entities like Supreme Court and National Human Rights Commission have recommended the government to end impunity and respect human rights of people. In the case of killings, abduction, disappearances, forced displacement affected by the armed conflict, extortion and torture, NHRC has made a series of recommendations and instructions to the government for arranging compensation to the victims and for taking legal action against the culprit of the past. However, contrary to the people's expectation the government has mostly failed to respect the instruments and recommendations of the NHRC and Supreme Court. NHRC and Commission for Investigation of Abuse of authority (CIAA) for its part, has been bestowed with much authority in investigating into the irregularities that occur in the cabinet, bureaucracy, judiciary, security forces, the private sector, NGOs/INGOs, civil society and even the parliament. But CIAA has had very few success stories along its course. Although the parliament has finally ratified the United Nations Convention against Corruption, that Nepal had signed as long back as 2003 CIAA has not been able to work ahead in the task of nabbing the corrupt and bringing them to book.

In the aftermath of 1990-2006 Jan Andolans, the commissions created to investigate human rights abuses- the Mallik Commission in 1990 and the Rayamajhi Commission in 2006– both produced detailed reports that were shelved without action. Little progress on transitional justice has taken place since hostilities ceased. The report of the Ministry of Peace and Reconstruction records that the families of the 1,027 disappeared persons remain ignorant of the fate or whereabouts of their relatives.[58] Compensation has not yet been received by all the wounded or all the families of those killed. In many instances, properties seized have not yet been returned.[59] Nepal has not acceded to the ROME statute of ICC that has hindered the country from fulfilling international obligations. Nepal, as a state party, although, has signed a significant number of international instruments pertaining to human rights and humanitarian law she has not been able to follow legal and constitutional measures to denounce impunity.

Transparency international (TI) has placed Nepal 146$^{th}$ out of 178 countries that were surveyed and ranked in its corruption perceptions Index (CPI) in 2010. This is the result of lack of rule of law, breakdown of the constitution, dysfunctional House and almost defunct government. Corruption in public offices, level of corruption, action against corruption and its output, government anti corruption initiatives, administrative corruption, political corruption, bribing in import and export and irregularities in contract awards have all contributed to making Nepal one of the most corrupt nations in the region with a score of 2.3.[60] Almost three years after the Comprehensive Peace Agreement (CPA), Nepal continues to remain a conflict zone. If the decade long insurgency cost around 13,000 lives the past two years and 10 months witnessed a total of 1,284 deaths, 2,100 abduction and mushrooming of around 109 underground armed outfits according to INSEC records

One distinct feature of post-CPA killings is that around 33 percent of them are committed by armed groups. While the two conflicting forces in the pre-CPA era— UCPN (Maoist) and the state seem less involved in the killings in the post CPA period, new forces are responsible for 90 percent of the deaths. While the Maoists and the state allegedly killed a total of 31 and 112 people, 1,141people were killed by new armed groups. Parties have also formed semi-armed youth wings. The establishment of 'youth wing' across the political parties and their tendency to flout rule of law for partisan interests is hitting the nerve of law and order. While the Maoists' YCL killed 10 and abducted 336 people, UML's Youth Force killed one and abducted 13.[61] Militarization of the youth wings of parties has caused a decline of human rights standards eroding the concept of public security which is vital for ordinary citizens to liberate themselves from primordial fears and basic needs deficits. Mostly unemployed youths between the age of 20 and 25, especially of poor economic status have been lured towards joining different underground outfits and armed groups. Government apathy and the parties' tendency to defend criminal activities of their youth wings have made a bad situation worse. There is no place for private armies in a democracy. But armed outfits, most of which consists of criminals are striking terror in the minds of the peace-loving people. The fragility of the Nepali government at the centre has been a reason why the armed outfits have succeeded in spreading around the country by virtually creating a statelessness situation. Incidents carried out by non-state actors reveal a strong nexus between crime and politics as well as the motivation for money, power and identity. The strength of the outfits is much related with the relative weakness of the government, which has paved the way for escalation of terrorist activities.

Some organizations of political parties and affiliated bodies are also found to be indulging in anti-social activities giving rise to much apprehension about real peace materializing any time soon. Nepal's democracy now rests on the commitment to civilian supremacy, political openness, people oriented republic. The Nepal Army has been brought under civilian control which is necessary for a long term security and stability of the nation. But, Nepal is being treated by the international community as the most insecure, fragile and weak state. As a result, the task of stabilization of national security and orderly participation of citizen's constitution- making and peace process in a satisfactory way remain tantalizing.

The Constituent Assembly (CA) election had broadened the social, gender and inter-generational bases of political power. But incapacity of ruling political classes to cope with multiple challenges has posed the problem of governability. The unstructured, fluctuating, unsystematic, anomic and multi-dimensional participation of Nepali citizens subsuming the absolutization of mini-identities of class, caste, ethnicity, region, religion rather than meta-identity of citizens has made conflict an open-ended exercise. These multiple identifications of citizens have weakened their loyalty to the state, eroded any respect to the rule of law and opened a new security problem. The deadlock created by the opposite conception of adjustment of armed forces, merger trust between civil and military and conflicting vision of democratic republic vs. people's republic have provided various armed groups to free ride causing security deficit and shrinkage of democracy, compelling us to say that government is unable to improve security situation in the country.

The recent rise of protests among marginalized groups and increasing lawlessness in the Terai already signal the risk of outbreaks of new form of hostilities if these root causes are not addressed. Of the 551 people killed in 2007, 127 came from 10 Terai districts of the East and Central development regions. Moreover, of the 1,700 people abducted, 343 were from those Terai districts. In 2008, 18 government officials were killed: 17 in the Terai and one in the Hills. The Nepal Human Rights Year Book 2009 reveals that 541 individuals were murdered and 729 abducted in 2008.[62] The series of extra-judicial killings in Terai, "published by the Democratic Freedom and Human Rights Institute (DFHRI) shows that the state was involved in 133 extra judicial killings, while armed groups were involved in 128 cases during the 2007-2010 period.

The impacts of the killings left the people with growing insecurity, brain drain, waning social harmony and reduction in agriculture as well. In the last few years, Nepal has increasingly being pulled to the centre of cross- border crime and terrorism and yet security establishments have been able to do little to control this trend. The open border with India remains a key challenge as the flow of weapons, ammunitions, cash and individuals is encouraging criminal activities and violence on both sides of the border. The open border culture has given leeway to armed groups in the Terai who coordinate with likeminded groups from India. The shooting incidents of businessmen, the murder of media entrepreneurs, the bombing incidents in the heart of Kathmandu in the day broad light indicate a trend that can tear apart the fabric of internal public security and strain international image. Buses are burnt, public property is looted, and the common man is put to great hardship and inconveniences. Even if the Maoists have silenced their guns formally, its effects on spreading gun culture are strong. These incidents have come to the people as a fear psychosis. People are losing faith on the state because the government has failed to provide even a semblance of security to them by maintaining law and order.

The fear psychosis that the lawlessness and governmental ineffectiveness have generated among the populace has also forced them feel the non-existence of the governance, where the leaders talk much about good governance. The way in which the police handled the explosions has exposed serious short comings in the state's security institutions, particularly the role of the National Investigation Department which is filled with political party affiliates. There is excessive political interference in the civil police who has weakened the efficiency of security institutions and promoted nexus between police, crime and politics. Among the non-state actors that work for debilitating the state are terrorists and their organizations within and outside the country. Now there has been a tendency to develop linkage between terrorists working inside the country and international terrorists gangs. It is "difficult to imagine a world without terrorism in the foreseeable future, for it would imply a world without conflict ant and tension… one must conclude that the world is now entering a new phase in its history, more dangerous than any before."[63]

Generally people resort to violent means when the state and government curtail freedoms or monopolize resources, denying other general people of every opportunity. The illegitimate state and government might then call such means as terrorist methods. The ten–year–long war of the Maoist against the state were branded as antinational and terroristic. The terrorist tag is still branded on the Maoist by the US, despite the Maoist transformation into a civilian party. However, in the given context, terrorism in various forms and objectives is taken as the potential force against the state. In Nepal too, doused in violence and indulged in criminal activities, violence gangs continue to pose threats to the state and society.

Generally, terrorist activities begin with public targets, but in course of time they tend to kill individuals without specifying any charge as has been happened in the country today. Nepal is under the international radar for terrorism because the country is being projected as a corridor for regional and international terrorism. Terrorism, for example, is one of such trends of threats that most countries of the world are facing. How terrorism at home and in interstate relations can be tackled is a great challenge. Nepal in particular is also singled out as one of the sites of terrorist activities that are allegedly carried out by some groups against India. It has been frequently said by India that terrorists backed by the Inter Service Intelligence (ISI) of Pakistan use Nepal as a conduit for terrorist mission in India. Now terrorism and the politics of violence or increasing trends of criminalization of politics have been able to sidetrack the major national agendas.

To what extent do the people believe that their newly acquired liberties are guaranteed and protected by the government is strongly related to the level of security and patterns of political behaviour.[64] Normally understood, to borrow Baral's words, democracy is a universal value centered on people-that inculcation of culture of moderation, tolerance, recognition of worth of each individual, struggle for justice, indomitable courage, end of all forms of exploitation, development of cognitive, and evaluative domains, change of government through legitimate constitutional and legal means and security and peace.[65] The greater the extent to which liberties are perceived by individuals to be guaranteed, the more likely the individuals are to exercise their civil liberties, a process which is essential for the functioning of civil society.

A civic political culture should consist of a set of beliefs, attitudes, norms, perceptions and the like, that support participation. But can the present situation provide people with that security? If not, how can a participant culture be expected? For a participant culture to arise, people must have the willingness to participate, but such a will also needs a sense of political security. The individual must feel secured enough to exercise civil rights without fear.

The strength of any democracy is its people. Without peace of mind and feeling of security, democracy can neither be practiced nor will it be sustainable. However, Nepal's 22.2 million people live in fear. The instability of national politics has shut the doors of democracy on the people, who are instead facing more insecure in every walk of life. The country's politics remain exceedingly tense and dangerous. The volatile and polarized nature of politics with its demons like public insecurity, frequent *hartals*, terrorist acts, toll collection and corruption makes life a daily survival struggle for the general people, The people are frightened at the manner in which violence has escalated in the Terai and the urban areas, including Kathmandu. The Special Security Plan enforced by the government since 2009 has yielded some results, but the trends of extortion, abduction and murder continue as if culture of violence has come to stay in Nepal. The muscle, money, and mafia have significantly contributed to prolonging the culture of violence.

Analyzing the wide spread violence and feeling of insecurity imprinted in the mind of people, some of the features of violence can be put forth: taking arms for political ends, for taking revenge, and for fulfilling selfish interest of others. Whatever the motivations these incidents are the by-product or fluid political situation that defies the very coercive power of the state. Neutral, speedy, and effective state mediation mechanisms are needed to deter the rise of self-help groups in the security sector. This calls for good governance, particularly in areas related to public security. For that the government must adopt a broader security policy and revamp the existing public security institutions. So politics in Nepal seems for own sake or for leaders sake, not for people. We see talking politics men to men, leaders-to-leaders, and party-to-party. No change has been experienced and seen in Nepali politics although politicians talk about democracy for the people.

Unstable and opportunist politics are more at the root of unbridled corruption at all points in time. So the present political culture of Nepal gives an unpleasant flavour of politicization of crime and the criminalization of politics, which gives birth to the culture of corruption, impunity and violence. Politicization of crime involves the competitive use of anti-social forces for the mobilization of party funds, for management of elections, for organizing meetings and conferences and even for recreating workers at lower levels from anti social elements. It also includes unethical behaviour of elected representative and the misuse of criminal intelligence as a political tool for blackmailing political leaders, the people and criminals. Crime has infiltrated politics and political parties on quite big scale that the lines of demarcation between crime and politics, criminals and politicians appeared blurred. Many established leaders employ goons and give political patronage to criminals and corrupt.

Succeeding governments have misused the provision of withdrawing criminal prosecutions to serve party interests. Political patronage to criminals these days is what has contributed to impunity growing to gargantuan proportions. Likewise, the protection of perpetrators of malpractices has led to a culture of disobedience and thus an increase in different sorts of crime. Among cases withdrawn by different governments is one against an elected member of parliament of the then ruling party, who was being tried for murder. Records also show that murder charges against a minister of a coalition government were withdrawn within 15 days of the accused person being appointed as Home Minister. The proposal to withdraw such cases is made by the Ministry of Law and Justice at the recommendation of the Home Ministry upon which the cabinet takes the final decisions. The decision to recommend withdrawal of charges is made by the Home Minister.[66] *Samakalin* mentioned that from 1990 to March 1997, the governments of the day withdrew 575 criminal cases from the court.[67] Another paper *Deshantar* reported that 25 cases related to the corruption were won by the accused.[68] Attributing to a summary of the Home Ministry report, *Deshantar* Weekly wrote that, most of the police and CID officials are supporters of the smugglers.[69] It is also reported that higher level dignitaries, top politicians have not been covered by the CIAA. Although high profile graft cases are deemed to attract immense public curiosity past experience has seen very few bureaucrats and leaders who have held public office being prosecuted on corruption charges.

Utterances like this coming out from the responsible quarters have made the national scene dismal. The erosion of faith in some constitutional organs, specially the commission for the prevention of abuse of authority, that are created for removing corruption etc. are in moribund state, despite widespread public concerns expressed against their inaction. The commission is resentful saying that it has not legal sanction to act against the corrupt authorities. But the governments have invariably turned a deaf year to its helplessness. Worse still, organized crimes transcend the national boundaries and failure to control it has badly affected the country's image internationally. Institutionalized corruption, criminalization in politics, and the nexus of the culprits with the power centers, have bolstered the culture of impunity. Political protection of the criminals which includes hiding crimes withdrawing legal charges, escaping legal punishment or giving undefined state pardon to the criminals is a major challenge in the fight against impunity.

Due to such culture of impunity, the political environment has been corrupted to such an extent that it is difficult to find instances of the abuse of law where some parties or individuals that identify with certain parties have not been involved. Abuse of authority by public officials, misuse of public resources by party leaders, workers and sympathizers and corruption by all and sundry to such an extent that the concept of the rule of law is now virtually only on paper. The infamous "Red Passport"[70] scandal in which parliament members have been accused of misusing diplomatic privileges is a case, where society has failed to punish both to responsible officials and other allegedly involved in the violation. A government committee was formed to "look into recommend ways to prevent the same in the future. Even though an inquiry was done, it came with built— impunity. However, the reports of those investigations have not been and are not expected to be made public, because of the possible involvement of powerful people from all major political parties." [71]It shows how the state authorities have been abusing their power while the high ranking accused have been operating through political nexus to get impunity in the country. This is in keeping with Nepal's classical aphorism, "law for the poor, impunity for the rich," *(Sana Laị Ain, Thula Lai Chain).* Paragraph 7.1.3 of the Comprehensive Peace Accord concluded between the government of Nepal and the UCPN (Maoist) on Nov. 21, 2006 states, "both sides express the commitment that impartial investigation and action shall be carried out in accordance with the law against persons responsible for creating obstructions to exercise the rights stated in the accord and ensure that impunity shall not be encouraged. Apart from this, they also ensure the rights of the victims of the conflict and torture and the rights of the family of disappeared persons to obtain relief."

The government issued its minimum programmer of consensus with the signature of the top leaders of eight political parties that crimes and anarchy shall be controlled by strengthening the situation of peace and security and rule of law shall be strengthened and made effective. Instead, those responsible for gross violation of human rights laws and serious violation of humanitarian laws have not been brought to justice resulting in increased impunity and decreased accountability. Of course, new assets of Nepal's democracy, which are evolving in the course of a gradual, civil-society backed expansion of democracy's participatory ethos, such as the 'Right to Information Act' introduced and an ever more assertive, well-fortified and watchdog-like media, with its notorious 'sting operations', make it more difficult for perpetrators to get away with their lapses.

The prevalence of corruption among political leaders is not a new phenomenon.[72] It is a common occurrence even in developed countries. What is new is 'speed money'. But arresting the lawmakers in the passport scam and incidents of former minister and present minister[73] by the Supreme Court on graft charge and sent to jail, might have increased the level of trust and also a definite shift in public perception in the judicial system. Still there are a number of powerful people who have been using and taking undue benefit from the state and government authorities, but the law is unable to punish them. They not only indulge in corrupt practices but agree to patronize the lawless. Black money and black deed, ensure status, social respect are plus point in the culture of politics today. The notorious criminals, smugglers and murders are swarming in politics. So unstable and opportunist politics are more at the root of unbridled corruption at all points in time. Formerly, they were on the periphery of Nepali political scene. Now they have considerably moved towards the centre to manipulate the gears and levers of political machine. The criminals who thrive on illicit money have penetrated the law enforcing agencies and political parties to an alarming extent. These evidences have fuelled the public view that the law is still biased towards them. This has led to the impairment of state authority and the eclipse of public morality and public interest. A valid point raised among the people is "a law breaker should not be a law maker from the parliament to local bodies."Law- breakers, persons with criminal records and corrupt individuals should be debarred from the political context.

Election means sanctity of a position to represent people. Losing this sanctity means devaluation of politics and politicians, which in turn, hampers the formation of civic political culture. Conversely when one or several of the functions are not performed effectively, a vicious circle begins: various centers of power vie for control, multiple decisions–making processes confuse priorities, citizens lose trust in the government, institutions lose their legitimacy and populace is disenfranchised. In the extreme cases, violence erupts. This negative cycle creates the "sovereignty gap"-a gap that fails to establish connection between citizens and the state, rulers and ruled.[74] The culprit is the weak state, unable to provide basic services to its population, unable to police its peripheries and unable to distinguish law abiders from lawbreakers. Weak, incompetent states unable to enforce the rule of law are dangerous. Under these conditions, civil war is profitable for potential insurgents, in that they can both survive and enjoy some probability of winning the state. Immunity from civil violence comes with building states with the power and the incentive to enforce the rule of law.

## A Perspective on the Spirit of Sacrifice

A civic society can be built only on a foundation of a class of sacrificial individuals who work for the common good of the whole society and not on a class of individuals who operate on selfish profit motives. But the spirit of sacrifice is rapidly disappearing from the political scene of Nepal. Sacrifice and hardships would no more guide politics as was observed during the long democratic struggle. All parties suffer from such trends. The present political culture especially after the restoration of multiparty has dragged the nation into the abyss of obscurity. The great leaders, martyrs, and the rulers of the past, who left them private fortunes, their occupation and even their family life to take part in the national movement are disappearing from public and are being replaced by them who stand for power and pelf in politics. They gave specific importance to the moral aspect of politics, to the purity of means, towards the attainments of ends, to the principle of national agenda.

When political parties and leaders start mixing ideology with strategies and petty partisan and individual interests, they flatter in their principal mission. But, now politicians are first concerned with their individual interest, (for e.g., the wrangling for the Home Ministry) next, they look for the interest of their group or people. They do not even look for the party interest. National interest is a distant thing. No one is concerned about the prosperity of the nation, strengthening of democracy and the elimination of poverty.[75] Political leaders so seem to be preoccupied with their own survival strategies making them too indecisive and vulnerable. Most leaders penchant for power (popularly known as *Kursi*). An intense factionalism within the governing party is based not on differences in policy but on competing personal loyalties and ambition. The party functionaries are less concerned with the specific policies, ideology and unity of the party than they are with access to power. May be with such issues the past and present governments have not been able to deal with the pressing issues of the nation. Such particular incidents have come to the people as a moral degradation of the leaders and governments though legitimately formed by the parliament. With the right to information in focus, the common people want to know where things have gone wrong. So it makes people to observe that for the majority of political leaders democracy has now become closely related to strong personal career interests and ambitions than to the pursuit of happiness of the citizens. The rulers have either ignored or suppressed public opinion, have distributed patronage in a narrow and selfish manner, have directed economic development for the profit of its kith and kin and usurped much of the public resources to sustain their oligarchy, ironically in the name of Loktantra.

At present the main agenda for Loktantrik Nepal is to end the structural and material conditions promoting conflict, inequality and injustice and to prepare the foundation for economic development and prosperity. Political parties in Nepal have been unable to push forward the key agenda. The main reason for the failure is the means they have adopted to come to power. By the time the political parties come to power they would have already sacrificed their moral grounds, and taken recourse to misuse of public resources, crime, violence and intimidation. Sacrificing moral grounds and sacrificing national interest for self and then party instead of common good have made the national agenda a distant thing. Indications that the fortunes of self and party are more important as compared to the interests of the nation are evident from this working culture.[76] This is what is called the individual political culture in the words of Daniel Elazar,[77] where private concerns are more important than public concerns. Like shrewd magicians, Nepali leaders have a proclivity to deceive citizens with skillful "optical illusions" fashioning their promises and painting often an idyllic picture of the national situation. One general evil of Nepalis habit is, says Nepal's great poet Laxmi Prasad Devkota, "we always first think of ourselves before we think of the nation in any of the schemes that we entertain."[78]

Over 60 years have passed Nepal's democracy still has not taken hold and Nepal's democratic culture could not flourish. This is why the country which saw the possibility of growth after the 2006 revolution in the year 2007-8 with a GDP growth rate of 5.8 percent has been staggering. The subsequent years have seen growth limited to around 3 percent every year. Last fiscal year, the government was unable to spend a huge chunk of the development budget creating further hardships for the common people. With the government formation held hostage by political mismanagement, this year's regular and development programmes are also likely to suffer, because as of yet, little progress has been made regarding plans for the next fiscal year.[79]

Nepal's development programmes always suffer from last minute political whims and culture of sharing of benefits among parties in power. With the integration and rehabilitation issue taking the centre stage, the most crucial task of getting over the contentious issues to move ahead the task of drafting the constitution is receiving scant attention. At the going rate, it seems next to impossible to have the constitution drafted and promulgated even by the next Constituent Assembly to be elected with the same culture and behavior of the leaders. The political process of Nepal revolves around powerful personalities rather than institutions. There must be more priority for the interest of people than the self interest of leaders, their family and friends, political parties, regional, ethnic groups and religious bodies. The crisis in promoting national interest and security are posing serious threat to the consolidation of democracy in Nepal. It is safe to say that both have not gained serious political attention as we know, issues do not have any important place in the traditional and individualistic style of politics as in the moralistic style of politics.

The election survey for studying the political beliefs and behaviours of the Nepali people in 1994[80] revealed that 61 percent (617) of respondents agreed that the politicians care too little about what the voters think, while only 21 percent (207) of them disagreed on it. The view corroborates with the public opinion surveys of South Asia 1999 which reveals that 92 percent of respondents in Nepal felt that political leaders had become more corrupt. The survey found that in Pakistan a mere 3 percent felt political leaders to be honest compared to 17 percent in India and Nepal and 24 percent in Bangladesh respectively.[81] This view also corroborates with the findings of an empirical study on political leadership in

Nepal based on field survey that the portraits of Nepali leaders are selfish and corrupt, power centric, deviation from norm and values, negligence of people and development and negligence of national interest.[82] Voters' attraction towards election largely is determined by the performance of MPs in the parliament and public life of the people.

During the election, party leaders promise to fulfill the flood pent-up demands of the citizens, igniting inflated hopes beyond the capacity of the democratic leaders to fulfill even if they are catapulted into power. The unfulfilled promise of the parties have turned the voters into cynics, on the one hand and brought about pathological side effects on social integration on the other. Since a tendency of promoting self-interest is rampant among them, they are consciously and unconsciously contributing to the erosion of value and ideology in politics. Poor presence of MP's during sessions, articulation without the necessary preparation, little encouragement to participate, tendency on the part of ministers to remain absent from parliamentary meetings, turning a deaf ear to the questions raised on public concern show how MP's have been more obsessed with the calculus of their own self-interest at large. The House has had to be adjourned for lack of a quorum several times, notwithstanding the fact that many MP's were found to be elsewhere with ministers doing business of their own. Party leaders are found to be sending MP's outside Kathmandu even when the parliament is in session. Attending the sessions only through the party whip does not augur well for bolstering the image of the MP's before the voters. Judged from this perspective Nepali leaders in general have failed to inject enthusiasm and hope in the people.

In Kathmandu, one columnist offered the epitome of all that's bad about Nepal as the definition of politicians described political leaders and parties "full of alcoholics, womanizers and school drop-outs." In a political culture resulted from such phenomenon it is difficult to inculcate a spirit of sacrifice, particularly when businessmen and politicians appeal to baser motives. It exhorts young people to develop the spirit of sacrifices, but there is the feeling that the spirit may wither away as the present generation of leadership disappears. Whereas, in the past these were important sources of the spirit of sacrifice and the sense of discipline, obligatory culture and the common good which explain so much of civic culture. But there is a wide spread feeling in Nepal that such attributes are now regarded as old fashioned and illogical. So, the manner in which the politicians are behaving under the present democratic dispensation portrays to the public that their motivation has changed. In the past, they were preoccupied with the politics of survival but today, their survival instinct has been generally transformed into an earning instinct giving rise to doubt in the minds of the people that democracy is only for them, not for the poor sections of the electorate.

For democracy to take firm root in Nepali mind, all the sectors of the society must uphold democratic ideas, norms and practices in the true sense, which is above individual and party interest. Nepali democracy, therefore, requires skilled, honest, educated and visionary political elites capable of making the essential legislative and administrative decisions in the interest of the public. But when such ideal attributes are absent, people become utterly frustrated.

## De-culturation of Politics

Culture is regarded as a complex phenomenon which includes knowledge, art, belief, morals, law, custom and other capabilities acquired by man as a member of society. The people of a society share a common human nature like emotional drives, intellectual capacities and moral perspectives. The common human nature expresses itself in the form of certain values, belief and emotional attitudes which are transmitted from one generation to another, though with greater or lesser modifications they constitute the general culture of that society. Culture, is therefore, a profound possession that ramifies throughout human life. Politics is one of the unavoidable circumstances/facts of human existence/relations.

Each political system is embedded in a socio psychological environment- the set of values, beliefs, orientation and attitudes of the people toward politics, i.e., the political culture. However, the political culture encompasses both the political ideals and the operating norms of a polity including not only the attitudes to the politics, political values, ideologies, national character and cultural ethos, but also the style, manner and substantive form of politics. The political culture of people gives them an orientation towards their polity and its processes. The way to learn about political beliefs is to observe the ways in which political structure operates. These beliefs affect and are affected by the way in which the structures operate and there is a close circle of relationship between culture and structure.

But what is found in Nepali political culture today is a corroding de-culturation of politics; a decline of tradition of civility. Political culture of the ruling class has deflected from the past beliefs, which is devoid of the norms of decency. The ruling class obeys no discipline, no rule, and no principle of public morality; display no sense of public awareness and show no concern for the public weal. The rulers are willfully clinging to power by hook or by crook. Morality, it seems, is the one thing missing in Nepali politics these days. It seems to be guided by the political doctrine of Machiavelli, (as also discussed in chapter four above) which denies the relevance of morality in political affairs and holds that craft and deceit are justified in pursuing and maintaining political power." To retain power, the hereditary prince must carefully maintain the socio-political institutions to which the people are accustomed; whereas a new prince has the more difficult task in ruling, since he must first stabilize his new-found power in order to build an enduring political structure. He believes that social benefits of stability and security could be achieved in the face of moral corruption. Aside from that, Machiavelli believes that public and private morality should be separate in order to rule. To do this, it is required that the prince should be concerned not only with reputation but that he is also willing to act immorally. As a political scientist, Machiavelli emphasizes the occasional need for the methodical exercise of brute force, deceit, and so on. The leaders and politicians in Nepal these days openly adopt Machiavelli's assessment to recognize the need for separation of morals from the power struggle; the irrelevance of morality in politics. But they have forgotten that politics devoid of morality is a sure road to disaster and morality is an integral part of any political culture. They do know less that morality if removed from politics, it is no better than chicanery and politicians no better than *thugs* (cheaters). Rising scenarios point to the fact that democratic commitment of leaders of even major parties is only a sham and pretentious since their own greed for power post and pelf and privileges have made them myopic and blind. Fatigued with such behavior, many people feel that the legacy of old game of horse trading is continued to be in the government by any means.

The culture of politics in Nepal has on one side depleted with a false sense of ego; the degradation of sentiments of justice, idolization of money and power; and adherence to lofty principles and spiritual ideas. On the other, it is marked by the rise of parochial elements in power, politics and political processes. The political elites keep on talking of good governance, welfare state, social justice, and equal opportunities for all, with the result that the rich at the top are annoyed by their talks and the poor are dismayed by its performance. Individual sense of self-importance, personal egos, and deep rooted instincts of self has become pervading features of Nepali political culture. But the erosion of value in politics is not arrested with seriousness.

Political culture has turned to business culture and not service. Well connected people with appropriate family background and convenient tags enter politics. To them politics is greed, an amoral greed for wealth. It has nothing to do with patriotism. This culture again lacks the sentiment of nationality which starts from the mind and judges from the heart. Nationalism is where both the heart and the mind must come together in the right way and for the right purpose. The spirit of nationalism can sustain itself only when it is guided by the right kind of vision and reasoning capacity i.e., to distinguish between right and wrong, good and evil, justice and injustice and moral and immoral.

The brute quest for political power, violation of constitutional norms and values, lust for money and unethical alliances, all indicate the populist trend in the Nepali political culture that leads to the deculturation of politics. It seems that the leaders of political parties have not taken the CA and the parliament seriously. Their absence from the CA sessions demonstrates how causal they are. A survey conducted by Martin Chautari has exposed their lack of seriousness as if the CA is like a platform for them.[83] Their consecutive absence from the CA is also a violation of the Interim constitution. According to the Article 67 of the Constitution, the seat of a member of the CA is said to be deemed vacant "if he/she remains absent from ten consecutive meetings without notification to the assembly." In the present context, non of the leaders had notified to the CA, a national daily broke out the news about their long absence, and they tried to show their presence in back dates in order to save their membership. It is totally alienated from the sense of responsibility or duty and transcendent truth, from the lore of philosophy, literature and art; so ceases to be the real political culture. It is self indulgent, self-centered and self-willed, where political activity is devoid of the norms of decency.

The Mps have become potential blackmailers and the norms of decency and decorum are more often flouted than respected. Abuse is now regarded by the ruling class as integral part of political dialogue. Abusive language has led to the vulgarization of politics. It denotes ideological bankruptcy. Apology is a part of parliamentary etiquette or culture. It is indeed to restore decency, but it has diluted now, so has become a thing of the past. Abuse is not madness, it is a calculated method adopted by the ruling class to insult and harass somebody. It is also intended to deceive and misinform the people.

The most recent trend in the political culture of Nepal is a tendency which indicates lack of refinement, good manners, which thrives on the heaping abuses on dissenters and opponents. It is abuse of language; a direct consequence of the abuse of power. It is foul-mouthed attack to discredit the opponents. It is the use of bad language in political dialogue or a game of rascally tricks without enough thoughts of the consequences. Disgraceful and vulgar words no matter whether in parliament or in street have been employed by the ruling class to frighten and hurt the opposition and vice versa. The personalized and bad language used by members of parliament especially between the position and opposition is creating and nurturing a culture of intolerance. Barring from airing views by snapping the microphone wires gives the clear picture of wild culture in the party and parliament. Both intra-and inter- party dog fight has not only ruined the system but also is inducing hopelessness in the society. As a result, polarized emotions and conflicts overtake the culture of rational argument. The incessant power struggles between the government and the opposition have also further polarized the civil servants and restrained their efficacy from being directed towards democratic governance of culture. It is because beneath the democratic set up, the elements of the feudalistic political culture still work against the true spirit of democracy and unity. Submissiveness of the masses to ministers is there. The old idea of personal rule has remained alive and well in government departments where even minor decisions would be referred up the long hierarchy to ministerial level. Such orientations have made politics more difficult to inculcate democratic culture. In the post-Rana years, powerful politicians, such as the prime minister and members of the cabinet on palace secretarial would have crowds of individuals gathering outside their homes before office hours. These people turned up and waited to ask personal favours or just show submission and loyalty. Now the trend is towards the political leaders and politicians. Such phenomenon has provided a new impetus to higher caste, community, religion in the social order because the professional politicians have made use of these forces as a means of catching votes. The result of new mass culture is that it has increased more stress and strains in our political culture on the basis of caste, community although ideology has nothing to do with it.

The political values based on caste and communities have given rise to political corruption, favoritism and culture of political alienation and dissatisfaction. The political culture resulted from such an experience is far from being a noble venture or a quest to fulfill people's hopes and aspirations. Irrationality has no limit-as Abraham Lincoln said," you can fool all the people some of the time and some of the people all the time but you cannot fool all the people all the time. Now people have become wiser. People have become more aware of their rights and duties. They are now actively involved in the process of democratic political functioning. They have learnt that they can't be fooled all the time by the exponents of the new political culture in the country. They have realized their intrinsic worth and given a befitting reply such opportunistic politicians time and again. This shift in the perception of the masses certainly raises the hope that out of the ashes of the present political imbroglio, a new political culture will arise phoenix like and the country will be proud of its traditions and conventions.

## Culture of Foreign Interference

Nepal occupies a central part of Asian geopolitics between two advanced technological super states China in the north and India in the east, south, and west each with over one billion population, leading infrastructure, software technology industries, high growth markets and highest engagement of multilateral institutions. This potentially makes it a transit corridor for increased Sino-Indian competition for trade and commerce. Its geopolitical location constitutes its strategic geography vital to their security, stability, progress and peace. An increasingly open and democratic Nepal in the future is more likely to be swayed by the ongoing geo-strategic competition between them and the great powers for their influence. History bears testimony to the fact that after the unification of Nepal in 1769 AD, Nepal's security was based on a policy of active defense.

The advent of Rana regime in 1846 modified this policy as it maintained special security relationship with British India and isolation from the rest of the world. After 1950 the state adopted the policy of diversification in international relations. So, strategic thinking on Nepal's national security assumes that National sovereignty and integrity will not be threatened until and unless some external powers do not play their negative role. It is also assumed that, however, the assessment or reassessment of national interest is conducted by whatever government in power, government directly headed by kings or Rana Prime ministers or different leaders of political parties, the ultimate goal has been to keep the foreign policy in balance, safe and vibrant.[84]

The ground reality of Nepal is such that it does not pose any threat to China nor India, but the two neighbors pose such a threat to Nepal. External players who often helped parties to restore democracy also played negative roles showing their own preference to parties and leaders. Their interventionist roles become active when parties leaders themselves become weak both psychologically and organizationally. Their temptation to be close to India and China, for example, has encouraged these powers to be more interventionist for influencing the internal politics of Nepal.

The disintegrating armed outfits are using weapons made in China and India. The Maoist insurgency received support and assistance from both China and India. For a decade long armed conflict, the Maoist rebels remained under Indian protection and information in Indian soil. Weapons are being supplied from China without any obstruction, which is weakening Nepal's internal peace and security and national integrity. Nepal government and political leaders have not drawn the attention of Beijing and New Delhi on the subject—either due to fear or with fear of losing the state power. Leaders' silence is suspicious as ever. China accuses and suspects that America, India and European nations are providing energy to Free-Tibet agitation through Nepal, while India accused China and Pakistan of posing a danger on Indian security by making Nepal a base. Nepali political leaders have never expressed concern before New Delhi and Beijing of the looming disintegration, anarchy and civil war. The political leaders have been assuring New Delhi and Beijing of security and welfare of both the nations, while the two neighboring governments have not satisfied from such assurances. Beijing and New Delhi want assurances and commitments from our political leaders to guaranteeing tight security from Nepal. But they are the one responsible for playing a decisive role in Nepal's politics, economy and security policy.

Nepal should be sensitive to the security concern of its neighbors and ensure that the challenge is how are we going to deal with immediate neighbors particularly with India and china when the bilateral relations between these two countries are rapidly changing for the better and friendly nation particularly with the US, the UK and the European union, Japan and other distant nations in the context of changing domestic as well as international scenario in the days to come. Moreover, when the west, particularly the US and UK, is coordinating their Nepal policy through India, under these circumstances it has become difficult for Nepal to conduct balanced foreign relations. There is a broader consensus in Nepal by maintaining balance in the relation of the two neighbours and taking benefit from the economic development of them. But in reality this policy has never been implemented particularly because of the reluctance from the part of our southern neighbor. Both China and India are likely to dominate world affairs in the days to come both in strategic and economic front and success and failure of Nepal's foreign policy depends, whether its leaders can take advantage of this 'boom' of the half-of the world or not.

Nepal neither has the strength to play one country against another nor does it have much choice and ambition left other than developing its capacity as economically viable state that can protect its citizen both outside and inside and create an environment where citizens can prosper with dignity. Moreover, Nepalis should not be worried in advancing relations with China merely because it is a communist state and retreat its relations with India just because some of the political parties blame it as an 'expansionist' power. What it has to do is to manage internal security and put its house in the order, prioritize foreign policy agenda and reap benefits from regional and global economic participation. Similarly, unavailability of clear national vision on foreign policy, other than the traditional values based on the principles of *Panchasheel*, non-alignment will not be able to address the changing global, regional and national political and economic challenges. Since international power balance has gradually being shifting towards this region, we have to redefine the traditional thought of Nepal as a yam between two boulders "laid down by King Prithivi Narayana Shah, (though it was contextual in that era) to the idea of a "Vibrant Bridging State of South Asia and East Asia."[85]

The heavy reliance of the country on foreign aid and foreign experts and an uncritical adoption of the policy of conditional ties of international capital markets have locked the nations into external dependence and undermined the role of the state in domestic and foreign policy making. In this context, Dahal has remarked that: "… the unfolding of harsh culture of dependence, debt and inequality led to the dis-empowerment of citizens".[86] The excessive reliance of the state on the external world for development has also weakened the prerogative of the parliament on public policy formation and consequently, stripped it of ownership of those policies. Pandey in his article, "A successful story on failed development" has commented- "… due to our begging culture, we have suffered in building competence on- "negotiation skill and deriving permissible benefits."[87] He further remarks: "Democracy is not and cannot be a "project" to be appraised, financed, implemented, monitored and evaluated at the behest of the external partners." [88]

The situation is reverse in present day Nepal. Policies come from abroad in the form of advice even when they are linked to conditional aid. The donor's intervention in policy making has become further intensified with an increasing emphasis on governance. A number of donors now feel free to ignore the state authorities, when they find it necessary to do so, mustering support from the corruption of the government and the inefficiency of its policies. The donors have bypassed the state sovereignty in policy decisions in the name of engaging civil society and grass root organizations. As a result, who is responsible for policy making in the country and who will be held accountable are questions that seem to have no answer at the moment. If foreign aid does not advance the cause of development and poverty alleviation, it has nothing to do with the condition of the grass level people. It does only encourage the culture of begging or a culture of dependency, or both.

The dependency thus imbues governance with the values of status quo and, consequently, unresponsive to citizens' concern. If this situation continues, the condition of nation and citizens are sure to worsen and political culture and behaviour to suit the present democratic polity hardly develops. Citizens are finding it difficult to settle with what democracy means to them, if the political process leads them to more dependency in psychological and economic terms. The purpose of foreign aid should be to liberate productive forces of society and enable the citizens to reap the benefits through their continuous participation and empowerment. With regard to Nepal's dependence on foreign aid, the dependence is not only limited to the need of development. Rather social peace and even the survival of the nation also increasingly depend upon it. This dependency culture and more seriously, foreign aid creating a fatalistic mindset has been highlighted by Dor Bahadur Bista in his book *Fatalism and Development.* He demonstrates how growing foreign/development aid has been so influential in the foreign policy and cultural dynamics of Nepal.[89]

Dependency and fatalistic mind set have been the overriding features of the socio-economic and political development of Nepal. He further quotes foreign aid donors as father –surrogates. … When this passive parental dependency is applied to foreign aid, the only active agent of development becomes the foreign party, who then must supply the resources, the administration, the imagination to plan and the motivation to make it all work. While Nepalese are slow to thank their foreign benefactors, they are quick to attribute blame to them for a host of real and imagined ills, while they themselves maintain a child- like innocence. This behaviour makes some foreign aid administrators and experts adopt an arrogant and condescending attitude towards their Nepali counterparts which in turn cause resentment towards foreign aid among some Nepali people. These various orientations to foreign aid with all their inconsistencies cannot form a positive receptacle for foreign efforts to support Nepalese development."[90] But current fatalistic beliefs have institutionalized the culture of dependency instead of generating its own process of growth addressing the needs of the people and raise the standard of living.

It would be naïve on our part to think that foreign influence in Nepali politics is a new phenomenon. In fact, it has always lurked and thrived in the shadow of Nepal's shimmering *Himals* from the unification days, to the days of superpower rivalry, right down to the unipolar world of today. It is now common knowledge that outside interference in our internal affairs has become a reality. Let us not forget that the more subtle and civilized form of interference in Nepal's internal affairs for matters of vested interest was deftly practiced by the British during the days of the Raj in bringing Nepal under its sphere of influence by propping up Rana autocracy for over a century. In today's times, however, blatant interference by regional and international powers clearly illustrate that the game is still afoot. External interference is partly responsible for not creating congenial environment for building political system. External penetration has increased significantly in the post-2006 period due to lack of confidence of leaders. It has been alleged that India's pressure has caused a series of splits within various Terai parties.[91]

Nepal's Geo-politics and increased interest of foreign powers have contributed to generating distrust among political forces. Due to multiple political centers, Nepal's two neighbours plus the United States and other Western countries try to reach out to each major party so as not to allow other competing powers to monopolize the political scene. Its impact has been felt in power configuration as well as in intra- party and inter- party alignment in respective lines.

Political instability is also the cause and consequence of external pressure to which parties can seldom resist openly. Political leaders themselves develop a psychology that unless they get support of India, their own survival will be in question. Other countries have also been playing their roles to influence the parties. International organizations are directly involved in constitution making activities or by pumping money to sell their own agendas through NGOs and individuals. Politicians are not free from such wide spread penetration.Nevertheless, in the globalized world where each country is exposed to other, such mutual interactions are natural. But it is up to the Nepalis themselves to develop their capacity to resisting all such pressures. Some examples have shown that external powers have also limitations because they cannot always show their individual or party preferences while forming a government nor can the present Nepali politics afford denial by keeping out certain parties out of power. What Nepali needs today is commonality of approach to certain key issues such as democratic stability, peace and development. Pursing these objectives need broad mindedness, vision, strong leadership and cooperative relationship among the political forces.

Nepal opening up to the modern world also means inviting outside interference in the name of democracy, development and foreign aid. The fact that this mountainous country geographically straddles two of the world's biggest nuclear giants, but more importantly, that it is also strategically– if not uncomfortably– wedged between Tibet (China's soft underbelly) and the vulnerable Indo-Gangetic plains (India's heartland) is reason enough for outside powers to have their stakes here. However, the intention here is not to blame outside powers for throwing diplomatic norms to the winds and aggressively pushing forward their agendas vis-à-vis Nepal's new leadership. Whatever is the reason, the reality; whether our democratic leadership accepts it or not, is that they allow it. If Nepali politics is remote controlled by outside powers we have nobody to blame but ourselves.

As Shakespeare in Julius Caesar puts it: "The fault dear Brutus is not in our stars, but in ourselves that we are underlings." Our leaders/politicians must have realized by now that blatant foreign interference is like the proverbial camel inching into the tent, and once in, the impossibility of getting him out. The blame needs to be borne entirely by political amateurs who have in the name of power politics been more careful of personal and party interests rather than the national cause. In recent years, such interference has become very blatant and this is indeed a matter of worry for any Nepali who wants to see an independent and sovereign Nepal. Narayan Man Bijukche[92] now is saying that virtually all the parties are fighting as pawns of outside powers. The people want to see a new constitution and peace, but these will mean nothing if they are subjugated by outsiders. They are ashamed by the constant interference from outside and they are angry at the failure of the government and the political parties to address the domestic interferences. Although external pressure has often been exerted on the political elites of Nepal, however it is not a new thing. It happened for the right cause insofar as it remained an advice. But the manner in which political leaders regarded less of parties started succumbing to external factors for taking decisions in the post-2006 movement is shameful.

The fault lies with leaders who, instead of becoming popular on the strength of the people, count on foreign power, particularly India, for being in power. Prachanda had severely criticized the foreign intervention in Nepal in his address to the nation on May 4, 2009. He said, "Various national and international regressive and status quo elements are inserting a conspiracy against the young republic, national independence, socio-economic transformation, and development." Although Prachanda severely criticizes the foreign forces on one hand, he seeks India's support to continue the government on the other side. It is seen that almost all the leading leaders, as long as they are in the power and government take foreign interference as cooperation. Once they ousted from the post the same governing elites blame it to be interference into internal affairs of Nepal. This culture is enough to give the clue of the nature of new political culture being developed that shows how leaders move on with double standard values even in the most critical national issues.

What we lack at present is consciousness among political parties. For e.g. - we complain about foreign interference in our internal affairs but we do not have any mechanism to counter these interferences. Neither have we had strategy that would guide us to deal with these emerging challenges nor coherence and common voice among political parties. In fact, it is we not them who are inviting this interference. Today, however, Nepal's politicians scramble for visiting New Delhi in particular for enhancing their prospects of power at home. When they do not draw as much attention from the Indian side as they expect they cry hoarse against India or grumble for being ignored. Similarly, Nepalis have been rising about border encroachment for the last so many years but leaders have not been able to develop any mechanism to counter this unabated encroachment nor have they seriously taken up issue at the political level. Foreign policy of Nepal is conducted on the basis of whims and vernacular media report that foreign power has captured key political figures from all political parties to serve their interests.[93]

The crucial days are ahead for Nepali policy makers. Internal situation is in a mess with the major parties responsible for bringing about a radical change quarreling for no substantive reasons. In the same way, foreign policy, which is supposed to articulate vital national interest, is now an abandoned area. All casual functions are discharged in absence of any developed institution headed by a foreign minister having minimum idea of foreign policy. A sound foreign policy based on ground realities should be the major concern of today's Nepal, but post 1990, political parties are not serious about projecting Nepal's international image. If Nepal fails to keep its own house in order by consolidating representative institutions, its aspiration to be an independent and sovereign nation would be undermined. Limitless transition and visionless politics may be more alarming when foreign powers start showing their active presence than ever before and when the political and other elites become too weak to manage them as the recent developments have demonstrated. It is particularly important when China and India are emerging as competitive powers whose future activities need to be appropriately balanced by Nepal. However, this needs both acumen and status of leaders.

Globalization process, larger economic factors, management of natural resources, security concerns have increased the need for better relationship between the two countries. Managing and running the relationship is about much more than making treaties, laws and rules. That is the easy part. The hard part is implementing, operating, monitoring, evaluating, fixing and spreading the best practices in a reciprocal way on the basis of equality, territorial integrity, sovereignty, mutual respect for each other and non-interference. At least Nepali leaders and people keep in mind that the theories and modalities applied elsewhere are not likely to be workable in Nepal. It is wise to think that Nepalis alone are the best judge for steering the course of Nepal.

**People's Satisfaction (Supply and Demand)**

The 1990 constitution guaranteed for nearly the first time political rights and civil liberties of the people. This means that the people could speak and freely express aspirations for their political, cultural and social rights. Nepal can take pride and some satisfaction in what the people have achieved in the course of the movement for democracy and peace. So it does not mean that no positive developments have taken place in democratic consolidation. Nepali people have always supported the political change. People are the strengths of democracy and through the electoral process they have demonstrated their commitment over and over again. The unprecedented participation and sacrifices by all section of the people in the movement not only ended the king's despotic rule, it has also helped to sideline the 240-year old institution of monarchy, hopefully for good. These achievements have earned the people much goodwill and confidence that when challenged, no matter how poor and disvantaged, they are capable of rising to the occasion and taking their destiny into their own hands.

For a long time, the people believed in the rhetoric of development and in the promises made to them that development, whatever that may be would deliver income and opportunities denied to majority of them through history. Collectively, they accepted what they were asked to believe by successive rulers in various régimes. The people's movement for democracy and peace is therefore, primarily about the people's right to equality, not only in accessing political power but also in realizing their social, economic and cultural potentials. But there is the real and perceived inability of the transitional or interim government to break away from the past, culturally and socially and to move forward according to the mandate of the people's movement. When we analyze and understand the events and achievements in peace building, we also observe the continuing disappointments and challenges in the country.

In particular, one should note that the Jan Andolan11 of 2005-06 receives the massive support of the people because of their hopes and expectation that the successful conclusion of the movement would provide not only with the answers to the questions just posed but also generate practical policies and actions as required. Overall, despite the continued inability of elected governments to deal effectively with the problems confronting their country, Nepalis were more strongly committed to democracy during Jan Andolan11 of 2005-06. Despite the fluctuations in the public confidence that democracy could solve their problems, support for democracy as a better system of governance remained consistently high and even increased than they had been in 1990. With the political leadership about to betray the people once again, it is feared that the process is in jeopardy and the country might be pushed into the vicious circle of political instability, anarchy, violence, resurrection of authoritarianism, poverty and continued misery. Such practices have made politics more difficult to inculcate democracy that would really deliver.

Nepali people thus almost separated their support for democracy as a political system from their evaluation of the performance of the leaders and political parties. This would mean the continuation of the hold of the traditionally dominant groups on political power and economic resources. It would also mean that the outcomes of the new uncertainty, political instability and possible violence will affect all strata of population. Yet, another belief of the people in Jan Andolon II will be belied. The people had told the leaders that they wanted the democratic movement and the peace process to end in such a way that no other Andolans big or small, would be necessary in the country again. Above all, performance legitimacy of the new order would also determine the protection of democratic values and norms. Nepali politicians, however soon forgot this mutuality of values and norms and institution building that can strengthen the delivery side of the system. Development experts assume that the state is there to provide services and that if it fails to do so it will face a crisis of legitimacy and the nation tends to feature high on the list of fragile or failing states.

The people have not seen any sign of change that affects their lives directly and positively. The living conditions of the people have not improved and there is no evidence that the government is even thinking about the ordinary people and their problems and anxieties. The Maoists' strategy of using militant, aggressive and obstructive methods-perhaps in an attempt to compensate for their political frustrations at the hands of their partner in SPA-is hitting the ordinary people hard. Strikes and closing down of schools, streets and even hospitals have become a routine affair. The law and order situation is in disarray. Social, political and economic crimes have become an everyday affair. That the state does not have its presence in most parts of the country is a refrain one comes across even in the otherwise privileged communities of the Kathmandu valley. And to add to all this uncertainty, there is the new round of political conflict. The country is oblivious to the difficulties that such an environment posed for the realization of the declared objectives of political freedom, social justice and development of the country. On the social side, the focus of attention was, at best, on the programmes for improvement in the delivery of the services by the social sectors. But service delivery, even when successful, is not the same thing as social change. So with all these reasons, people's euphoria and enthusiasm awakened by the successful mass movements has turned into the culture of indifference, frustration and disillusionment towards the political parties, leaders and government. Too much partisanship, the rise of bitter opposition among factions, unstable coalition government, and deficits in internal democracy and unhealthy inter-party relations made the government supply side almost nil. Enthusiasm for democracy, participation in electoral politics and popularity of democratic leaders all declined significantly.

The frustrations and disappointments with the corrupt governments ran deep. The high level of frustration is not channeled into legal, peaceful system maintaining mechanisms and processes, rather in illegal and violent political activism. This may well have resulted in decreasing voter turnout, despite some rise in the 1999 election, over that of 1991. Although after the abolition of monarchial system, the country was declared as a federal democratic republic making the people sovereign and elected a CA for a new federal republican constitution, the pangs of long transition caused by the irresponsible political leaders have despaired people. The people are worried that the transition is already too long. The scenario I have presented does not make people confident about the future of democracy and political system. Spirit of democracy and culture of rule by the people is what is missing in the political parties and its leadership in Nepal.

The democracy deficit system is indeed an irony for Nepal. Nepali culture and politics are, in fact, quite enmeshed. The state of politics in Nepal is well reflected by a proverb in Nepali popular culture which says *kam navae rajniti garne,* one who does not have any principles does politics. Fewer people than in 1990 believed that the government would be better without politicians and those politicians were indifferent to the country's problems. One cannot blame the general people for such a perception or judgment. The people have watched with frustration the confrontationist nature of politics with continuous boycotts of the parliament by the MPs and opposition. Such understanding of democracy that fails to deliver would make people disillusioned and the reverse trend begins to unfold. The Nepali state is becoming weaker by every passing day. Development is hard-hit due to more than 15 hours of load shedding, lack of regular water supply, closure of industries because of the uninterrupted strikes, threats and extortions.[94]

The domestic mess and inaction has also been reflected in foreign policy and diplomacy. Observers believe that no serious efforts were made to redefine Nepal's policy in the changing national, regional and global context. There has been a steady decline of the role of both government and state. The pre-CA in 2008 did convince people that Nepali political parties were together in so far as ideological framework was concerned. The election manifestos, barring some political rhetoric, have provided the contours of politics of delivery. Such manifestos have all been remained on papers or as propaganda materials used for election campaigns. So only hopes and rhetoric promises are being delivered. Manifestos are matters of rites for them. This hiatus between proclamations and performances is fundamental feature of the culture of politics in Nepal. All these have impacted on the overall productivity of nation.

Since governance is related to delivery capacity, which is legitimacy besides constitutional-legal legitimacy, the non–functioning organ cannot meet the requirements of a legitimate government. But the post-movements situation demonstrated that democracy for which the unprecedented movement was launched is turned into a chimera. The hyper inflation, the alarming level of criminal activities and so many other problems faced by the people are simply being ignored. Crisis of governance, misunderstanding of vital issues raised for restructuring of the state and failure of leaders of parties to sit together in finding a way out for settling down the pertinent issues and failure of the parties to agree on setting parameters for writing the constitution is likely to reverse the process of democratization.

Needless to say, the political parties have failed to deliver on the most important of the key promises since signing the comprehensive peace agreement in November 2006 and holding the CA election in April 2008: framing a new constitution keeping in view the aspirations of the people. The CA elected for a term of two years, has had its term extended as many as four times. As if it was not enough, instead of promulgating the constitution, they forced the Constituent Assembly to die on May 27, 2012 and send the country to a never-ending political transition. Never in the history of the country, were the political parties so weak to deliver what they have promised. The Maoists have used the power to hijack the economy and captured the state as they have been repeatedly claiming, but the Nepali Congress and CPN-UML never took it seriously, adding to the woes of the people further. Government's motion to hold election of the CA in November 22, 2012 disappoints the people yet again. It is important to note that in the absence of a parliament, political parties do not represent the people, they only represent themselves.

Prior to declaring Nepal into a republican country, political leaders injected into the minds of the Nepalis that all the miseries of the people under the monarchy of the past would be wiped out by going into republicanism. Prior to the last election to elect the CA political leaders injected into the minds of the common Nepali people that CA elected by the people would transform Nepal into a *Ram Rajya* (where the people's needs are met with top priority). The birth of the CA would be the dream of the Nepalis fulfilled. Soon after the birth of the CA, political leaders injected another item into the minds of the people that federalism would reverse all the roots of the inequalities of the centuries past by igniting prosperity into the most remote of the country and writing of the constitution would transform Nepal by correcting all the misfortunes of history. People do not seem to believe that a misfortune would have come to them if the CA had promulgated a wrong and irresponsible constitution prior to its demise. Nepal has gone through many changes but the dreams of the people are not only unfulfilled, on the contrary people are experiencing more injustice against them by the augmentation of corruption, impunity and general feeling of insecurity and terror resulting in a general apathy and total disappointment with the behavior of the leaders. In fact, it was apparent to all that the political parties were more involved in the game for power than in performing the task that they had been mandated to do.

The country is now at a cross roads. The present government now regarded as care taker one has set for fresh polls in coming April 2013. The situation is thus the result of the Nepali leaders' attachment and too much importance to the political process that made them ignore issues that have greater and more tangible impact on people's day to day life. The past five years since signing the Comprehensive Peace Agreements has been obsessed without the political process. Day in day out, the focus was on completing the twin task-concluding the peace process and writing a new constitution- at the expense of delivering government services, maintaining law and order and enhancing economic development. Since democratic institutions are weak, the service delivery mechanism is a complete failure and the people are deprived of the fruits of development that was supposed to percolate to the grass root level.

What determines, whether or not new democracies survive is not primarily the severity of the problems they face or their ability to solve those problems. People are appalled at the way the politicians are so nonchalantly involved in a power struggle even as the nation is tottering towards political disaster. They are angry at the failure of the government and the political parties to address the different difficulties faced by them. Yet, no plans or policies seem to have been formulated by any of the parties or the government to solve such problems. Moreover, the capacity of the state is further on the decline due to lack of political direction in all areas of public life. The governments headed by prime ministers are hamstrung by the chains put on them by their own parties as well as the coalition partners. It is the way in which political leaders respond to their inability to solve the problems confronting their country. So the dissatisfaction of the people remains more pronounced on the dimension of the output effect rather than the system effect. There is in other words more dissatisfaction with the specific performance of government and leaders than with the system as a whole. Unfortunately, politicization of crime, unethical behaviour of elected representatives, lack of co-operation between ruling and opposition party, de-culturation of politics, lack of spirit of sacrifice of the leaders and frequent fall of governments and excessive foreign interference in the internal affairs of Nepal have severely delinked and alienated people's aspiration and expectations that has taken the culture of politics in Nepal on a reverse gear. These incidents also have created the major source of dissatisfaction of the general public towards their system.

The very negative impact of this political culture let reduce the possibility for system stability and output efficiency. The democratic culture issue focuses attention on the relation between the performances or effectiveness of new democratic governments and their legitimacy-in other words the extent to which elites and public believe in the value of the democratic system. In an essentially pessimistic argument about this relationship Diamond Linz and Lipset held that a primary reason for the instability of democratic and other regimes in the Third World ,was the "the combination and interaction of low legitimacy and low effectiveness."Regimes begin with low legitimacy and hence find it difficult to be effective, and regimes which lack effectiveness, especially in economic growth, tend to continue to be low in legitimacy.[95] A growing literature on democratic governance supports that the legitimacy of particular rulers or governments may depend on what they can deliver. The legitimacy of the regime derives from the electoral processes by which the governments are constituted. The legitimacy of democratic regimes clearly rests on processes and procedures and strongly on performance. If performance legitimacy plays a strong role in democratic regimes, there is a less gap between the performance (supply side) of the government and expectations (demand) of the people in Nepal.

Now, the new political environment and trends created have given rise to serious questions regarding the sustainability of democracy itself. If this is how things move, nothing better can be expected in the days to come. This has been the aura haunting Nepali politics, which leaves the people more pessimistic rather be optimist. Despite the completion of three national elections, Nepal is, however, a country in democratic transition rather than a state featuring democratic consolidation. In sum, the political culture of Nepal after the restoration of democracy has been dominated by the weakening of norms and value based politics, erosion in leadership quality, and cynical manipulation of constitutional provisions, mismanagement, irresponsibility and unaccountability in the public sphere. It has made the culture of democratic consolidation difficult in Nepal not because people have lost faith in democracy but because of the faltering interests of the political parties in being responsive to their primary mission rather than national interest. Past studies and reports including that of Annan, 2005 reveal the high risk of peace processes relapsing to conflict.

In a report entitled *In Larger Freedom*, the former Secretary-General of the United Nations, Kofi Annan, notes, "Roughly half of all countries that emerge from war lapse back into violence within five years." The sign of erosion of democratic ethos making consolidation of the political order more difficult makes one to say that even after nearly two decades of democratic governance, the people have realized no substantive change. The history of all democracies has shown that good institutions which are accepted function well and also adjust to the special conditions of a country are the most important factors for success. However, this phenomenon has come as the established political culture in Nepal where democracy is being primarily taken as machinery made of institutions which does not live with the spirit and expectations of Nepali people.

The negative effect of this political culture on institutional performance has thus damaged the base for a secular political culture. It cannot go on like this forever. It has foreclosed the opinion that could only be changed through extra-constitutional means or what John Locke had suggested the right of people to revolution in case the contract broke down. At this stage we need to look ahead and let the past be the past and think about how to secure our future. Effective and efficient government systems promote sound policy implementation and keep countries on track to reach desired development goals. While we deal with political transition, parallel efforts should be made to deliver good governance, political stability, public security and economic development.

## NOTES

1. *1999 General Election Opinion Poll: How Voters Assess Politics, Parties and Politicians*, (Lalitpur: Himal Association, 1999), p. 28.
2. *Public Political Opinion Survey in Nepal,* (Kathmandu: SEARCH (NGO), 1994), p. XXII.
3. Dev Raj Dahal, *Civil Society in Nepal; Opening the Ground for Questions,* (Kathmandu: Center for Development and Governance, 2001), pp. 45-45.
4. Public Political Opinion Survey in Nepal," *SEARCH,* (Kathmandu: November, 1994), pp. 24-25.
5. POLSAN, *Political Parties and the Parliamentary Process in Nepal-A Study of the Transitional Phase,* (Kathmandu: Jeewan Printing Support Press, 1992), p. 152.
6. *The Himalayan Times,* (January 1st, 2011).
7. *The Himalayan Times,* (May 24, 2011).
8. *The Himalayan Times,* (June 19, 2012).
9. Clientele politics de-links citizens from state and system undermining citizenship values. It patrimonies the personal links and promotes the culture of sycophancy. The benefits and opportunities are available to the clients not to the citizens that weaken both state-building and political process. For detail see,

pp. 94-96. Chandra Dev Bhatta, *Challenges of State Building in Nepal,* (Kathmandu: Friedrich-Ebert-Stiftung, Nepal Office -FES, 2008).

10. Political differences among top three officials of Tribhuvan University, and their acts to please the ideologically close staff have taken a toll on the country's oldest university. Vice-Chancellor (VC), Rector and Registrar under the quota of CPN-UML, Nepali Congress and UCPN (Maoist) respectively acting primarily in championing the cause of the party they belong to have led politicization and polarization of TU, *The Kathmandu Post, (*January 7, 2011).
11. National flag carrier Nepal Airlines Corporation (NAC) since long a victim of politics is now with just two age old Boeing 757s on its international routes that mostly face maintenance problems and only four air crafts in domestic routes, efficiency down by 50 percent, 1,400 staff facing an uncertain future with its top management in a legal tussle, all figure in the corporations' dismal situation, *The Himalayan Times,* (January 2nd, 2011).
12. *The Kathmandu Post,* (March 26, 2011).
13. Public Political Opinion Survey in Nepal," *SEARCH Op cit.* f.n. No. 4, p. 158.
14. Dahal, *op cit.,* f.n. No. 3, p. 46.
15. Myron Weiner, "Political Participation: Crisis of the Political Process" in Leonard Binder et al., *Crises and Sequences in Political Development,* (Princeton: New Jersey, 1971), p. 159.
16. Sills David L., *International Encyclopedia of Social Science,* Vol. II, (New York: The Macmillan Company and the Free Press, 1972), p. 223.
17. Robert D. Putnam, *Making Democracy Work: Civic Tradition in Modern Italy,* (Princeton: Princeton University Press, 1993), p. 167.
18. Joseph A Schumpeter, *Capitalism, Socialism, and Democracy,* (New York: Harper and Row, 1942), pp. 289-296.
19. Gabriel A. Almond and Sidney Verga, *The Civic Culture: Political Attitudes and Democracy in Five Nations,* (Princton: Princton University Press, 1963), p. 493.
20. *Ibid,* p. 490.
21. Dev Raj Dahal, "Reforms in the Electoral Process of Nepal," *Comparative Electoral Process in South Asia,* Devendra R. Pandey,

Anand Aditya, Dev Raj Dahal (eds.), (Kathmandu: NESAC, July 1999), p. 147.

22. Puspa B. Pradhan, "Government and the Opposition: The Pivot of Polity" in *Political Parties and the Parliamentary Process in Nepal: A Study of the Transitional Phase,* (Kathmandu Jeewan Printing Press, 1992), pp. 154-55.
23. "Interview in", *The Telegraph Weekly,* Vol. 16, No. 46, (Kathmandu: Animesh Publication, January 26, 2000 Wednesday).
24. Pareto and Mosca's, *Approaches to Leadership in Peter Bacharach, The Theory of Democratic Elitism: A Critique* (London: University of London Press Limited, 1969).
25. Devendra Raj Pandey, Governance and Political Corruption: A Perspective on Prospects of Regional Cooperation in South Asia, p. 302. In *South Asia 2010: Challenges and Opportunities* K.K. Bhargava, Sridhar Khatri (eds.), Friedrich-Ebert-Stiftung, (New Delhi: Konarch Publishers, 2001).
26. Lok Raj Baral (ed.), *Constitutional Government and Democracy in South Asia*, (Kathmandu: Nepal Centre for Studies Contemporary-NCCS, Nepal, 2011), Introduction: Democracy in Twilight Zone, pp. 33–34.
27. *Ibid.*
28. Lok Raj Baral, Krishna Hachhethu and Hari Sharma, *Leadership in Nepal,* (Delhi: Adroit Publishers, 2000), p. 6.
29. *Ibid,* p. 7.
30. Samuel P. Huntington, *The Third Wave: Democratization in the Late Twentieth Century*, (Norman: Oklahoma Press, 2010), p. 45.
31. K.K .Bhargava and Sridhar Khatri (eds.), "Governance and Political Corruption: A Perspective on Prospects of Regional Cooperation in South Asia," *South Asia 2010: Challenges and Opportunities,* Friedrich-Ebert-Stiftung, (New Delhi: Konark Publishers Pvt. Ltd., 2001), p. 302.
32. Lok Raj Baral, *Nepal-Nation-State in the Wilderness; Managing State, Democracy, and Geopolitics*, (New Delhi: Sage Publication, 2012), p. 232.
33. *The Himalayan Times*, (September 4, 2011).
34. *Ibid.*

35. Krishna P. Khanal, "Democracy and Federalization of the Nepalese State Challenges and Opportunities," *Sangam Journal* Quarterly, Vol. 1, (Kathmandu: Publication of Sangam Institute for Policy Analysis and Strategic Studies, 2009), pp. 15-16.
36. *The Himalayan Times*, (May, 29, 30, 2011).
37. Prayag Raj Sharma, *Restructuring the State in South Asia: Some Impressions and Ideas,* Lok Raj Baral (ed.), (New Delhi: Adroit Publication, 2008), pp. 156-57.
38. World Food Programme, (WFP) 2009, "Struck Out: The Everyday Economic Livelihood Impact of Bandhas and Strikes in Nepal," *WFP Nepal-Food for Thought*, Issue (1, March 2009).
39. *The Himalayan Times*, (January, 8, 2011).
40. Dev Raj Dahal and C.D Bhatta, "Is Culture of Constitutionalism the Agenda," *Multiverse of Nepal's Democracy; Contents and Discontents,* Tone Bleie and Dev Raj Dahal (eds.), (Kathmandu: Modern Printing Press), pp. 30-31.
41. John Galtung is an award winning Norwegian founder for peace studies, generating a unique conceptual toolkit for empirical, critical and constructive inquiry into the study of peace. For detail see, *nepaltimes.com/2012.10.15/ interview/1970#UTB FrIgdD s*.r demands.
42. *The Himalayan Time*, (Tuesday, December 20, 2011).
43. S.M. Rahman, *http:www.friends.org. PK/rahman/building/20 political htm, building political culture*,
44. The districts affected by armed outfits are Morang, Sunsari, Saptari, Siraha, Jhapa, Udayapur, Khotang, Parsa,, Sarlahi, Kapilbastu, Rupandehi, Banke, Bardiya and Dang. Kathmandu is also a soft target of dispersed armed groups. *The Himalayan Times,* (January 17, 2011).
45. Quoted in *http://www.friends.org.PK/rahman/building%20 political. htm* "Building Political Culture Anew," Dr. S.M Rahman.
46. Samuel P. Huntington, *The Third Wave; Democratization in the Late Twentieth Century,* (New Delhi: Adarsha Books, 2010), p. 107.
47. Mihir Kumar Thakur, "Corruption in Public Administration", *Nepalma Prajatantrako Ek Dasak* Achyut B. Rajbhandari, S. Srivastav, I.P. Pokhrel (eds.), (Kathmandu: Centre for Democracy and Good Governmance, (FES, 2057), p. 217.

48. Rishikesh Shaha, *Nepali Politics: Retrospect and Prospects,* II ed., (Oxford: Oxford University Press, 1978), p. 4.
49. *Janadesh Weekly,* (Kathmandu, March 30, 1999).
50. Dev Raj Dahal, *Weak State, Social Classes and Social Transformation in Nepal,* (Kathmandu: FES, Nepal Office, 2007), pp. 24-26.
51. Joseph La Palombra (ed.), *Bureaucracy and Political Development*, (New Jersey: Joseph La Palombra Princeton, 1963), p. 4.
52. The move by Finance Secretary Rameshowr Khanal to disaffiliate himself from Nepal's bureaucratic set up with regard to the issues of fake VAT bills has certainly caused a few ripples. Bharat Mohan Adhikari, former finance minister-Khanal incident is observed by the bureaucrats as an addition in the series of tussles as they have seen war of words between former energy minister Prakash Saran Mahat and secretary Shankar Prasad Koirala, former minister for labour and transport management, Mohammad Aftab Alam and secretary Dinesh Hari Adhikari, former forest minister Deepak Bohara and secretary Yubraj Bhusal and former deputy Prime minister Sujata Koirala and secretary Madan Kumar Bhattarai during Madhav Kumar Nepal-led government.
53. Dor Bahadur Bista, *Fatalism and Development: Nepal's Struggle for Modernization,* (Calcutta: Orient Longman, 1991), p. 98.
54. The direct telephone interview by The Global Corruption Barometer (GCB) of Transparency International (TI) with 7,500 respondents in Nepal, Bangladesh, India, Maldives, Pakistan and Sri Lanka carried out between 2010 and 2011 shows that paying bribe was a must while dealing with a police, land revenue offices and custom services. The survey also found political parties and police the most corrupt institutions in all six countries. *The Himalayan Times*, (December 23, 2011).
55. Binod Bhattarai et al., *Impunity in Nepal: An Exploratory Study,* (Kathmandu: The Asia Foundation, Nepal, 1999), p. 2.
56. The colour of the cover of the diplomatic passports issued by the government of Nepal is red. That explains the name the media coined for the scandal.
57. Bhattarai, *op cit.*, f.n. No. 55, p. 21.

58. Ministry of Peace and Reconstruction, Nepal 2007A, *Agreements and Understandings on Peace Negotiation of Nepal*, 2nd ed. (2008, GON).
59. *Kantipur*, (15th December, 2008).
60. Obtaining 5.7 score, Bhutan ranked comparatively less corrupt than India 3.3, Sri Lanka 3.2 Bangladesh 2.4 and Pakistan 2.3. With a score of 1.4 Afghanistan ranks the most corrupt nation in Asia. It occupies the 176th position out of 178 countries and Somalia is the most corrupt country in the world. Though Nepal is less corrupt than 35 countries, the level of corruption has been going up steadily. It ranked 143rd in 2009, 121st in 2008,131st in 2007, 121st rank in 2006, 117th in 2005 and 90th in 2004. The report ranked war affected countries like Somalia with a score of 1.1 as most corrupt, followed by Myanmar obtaining 1.4 and Afghanistan 1.4 and Iraq 1.5. According to the report, Denmark, New Zealand and Singapore are the cleanest countries with 9.3 scores. *The Himalayan Times*, (October 27, 2010).
61. *Ibid.*
62. *Nepal Human Development Report: State Transformation and Human Development*, (Kathmandu: UNDP, Nepal, 2009), p. 115.
63. Walter Laquer, "Left Right and beyond: The Changing Face of Terror," *How Did This Happen? Terrorism and New War,* James F. Hodge Jr and Gideon Rose (eds.), (New York: Public Affairs, 2000), pp. 81-82.
64. *The Kathmandu Post*, (September, 22, 2009).
65. Baral, *op cit.,* f.n. No. 32, p. 118.
66. *Ibid*, p. 18.
67. *Samakalin,* (May 22, 1997).
68. *Deshantar,* (August 19, 1998).
69. *Deshantar,* (September 27, 1998).
70. The colour of the cover of the diplomatic passports issued by the government of Nepal is red. That explains the name the media coined for the scandal.
71. Bhattarai, et al., f.n. No. 55, p. 21.
72. The CA members Gayatri Shah and Bishwanatha Prasad Yadav representing Nepali Janata Dal and MJF-Nepal, respectively had indulged in selling their red passports for undue financial benefit

and misuse of their honorary positions as drafter of the constitutions has come as a shock to the people. The arrest of former minister and member of the CA Shyam Sunder Gupta for ordering kidnapping of a Kathmandu-based business man speaks volumes about the nexus between organized crime and politics in Nepal. This is not the first time; politicians of national stature have been found involved criminal activities: nor is Gupta going to be the last one in the series. While some have been able to make big gains from criminal activities, there have been some who have had to pay the ultimate price of indulging in crime, corruption and varied unlawful activities. *The Himalayan Times*, January, 18, 2012. The historically elected Constituent Assembly even boasts of a member convicted by the Supreme Court in Bal Krishna Dhungel and there are others who are widely perceived to be involved in criminal activities. This particular incident made general people to perceive that their nomination in the parliament was basically due to the political set up rather than their eligibility to draft a constitution and play a role of Member of Parliament. *The Himalayan Times,* April 20, 2011. But arresting the lawmakers in the passport scam and incidents of former minister, Chiranjibi Wagle as convicted by the Supreme Court on graft charge and sent to jail, and UML's CA member Dol Bahadur Karki receiving six months jail term for his involvement in accepting bribe might have increased the level of trust among the public in the judicial system because the law has been impartial. Recently, the conviction of J.P Gupta, present minister for information and technology by the Supreme Court is again a clear indication that the fight against graft continues on a firm footing. *The Himalayan Times,* February 23, 2012. That the Supreme Court (SC) came up with a fair and impartial verdict has to be commended. This particular SC judgment has once again highlighted the fact among the public that it is committed to punish the wrong doers at any cost. However, there are a number of similar corruption cases lined up and speeding them up is of utmost necessity for the people's faith in the judiciary to be retained. Individuals who hold high posts had tended to skirt around such graft charges earlier that constituted impunity. Earlier records are very scanty on convictions in corruption charges, which may be the reason why even now corruption has become endemic. So it makes imperative that the anti-graft body be further strengthened, so that it can fight corruption on a wider scale than it has been doing at present. Meanwhile, the Supreme Court (SC) must continue its role of being stern in punishing the corrupt.

73. *The Himalayan Times,* (February 23, 2012).
74. Ghani Ashraf and Lockhart Clare, *Fixing Failed States*, (Oxford: Oxford University Press, 2008), p. 163.
75. Mahesh C. Regmi, *Kings and Political Leaders of the Gorkhali Empire 1768-1814*, (Calcutta: Orient Longman, 1995), p. 4.
76. With the formation of the full-fledged government turning out to be a conundrum for Prime Minister Jhala Nath Khanal, the Maoist Party is also in a fix as to how to go ahead now without being given the home ministry. The secret seven point deal had the supposed point therein, but CPN (UML) has put a spanner on PM Khanal not to let go the home portfolio in the name of the deal. Because the task of rehabilitation and arms integration of the Maoist combatants are yet to take off in earnest. The former Maoist combatants are under the special committee (SC), so giving the Maoist the home portfolio is looked upon with suspicion. *The Himalayan Times*, March 1st, 2011.
77. Daniel J. Elazar, *American Federalism: A view From the States,* (New York: Thomas Y. Crowell,), p. 30.
78. Laxmi Prasad Devkota, "We Think Ourselves First" *Janmotsab,* Brijesh Shrestha (ed.), (Kathmandu: Projal Maleku, 1997), p. 37.
79. *Ibid.*
80. Ole Borre, Sushil R. Pandey and Chitra K. Tiwari, *Nepalese Political Behaviour,* (New Delhi: Sterling Publishers Pvt. Ltd., 1994), p. 188.
81. *Human Development in South Asia,* The Crisis of Governance, published for the Mahabab Ul Hoff, Human Development Center: (Oxford: Oxford University Press, 1999), p. 130.
82. Baral, Hachhethu and Sharma, *op cit.,* f.n. No. 28, pp. 122-124.
83. Baral, *op cit.* f.n. No. 32, p. 256.
84. Sushil Raj Pandey, *National Interest-NI and National Security-NS. Theory and Practice in Nepal*. Paper presented at a seminar on National Interest and National Security of Nepal by Sangam Institute in association with Central Department of Political Science, Tribhuvan University, (Kathmandu: 21 August, 2009).
85. PM Bhattarai has shared the idea of a "Vibrant Bridging State of South Asia and East Asia". The concept has pulled itself out of the

long standing traditional foreign policy concept of the buffer and redirects its effort to making the country a vibrant bridging state of south Asia and South East Asia due to its specific strategic location. *The Himalayan Times* (Kathmandu: January, 17, 18, 2012).

86. Dev Raj Dahal, "Nuggets of Nepali Political Culture" *The Telegraph Weekly,* (Kathmandu: Animesh Press, December, 1999), p. 2.
87. Devendra Raj Pandey, "A Successful Story on Failed Development," *The Kathmandu Post,* (Kathmandu: Kantipur Publication, June 6, 1999), p. 3.
88. *Ibid.*
89. Bista, *op cit,* f.n. No. 53.
90. *Ibid.*
91. Prashanta Jha, "A Fine Balance," *Kathmandu Post* , (Kahmandu: June 15, 2011), and also see Pramod Mishra, "Cry Beloved Madhes," *Kathmandu Post,* (Kathmandu: June 15, 2011).
92. Narayan Man Bijukche, President of the Nepal Workers and Peasants' Party was one of the signatories of the 12 — Point Agreement between the Maoists and the then Seven Agitating parties. Bijukche, lambasted all the three major parties in the Constituent Assembly for working in the interest of one foreign power or the other, even for instance in the case of the United Nations Mission in Nepal (UNMIN). In a TV talk programme, he said "he regretted signing the 12-Point Agreement in New Delhi. No more the people here need to be told about such foreign interference. Just reading, seeing or hearing in the media outlets about the constant meetings by the foreign envoys with none less than the Prime Minister, ministers and party heads, the regular statements from foreign agencies telling Nepali politicians what they should do, a virtual order from the UN headquarters in New York on what decision the Nepal government must take on UNMIN and so on makes the picture clear for any sensible Nepali citizen on how much we are being dictated."
93. Chandra Dev Bhatta, *Challenges of State Building in Nepal,* (Kathmandu: Friedrich-Ebert Stiftung (FES), 2008), p. 90.
94. Nepal faces the worst national electricity crisis in Asia, with power cuts lasting up to 16 hrs. a day which is having serious impact on

economy. Although first electric lamp was lit some 100 years ago and during this period Nepal has produced less than 600 MW.

95. Larry Diamond, Jaun J. Linz and Seymour Martin Lipset, "Democracy in Developing Countries: Faciliating and Obstructing Factors," *Freedom in the World: Political Rights and Civil Liberties* 1987-1988, Raymond D. Gastil (ed.), (New York: Freedom House, 1988), p. 231.

# 6.

# Conclusion and Suggestions

Nepal is the one amongst some 120 states in the world of democracies. It is in democratic transition, so the country is focusing on democratic consolidation. Countries generally confront three types of problems while developing and consolidating their new democratic political system. The heart of the matter is how the ruling elites and publics respond to the inability of the new democratic governments to solve the problems. The key transitional problems in many countries in the process of developing democratic political institutions according to Huntington are transitional, contextual and systemic problems. This chapter concludes the book by giving the way outs or toolkits required for a dynamic and positive political culture essential for democratic consolidation in Nepal.

***Transition problems:*** Transition problems stem directly from the phenomenon of regime change- from authoritarian to democracy. They include the problems of establishing new constitutional and electoral systems, weeding out pro authoritarian officials and replacing them with democratic ones, modifying laws unsuitable for democracy, and changing authoritarian agencies.

***Contextual problems:*** A second category of problems stem from the nature of the society, its economy, culture, history, and are in some degree endemic to the country, whatever its form of government. The authoritarian rulers do not resolve these problems. As these problems are specific to individual countries and not to the common phenomenon of transition, they differ from county to county. Among those problems prevalent among third wave democracies, however are insurgencies, communal conflict, regional antagonisms, poverty, socioeconomic inequality, inflation, external debt, and low rates of economic growth.

***Systemic problems:*** Finally, as the new democracies become consolidated and achieve certain stability, they would confront systemic problems stemming from the working pattern of a democratic system. Authoritarian political systems suffer from the problems of overly concentrated decision making, deficient feedback, and dependence on performance legitimacy. Stalemate, the inability to reach decisions, susceptibility to demagoguery, and domination by vested economic interests are other problems.

Democracy would not be immune to transition, contextual and systemic problems. It is a natural process and a general phenomenon that a nation will most likely to suffer from these problems in transition. But it does not mean that those countries cannot consolidate their newly democratic political system or they cannot come out of transition. My point here is that democratic consolidation takes place in those countries if they manage to generate development, reduce inequality, establish new and functional constitution, electoral system, abolish authoritarian agencies, root out feudal cultures and maintain rule of law. Moreover, they need to change existing working pattern, behavior, norms, values and perception.

In third countries, these problems have afflicted democracy. In Nepal too, political culture for the consolidation of democracy cannot be immune to such problems. The clash of old and new values are embedded in every new democratic system. But the problems become acute when the feudal, authoritarian culture and practices go from strength to strength and dominant than the universally acknowledged values of democratic culture. Some significant variables such as the leadership role, parties' performance, and elite behaviours have been identified for making possible as well as showing caveats for democratic culture. Some crucial variables that work against democratic culture can broadly be identified as lack of ideological clarity, split political culture, the negative leadership role, the rise of ethnic-nationalism and regionalism, crisis of governance, apolitical mass, disoriented new generation and lack of faith in the overall capacity of Nepali state. Culture of dependency on external sources, increasing culture of political interference in internal affairs and lack of confidence to insulate politics from a variety of external penetrations have also added to the woes of transition.

There is widespread deterioration of values due to negative culture. So development indications show dismal changes even after more than two decades of multi-party democracy in Nepal. The legacy of the past in terms of the process of governing has continued. The relation between those who rule and those ruled has not been a two-way street in terms of democratic norm. The defenders of democracy themselves have shown their split political cultures inheriting both traditional authoritarian culture along with the invocation of participatory culture. But the ubiquitous presence of the former has made them incapable of freeing themselves from the same flaws of feudalistic and authoritarian culture as were experienced in the past. This has made people to notice that people's movements have brought about changes in political regime but not in the behaviour, culture, structure and leadership traits of leaders on one side. The dominant groups in politics and society are not ready for reallocation of power and resources. The social and intellectual consciousness has not changed for many decades. Over the 50 years of development efforts, inadequate movement of social tradition of social movement left the state free to continue doing what it does best maintaining the status quo, which serves the traditionally dominant interest in the name of development and democracy. The dominant conservative culture in the established political parties wants to maintain the status quo with which they see their own political and economic interests attached.

The diffused, rigid, ascribed, parochial culture instead of secularized political culture has not come to be overridden by a set of codified and universalistic rules. The result is that the secularization of political culture, that is increasing political awareness of the people by enabling them to have growing information about their political system and their role as a political actor have not been in ascendancy. It is because of secularization process that bargaining and accommodative political actions become a common feature of the society, hardly found in the political culture of Nepal. The present situation is not conducive to democratic culture; rather in many cases it has deteoriated. As the political transition process was less brutal than is usually witnessed in other circumstances, it could not sweep away the shibboleths of thirty years rather it has inherited many characters of the Shah, Rana and Panchayat political culture that is dominated by familial core, pyramidal social structure, social stratification, authoritarian trend, strange superstitious and religious ethos and poor economy.

The present political culture is still the reflection of the past Rana, Shah, and Panchayat rule – dominated by legacy, the older elites in all institutions and in the new forms they are the cadres of all political parties as elites of Nepali society. In the post- 1950 Nepali society and polity, the end of Rana and Panchayat system could not end the Rana and Panchayat political culture. But the country has undergone multiple transactions from authoritarianism to democracy, monarchy to republic, human rights, inclusion, participatory system of governance and secularism. However, such substantial changes have not made any dent in political behavior and culture.

The recent democratic political structure has become even worse in sharing the power and resources among the ordinary people. It has not dismantled that older social stratification, the traditional structures of power and authority. The few leaders of similar family background dominate politics and political parties are functioning according to their interest and preferences. Neither all ingredients of many spectacular events including the end of monarchy and the advent of the Maoist party after its 10-year- long insurgency could make a dent in the entrenched culture, nor could the pro democratic outpourings of the old major parties such as the NC and the CPN-UML show any significant departure from the past. Traditional and familial culture and elite behaviour add more woes to the democratic culture. The institutions are a hangover of the past that imprison new aspirations. It was not only during the Shah, Rana and Panchayat period (1769-1990 AD), but also during the decade of renewed democratic period the personalized system of governance has become a regular feature.

During the Shah and Rana systems, the exercise of authority was characterized as rule by *Hukum* or peremptory command, a more patrimonial rather than a feudal feature. The only difference is the distinct motivations of the public while fighting for democratic rights in each regime. For example, during the Rana regime, the democratic fight was against a hegemonic social class of the state. During the Panchayat, it was against the primacy of the limited political class of the system. Now it is against the leadership and pressure of interest groups that constitute the new political class. Contrary with the past, today's governance process is, nevertheless, more transparent but not necessarily accountable because of failure of both political parties and leadership for effectively articulating and aggregating the agendas of efficient and accountable governance. As a result, whichever parties come to power, they are casually attending to peoples' cause resulting in perpetuating the trends of old regimes. The result is a non-responsive culture that marks departure from the liberal political culture of the past. Associational life- the heart of democracy for the sake of communal benefit motivated people and ruler towards social, economic and political co-operation prevailed during the period. Money and power, the most important ingredients that are common in politics now at least had less influence during ancient and medieval Nepal.

The continuation of feudal values and ethos without a democratic norm are the cases of unchanged pattern that have dominated Nepal's political culture since long. Obviously, the development elite that emerged during the movement has espoused the same governing logic and reconstruction of the political culture into the state, as did the old elite. The feudal political culture is not being replaced by a new sense of direction and feeling of responsibility. Democracy thus turned to be a facade dashing all hopes of being inclusive and substantive. All these evidences indicate that although the Jan Andolans have repeatedly been portrayed as a glorious revolution which was supposed to give birth to a people-oriented culture, the new political system has failed to alter the lives of ordinary people. So even after two decades of democratic governance, the people have realized no substantive changes in life.

Political culture is a dynamic concept and responds to the needs generated from within the political system. Mere changes in system and constitution do not automatically bring a necessary change in people's orientation. The political culture of a society, thereby changes slowly. Democratic norms in the society tend to develop in the course of several generations only. Democratic experiments in Nepal so far suggest that there has not been much tangible change in Nepali socio-psychological dimension of power. The Nepali political culture assumes a model of hierarchic and authoritarian trends. It has not facilitated political ethics and a cultured mode of political behaviour in the country because the socialization process can not change as rapidly as the political system. It has not been attuned to civic norms, values and spirits.

A sudden jump from one system to another does not necessarily help people in giving up their past behaviour and attitude in a traditional society. It is so much imprinted in their psyche from centuries that political acculturation to democratic norms becomes difficult. It is observed that the change in 1990 confirmed the fact that a political system can not sustain itself only on the winds of change blowing from without. Instead it reaffirmed the need for a genuine awakening rooted in the minds and hearts of the people. The changes in Nepali political culture are produced by short term issues and events rather than fundamental changes in Nepali people, society, leaders and institutions. Although the growth rate of higher education and development of mass communication media have contributed to a gradual secularization and homogenization of Nepali political culture, these gradual changes in the society and culture cannot account for the rapid shifts in political attitudes, behaviour and perception of the leaders. So Nepalis today are more cynical about politicians, less confident in political institutions. Dissatisfaction with government policies and political leaders has resulted in a massive erosion of public support. The current period appears to be one of low trust and confidence in leaders and institutions.

Governments in Nepal have failed only because they have not been able to perform in accordance with the expectations of the people, also their failure is related to the destruction of democratic sanctity with the criminalization of politics for personal advancement. People had simple expectations that the political parties having had a long and arduous struggle for democracy will at least govern with accountability. But the leaders made politics an earning source at the cost of people's expectations for a better life. The simmering discontent towards the political parties and the political leadership in general has, therefore been the cause and consequence of the growing sense of betrayal among people. As the leaders of several parties have not been able to internalize the democratic belief system, it retarded the development of a political culture in which tolerance, accommodation and consensus thrive. Instead the habits of imposing one's own belief on others have led to widespread political polarization.

Consequently, leaders lost their visions in the blind race for power and money. This has created a situation in which leaders become corrupt and dictator failing to appreciate opposition and political dissent which are the prerequisites of democratic culture. Contrary to expectations, democracy in its functional attributes is overwhelmed by power centric intra-party and inter-party conflicts. Political parties are themselves becoming an impediment to democratic consolidation because of the promotion of their petty interests in the government. The level of political corruption they have encouraged and nurtured within the decades of democracy has been prominent factor in contributing to political instability. The undemocratic culture of leaders and the frequent changes in the government have proved the degenerating nature of Nepali political culture transforming itself into nothing but a naked power struggle. In recurring plots of government making and unmaking, the power contenders spare no foul tricks, i.e., bribe, horse trading, blackmail, adduction of some unreliable incumbent ministers and law makers, conspiracy, manipulation of constitutional loopholes etc.

De-culturation of politics, amoral and unethical attitudes of leaders, low trust and tolerance between the ruling and opposition and the administration based on conspiracy, mockery, nepotism, favouritism, sycophancy, authoritarianism, commissionary, abuse of power and authority have made confused, whether, Nepali political culture has become culture oriented politics or politics oriented culture. When political culture results from such an environment, much that is experienced politics today is an end in itself because culture has become an oppressed conceptual variable to politics. In such a situation, culture comes to be secondary on the one hand and politics on the other has not been the sustainer and protector of the cultural context. The cultural symbolism also has the capacity to counteract and counter balance the distorted images of men-distorted by the self-aggrandizing modes of politics. Concerning culture as a contributory to politics, Sidney Verba defines political culture as the 'system of empirical beliefs, expressive symbols and values which define the situation in which political action takes place.' Verba is not alone in so defining the political culture. He is in perfect communion with Lucian Pye, Gabrial Almond and many other illuminates like Samuel Beer, Adam Ulams, Dennis Kavangh, belonging to the fields of political science, political sociology, and political psychology. Conceptually, this view implies culture as contributing to political process as a result of which political development gets facilitated. Since cultural criteria guide, regulate and control many human endeavors, their superiority over all other categories of life is of utmost significance.

But the dissociation of politics from the moorings of culture has imparted to Nepali politics a typical cultural and anomic character within which culture-oriented politics has given way to a politics oriented culture.

The dissociation of politics and culture is alone responsible for making the politics a lucrative business and fostering a typical "*neta culture*" in the country. The politics of culture can not facilitate political ethics and a cultured mode of political behaviour conducive to democracy. Consequently, the assumed conceptual niceties of the political culture have simultaneously co-existed with the degenerated state of political affairs. Such politics of culture has made people and actor less orient to national integration- the heart of liberal democratic culture. Instead, the growing culture of violence in the society and the lack of rule of law have sapped both civic tradition and democratic norms to ignoble depth of domination, corruption, fragmentation, and disruption in governance. Accordingly, politics has not only turned out to be the end – product of all individuals and social pursuits but has also acquired a dangerous and menacing scenario. In this context, it is now more appropriate for Nepali political culture to be called the politics of culture rather than the culture of politics.

Today, every aspect of national activity, i.e., agriculture, industry, commerce, administration, local institutions and even sports and literature– has a political projection. Politicization in bureaucracy, educational institutions and other areas has destroyed the professional ethics, thus impeding democracy, governance and development. Politics thus has thrown overboard the transcended values of traditional political culture but has become amoral and unprincipled. It regards culture rather as epiphenomenon of politics. It is totally alienated from the eternal varieties and transcendent truth, from the lore of philosophy and morality. It acquires an ethos and style of its own and ceases to be the real political culture. It is self-indulgent, self centered and self-willed where political activity is devoid of the norms of decency. It is this uncultivated approach to politics that has led to the growth of politics of culture in the shape of mass upheavals, extremism and violence in society.

A growing body of academic works find that heart of the matter is how publics respond to those problems on one side and how political parties, leaders and governing elites effectively articulate and aggregate the agendas of efficient and accountable governance on the other. This book concludes by pinning its hope on the people and their belief that a system based on the culture of politics would emerge out of the imperfections. The suggestion for a need to restore civic ethics and culture in leadership for quality democratic governance has now become a necessity to reconcile the principle of social justice with the legitimacy of political order. National leaders have to take responsibility to restore ethics and culture to politics and build a sense of civic competence among the ordinary citizens. Attention is required to raise the moral standard of the leaders and bureaucrats to let them realize that they are part and parcel of democratic polity. The book suggests that political culture is more important than the model of governance for democrats. There is need to create such a culture to develop the feeling among the players that politics is a moral act and they are the moral agents to carry it out which they derive it from the nation's culture and social values.

Efficiency, ethics and morality on one side and co-operation, consensus and compromise are some generic attitudes evident in both authoritarian and democratic culture depending on the commitment and vision of political decision makers. Authoritarian regimes are not naturally endowed with quality of efficiency, nor do democracies always prove to be worthless. The book also suggests that commitment, sincerity and confidence of hardcore leaders of democracy are needed for a political culture to be conducive for democracy. The culture of morality, honesty, and integrity in the society which have reached the lowest point, if adopted once again, can save the nation and society from crumbling down. The future of Nepali political culture depends largely on the future performance of Nepali leaders and political institutions in dealing with the problems of economic stagnation, leadership crisis, ethnic issues, criminalization of politics and rampant corruption. If economic development makes democracy successful political leadership makes it real. The future of Nepali political culture depends on the performance of leaders and political institutions in dealing with the problems on the negative effects of political culture, which has damaged the base for a secularized political culture.

Nepali society is endowed with rich potential to promote political culture conducive to democracy, if the subcultures, thriving on regionalism, sectarianism and the money baron, who misuse the system for amassing wealth, are rendered weak and relatively ineffective. For democracies to come into being future political elites will at a minimum have to believe that democracy is the least bad form of government for their societies and for themselves. To make democracy more functional, cultural issues of politics like policies of inclusiveness, enthusiastic, participation of people in the polity and capacity to deliver goods and services are particularly to be taken care of by the democratic state. Society based on class and caste hierarchies with a tendency of perpetuating the same within the democratic system needs to be changed in order to make democracy strong and vibrant. So the heart of the matter is how political elites and publics respond to those issues and to the inability of the new democratic government to solve those problems.

A period of two decades may be short term in a country's history and culture changes slowly and requires the passage of further time to have an impact on the political culture. But it is not all the solution of the problem. The findings in the area is open to suggest that time alone does not free a political culture from the grip of the past and transform domination into the rule of reason and law. In this context, constitution making is not only the solution because culture is not that aspect which needs to be legislated so far. Crisis in Nepal is not due to the constitution and constitution making but the constitution and constitution making has been put into trouble by undemocratic culture of the leaders. Under the circumstances of this short, a more productive thing to do would be to go into the basis of a democratic regime and nurture its important component from all quarters. What remains to be done is to encourage the constitutional organs and political institutions to bring their behaviour closer to what is anticipated by the spirit and mandate of the people's movement.

Democratic culture cannot be institutionalized simply by the constitution and preaching of leaders; it must be adopted as a way of life that requires a vast process of social learning and energy for civic concern and action too. Citizens must have faith in themselves as agents of history and learn democracy by practicing in it. Then only it can be hoped that new emerging political culture will be more responsible towards the desire of the people and that it will act as a catalytic agent for change and progress in an evolving democracy. Only then the desire to have Nepal move from a parochial subject and subject participant culture to a participant civic one and from unitary to federal can be realized which will be conducive to democratic culture for New Nepal.

Political culture denotes the entire knowledge, instinctive attitudes, and moral and ethic values in relation to politics. So it especially requires the development of the following skills and habits:

- Sufficient knowledge of own political system,
- Emotional attachment and ethical support of the basic values of democracy and political institutions.
- A positive and active understanding of one's own role as a responsible citizen of the nation.

Beyond this basic orientation, an additional orientation is of particular importance for a stable democracy. Democratic culture also means the interplay between consensus and conflict, the willingness to reach a good compromise, agreement on the basis of dialogue and debate on political programs and understanding joint interests as the normal situation in the political activities of democracy according to Thomas Meyer, a German Political Scientist.

No matter which party temporarily holds control of the government, the basic rights of everyone are guaranteed and as many legitimate interests as possible are integrated into the process of developing objectives. Empirical researches have shown again and again in various cultures of the world that trust is one of the most important elements in a working democracy. Dialogue builds trust, which in turn steers a smooth transition towards participatory democratic culture. Cooperation is the success to this process. In this political culture three things in particular are meant by trust:

- The assurance that almost all people are willing to take the concern of the nation seriously.
- The expectation that binding agreements are kept.
- The assumption that these two attitudes are widely spread regardless of gender, ethnic heritage, social group, and religious affiliation.

The spiral of trust grows where institutional habits and experience support and nurture it. Only there where human trust exists to a sufficient extent, can a democratic culture develop on which functioning democratic institutions are based to a significant extent.

Viable political culture must necessarily be democratic for promoting respect for human rights, responsibilities and fundamental freedoms. Establishing democratic institution is always the safest means of developing a political culture for the large section of the population. Although establishing democratic institutions governed by the rule of law is the best prerequisite for developing a democratic culture, it is no guarantee for it. The best prerequisite for developing and gradually stabilizing a democratic political culture is the friendly democratic behavior of public and leading political class of the country. Their adherences to rules of the law will help develop an active civil society. If these factors come together, the emergence of a democratic culture is possible. For that we need to develop certain behaviours to set a productive and constructive political culture. Here are some toolkits required for a dynamic and positive political culture:

- Respect and recognize the existence and feelings of other people.
- Seek power with others rather than power over them.
- Dialogue with all parties, explore their goals and earn their confidence.
- Agree to disagree mentally rather than through violence.
- Believe in constructive criticism instead of mere criticism.
- Develop a win-win mentality.
- Whatever we demand from other parties, we must be willing to grant to others as well.
- Remain unbiased and impartial.
- Discussion should be issue based, focusing on agenda and vision.
- People's sacrifice and their suffering should be exposed and the responsibility of the state and its agents for causing that suffering be made clear.
- Develop tolerance and broad-mindedness to cope up with the situation.
- Understand other's point of view rather than imposing view on others only.
- Develop appreciative culture. The philosophy of this culture is about understanding fact finding and considering the situation from other person's perspective. It is about putting oneself in that person's position to evaluate and look at a situation.
- Learn from each other in an exchange of ideas, thoughts and experiences, and find out possible solutions together.

Practicing the toolkits mentioned above helps nurture the civic culture. The civic culture helps build tolerance, compromise, consensus, cooperation, trust in the political atmosphere- an environment where political players feel comfortable for expressing their thoughts without fear of getting into conflict. This makes the environment conducive for coexistence, and the synergies of it will help in building political culture in Nepal.

# References


## Development Reports

*Human Development Report.* Published for the United Nations Development Programme (UNDP). New York: Oxford University Press, 1992.

*Human Development Report.* UNDP, New York: 1996.

*Human Development in South Asia. The Crisis of Governance,* Published for The Mahabab Ul Hoff, Human Development Centre: Oxford University Press, 1999.

*Nepal Human Development Report.* Kathmandu: Nepal South Asia Centre (NESAC), 1994.

*Nepal Human Development Report.* Kathmandu: Nepal South Asia Centre (NESAC), 1998.

*Nepal Human Development Report: State Transformation and Human Development*, UNDP, Nepal, 2009.

*World Development Report*. The World Bank, Washington D.C. 1997.

## Articles

Adhikari, Dhruba. "Respect for Elderly Left Behind on Path to Modernity." *South China Morning Post*. Hong Kong, Monday 7, August 2000.

Baral, Lok Raj. "Party-Like Institutions in Partyless Politics: The GVNC in Nepal." *Asian Survey*. Vol. XXI, No, 7, July 1993.

— "Consensus, Parties and Governance." *The Kathmandu Post.* October 12, 1998.

— "Bartaman Rajya Byabastha: *Bhram Ya Satya*?" *Kantipur.* December 24, 2000.

Barth, Klaus. "Political Socialization: How to Teach Young Generation about Democracy." *The Telegraph Weekly.* Kathmandu: May 20, 1998.

Bhattachan, Krishna B. "Nepal in 1993: Business as Usual". *Asian Survey.* Volume 34, No. 2, February 1994.

Dahal, Dev Raj. "Nuggets of Nepali Political Culture". *The Telegraph Weekly.* Kathmandu: December 15, 1999.

— "Nepal: Tossed Into a New Political Future", *The Telegraph Weekly,* Kathmandu: January 12, 2000.

— "Samajik Naya Nepalko Prasangama." *Gorkhapatra.* January 1, 2000.

— "Vikas Nitiko Antarikikaran". *Gorkhapatra.* January 14, 2000.

Deuba,Arzu Rana. Open Letter to Political patriarchs, *The Kathmandu Post,* April, 29, 2012.

Gyawali, Dipak. "Riding The Bureaucratic Tiger". *The Independent.* February 20, 1991.

Jackman, Robert W., Miller, Ross A. "A Renaissance of Political Culture?" *American Journal of Political Science.* Vol., 40, Issue 3, August 1996 pp. 632-659.

Khadka, Narayan. "Effects of Negative Psychology." *Kantipur.* July 20, 1998.

Kharel, P. "Risks and Rewards". *The Kathmandu Post.* June 23, 1998.

Kumar, Dhruba. "What Ails Democracy in Nepal?" *The Telegraph Weekly.* Kathmandu: November 25, 1998.

Mishra, Birendra P. Constituent Assembly without Constitution: Last Court of Appeal, *The Himalayan Times*, May 30, 2012.

Pandey, Devendra Raj. "A Successful Story on Failed Development". *The Kathmandu Post.* Kathmandu: June 6, 1999.

— "Matching Democracy and Development Policymaking in an Aid –Dependent Country: An Illustration from Nepal." *Harvard Asia Quarterly.* 1999-2000.

Sangraula, Khagendra. "Bigat Ek Dasak Ko Sanskritic Yatra" (A Cultural Journey of a decade). *Jan Ekata Weekly.* Kathmandu: March 27, 2000.

Shaha, Rishikesh. "King Birendra as a Constitutional Monarch". *The Telegraph Weekly.* Kathmandu: June 24, 1998.

Sharma, Prayag Raj. "Values in the Doldrems Does the West Meet the East in Nepal?" *European Journal of Sociology.* Vol. xxx, 1989.

Shrestha, B.P. "Restructuring of Nepalese Economy and Its Governance." *The Telegraph Weekly.* Kathmandu: October 2, 1996.

Walton, Neil. "Nepal is in Worse Position than it was 10 Years Ago". *Khula Bazar. Nepali National Fortnightly,* Year 2, Number 4, Shrawan 16-30, 2056.

## Seminar Papers

Dahal, Dev Raj. *The State, Society and Development in Nepal,* paper submitted to IIDS, Center for Governance and Development Studies (GDS), Kathmandu: January 31, 1998.

— *The Nepalese Political Elites.* paper submitted to Enabling State Program (ESP), Department of International Development (DIID), Center for Governance and Development Studies (GDS), Kathmandu: September 2, 1998.

Khanal, Krishna. *Constitution and Political Parties in Nepal,* a report submitted to Friedrich – Ebert – Stiftung Nepal Office, 1997.

Khanal, Rabindra. *Political Institutionalization and Political Culture in Nepal,* paper presented to one day National Seminar, organized by Department of Political Science, TU, in cooperation with FES, 1998.

Kramer, Karl – Heinz. "Political Parties and the Development of Civil Society in Nepal" paper presented at the panel on *Political Parties and Civil Society in Asia,* organized by the International Political Science Association, Seoul: August 17-21, 1997.

Malla, Meena Vaidya. *Democracy, Security and national Interest*, Seminar conducted by Sangam Institute on National Security of Nepal: Thinking Ahead, Hotel Soaltee, Kathmandu, 24th September, 2009.

Meyer, Thomas. "*Mass Communication, Political Culture and Democracy",* paper presented at a seminar "Role of Media in Enhancing Political Culture in Democracy", Jointly Organized by *The Telegraph Weekly,* in cooperation with Friedrich– Ebert Stifoung, Kathmandu: September 17, 1998.

## Books

Acharya, Babu Ram. *Aba Yasto Kahilya Nahosa***.** Kathmandu: Offset Printing Press, 2056 BS.

— *Nepalko Sanskritic Parampara.* Kathmandu: Kathmandu Printing Press, 2054 BS.

Almond, Gabrial A. and G. Bingham Powel. *Comparative Politics Today: A World View,* Boston: Little Brown and Company, 1980.

Almond, Gabriel A. and Sidney Verba. *The Civic Culture: Political Attitudes and Democracy in Five Nations.* New Jersey: Princton University Press, 1963.

— *The Civic Culture Revisited.* London: Sage Publication, 1989.

Baral, L.R. *Oppositional Politics in Nepal.* New Delhi: Abhinav Publications, 1977.

— *Nepal's Politics of Referendum: A Study of Groups, Personalities and Trends.* New Delhi: Vikas Publication, 1983.

— "Political Culture and Political Process in Nepal." Malla K.P. (ed.), *Nepal: Perspectives on Continuity and Change.* Nepal: Centre for Nepalese and Asian Studies (CNAS), 1989.

— "Democracy: Problems of Adjustment." Khadga, K.C. (ed.), *The Institutionalization of Democratic Polity in Nepal.* TU, Department of Political Science/Sociology, in cooperation with FES, 2000.

— (ed.), *Nepal Quest for Democracy.* New Delhi: Adroit Publishers, 2006.

— (ed.), *Constitutional Government and Democracy In South Asia.* Nepal Centre for Contemporary Studies (NCCS), Nepal, 2011.

— *Nepal-Nation-State in the Wilderness; Managing State, Democracy and Geopolitics,* New Delhi, Sage Publication, 2012.

Baral, Lok Raj, Krishna Hachhethu and Hari Sharma. *Leadership in Nepal.* Nepal Centre for Contemporary Studies (NCCS) In Corporation of the Embassy of Finland, Kathmandu, Nepal: ADROIR Publishers, 2001.

Bhattachan, Krishna B., "Globalization and Its Impact on Nepalese Society and Culture." Madan Kumar Dahal (ed.), *Impact of Globalization in Nepal*, Kathmandu: Nepal Foundation for Advanced Studies (NEFAS), Friedrich–Ebert– Stiftung (FES), 1999.

Bhattachan, Krishna B., et al., *NGO. Civil Society and Government in Nepal.* TU: Central Department of Sociology and Anthropology in cooperation with FES, 2001.

Bhattarai, Binod, et al. *Impunity in Nepal: An Explorative Study.* Kathmandu: The Asia Foundation, 1999.

Bista, Dor B. *People of Nepal.* Kathmandu: Ratna Pustak Bhandar: 1967.

— *Fatalism and Development: Nepal's Struggle for Modernization.* Calcutta: Orient Longman, 1991.

Bongortz, Heinz and Dev Raj Dahal. *Development Studies: Self–Help Organizations. NGOs and Civil Society,* Nepal: NEFAS, 1996.

Borre, O., S.R. Pandey and C.K. Tiwari. *The Nepalese Election of 1991.* Electoral Studies, 1991.

— *Nepalese Political Behaviour.* New Delhi: Sterling Publishers Pvt. Ltd., 1994.

Brown, T. Louise. *The Challenge to Democracy in Nepal: A Political History.* London: New Fetterlane, 1996.

Burghart, Richard. "The Political Culture of Panchayat Democracy." Michael Hutt (ed.), *Nepal in the Nineties.* Oxford: Oxford University Press, 1993.

Central Bureau of Statistics. *Intercensal Changes of Some Key Census Variables – Nepal.* 1952/54-81, Kathmandu: 1985.

— *Nepal Census of Population.* Kathmandu: 1993.

Chalise, C. Suresh. *Sociology of the Legislative Elite in a Developing Society.* Kathmandu: NEFAS, 1995.

Chatterji, B. *Palace, People and Politics: Nepal in Perspective.* New Delhi: Ankur, 1980.

Chauhan, R.S. *The Political Development in Nepal 1950-1970: Conflict between Tradition and Modernity.* New Delhi: Associated Publishing House, 1971.

Dahal, Dev Raj. "Role of Political Education in the Democratization Process of Nepal." In *Nepali Political Science and Politics.* Vol. 5, Political Science Association of Nepal (POLSAN), Kathmandu: Modern Printing Press, 1996.

— "Political Socialization and Democracy in Nepal." Mohan Prasad Lohani and Bikas Lohani, (eds.), *His Majesty King Birendra: Multi Dimensional Personality.* Kathmandu: Silver Jubliee Celebration Committee, 1996.

— "Social Development in Nepal: Political Perspective." Bishwa Keshar Maskey (ed.), *Social Development in Nepal.* Kathmandu: UNAV, 1996.

— *The Challenges of Good Governance: Decentralization and Development in Nepal.* Kathmandu: Center for Governance and Development Studies (GDS), 1996.

— *Civil Society in Nepal: Opening the Ground for Questions,* Center for Development and Governance, Kathmandu: Modern Printing Press, 2001.

Dahal, Dev Raj, Bhatta, C.D. *Multiverse of Nepalese Democracy: Contents and Discontents,* Friedrich Ebert Stiftung (FES), Nepal, 2010.

— *Building Bridges of Peace in Nepal*, Friedrich Ebert Stiftung (FES), Nepal, 2010.

Devkota, Laxmi Prasad. "We Think of Ourselves First." Brijesh Shrestha, (ed.), *Janmostab,* Kathmandu: Prajol Maleku, 1997.

Faizal, Farah, Rajagopalan Swarna (ed.). *Women Security, South Asia: A Clearing in the Thicke*t, Sage Publication, New Delhi, 2005.

Gaige, F. *Regionalism and National Unity in Nepal,* Berkeley: University of California Press. 1975.

Galtung, John, Jacobsen, Carl G. and Frithjof, Kai, Jacobsen, Brand– *Searching for peace: The Road to TRANSCEND*, London: Pluto press. 2002.

Gellner, David N. and Joanna Pfaff – Czarnecka and John. Whelpton. *Nationalism and Ethnicity in a Hindu Kingdom: The Politics of Culture in Contemporary Nepal.* Amsterdam: Harvard, 1997.

Ghani, Ashraf, and Lockhart, Clare, 2008, *Fixing Failed States,* Oxford, Oxford University Press, 163.

Gupta, A. *Politics in Nepal: A Study of Post Rana Political Developments and Party Politics.* Bombay: Allied Publishers, 1964.

Gurung, Harka. *Nature and Culture.* Kathmandu: Jeewan Printing Support Press, 1989.

— *Nepal: Social Demography and Expressions.* Kathmandu: New Era, 1998.

Hachhettu, Krishna (eds.), *Nepali Rajyako Naya Sworupa ra Charittra.* Nepal Centre for Contemporary Studies (NCCS), Lalitpur, 2011.

— *Party Building in Nepal: Organization, Leadership and People*, Mandala Book Point, Kathmandu, 2000.

Hague, Rod., Harrop, Martin and Brislin, Shaven. *Comparative Government and Politics.* III Edition, London: Macmillan, 1992.

HMG. *The Constitution of the Kingdom of Nepal 2047 (1990).* Kathmandu: Ministry of Law, Justic and Parliamentary Affairs, His Majesty's Government of Nepal, 1990.

HMG, *Population Census 1991.* Kathmandu: Central Bureau of Statistics. His Majesty's Government of Nepal, 1992.

Hofteen, Martin. "The Dynamics and Chronology of the 1990 Revolution." Micheal Hutt (ed.) *Nepal in the Nineties.* Oxford: Oxford University

Press, 1993.

Hoek, Bert Van Den. "Does Divinity Protect the King? Ritual and Politics in Nepal." *Contributions to Nepalese Sutdies.* Vol. 17 No. 2, 1990, pp. 147-155.

Haftun, Martin, Reeper W. and Whelpton John. *People, Politics and Ideology: Democracy and Social Changes in Nepal.* Kathmandu: Mandala Book Point, 1999.

Huntington, Samuel P. *Political Order in Changing Society.* New Heaven: Bombay: Feffer and Simons 1968.

— *The Third Wave :Democratization In The Late Twentieth Century.* University of Oklahoma Press, USA, 2010.

IIDS. *The Second Parliamentary Election: A Study of the Emerging Democratic Process in Nepal.* Kathmandu: Institute for Integrated Development Studies, 1993.

— *The Third Parliamentary Election; A Study of the Evolving Democratic Process in Nepal.* Kathmandu: IIDS, 1996.

Jain, B.M. *Strategic, Military and Economic Concerns in the Age of Nuclear Diplomacy: India in the new South Asia.* Daryaganj: New Delhi, 2011.

Jaitly, Anam. *India's Political Culture-In Search of a Framework.* Jaipur: Aalekh Publication, 1991.

Joshi, Buvan Lal and Leo E. Rose, L.E. *Democratic Innovations in Nepal: A Case Study of Political Acculturation.* Berkeley: University of California Press, 1966.

Kamrava, Meheran. *Politics and Society in the Third World,* London: New Fetterlam, 1993.

Karim, Arshad Syed. "Political Culture of Pakistan: A National Policy–Decision Process." L.R. Baral, (ed.), *South Asia – Democracy and the Road Ahead.* Kathmandu: POLSAN, 1992.

Khanal,Rabindra. *Donors' Policies against Corruption in Nepal*, Transparency International Nepal (TIN), Kathmandu, 2005.

— *Local Governance in Nepal: Democracy at Grass root.* Smriti Books Lalitpur, 2006.

Khanal, Yadu Nath. *Nepal: Transition from Isolationism.* Kathmandu: Sajha Prakasan, 1977.

Khanna, Parag. *How To Run The Government: Charting A Course to the Next Reniassance.* Random House: New York, 2011.

Koller, Arnold, *Federalism in a Changing world –Learning from Each Other.* Montreal and Kingston: McGill Queen's University Press, 2003.

Kumar, Dhruba (ed.). *State, Leadership and Politics in Nepal.* Kathmandu: CNAS, 1995.

— (ed.). *Domestic Conflict and Crisis of Governability in Nepal.* Kirtipur, Centre for Nepal and Asian Studies, 2000.

Kumar, S. *Rana Polity in Nepal: Origin and Growth.* New York: Asia Publishing House, 1967.

Laitin, D. David, *Nations, States and Violence,* Oxford University Press, Oxford, 2007.

Malla, Kamal P. (ed.), *Nepal: Perspective on Continuity and Change.* Kathmandu: CNAS, 1989.

Malla, Meena Vaidya. *Political Socialization of Women in Nepal.* Adroit Publication, New Delhi, 2011.

Manandhar, Laxmi Keshari and Krishna B. Bhattachan (ed.). *Gender and Democracy in Nepal.* Central Department of Home Science, Woman's Studies Programme, Tribhuvan University in Cooperation with Friedrich – Ebert Stiftung (FES), 2001.

Manandhar, Tirtha Bahadur. "Educational Development, Population and Literacy." *Population Monograph of Nepal.* Kathmandu: CERID, 1995.

Mauzy, K. Daine. *Politics in the Asian States.* Kula Lumpur: Marican and Sons, 1983.

Mishra, Indra, Deo. *Understanding a Political System; In Reference to Nepal.* Varanashi: Vijayashree Enterprises, 1985.

*Nepal Opinion Survey Center, Political Opinion Survey of Kathmandu Valley.* NOSC, Kathmandu: Himalayan Institute of Development, 1993.

Pandey, Bhim Bahadur. *Teysa Bakhata ko Nepal* (Nepal of that time). Kathmandu: CNAS, 1982.

Pandey, Devendra Raj. *Nepal's Failed Development Reflections on the Mission and the Maladies.* Kathmandu: Nepal South Asia Centre (NESAC), 1999.

— Devendra Raj. Ed by Seira Tamang *Looking at development and Donors: Essays from Nepal.* Martin Chautari, Kathmanu, Nepal, 2011.

Parish, M. Steven. *Hierarchy and its Discontents: Culture and the Politics of Consciousness in Caste Society.* Oxford: Oxford University Press, 1997.

Political Science Association of Nepal (POLSAN). *Nepalese Voters: A survey Report.* Kathmandu: POLSAN, 1991.

Poudyal, Ananta Raj. "Ethnicity in Democracy." L.R. Baral (ed.) *South Asia– Democracy and the Road Ahead.* Kathmandu: POLSAN, 1992.

Poudyel, Bishnu P. Jha Hari Bansh (eds.). *The New Dynamics of Conflict In Nepal.* The national Advisory Council-South Asian Affairs and the Centre for Economic and Technical Studies (CETS) in Corporation with *Friedrich* Ebert Stiftung (FES), Nepal, 2009.

Pye, Lucian, W. "Introduction: Political Culture and Political Development." Lucian W. Pye and Sidney Verba (eds.). *Political Culture and Political Development.* New Jersey: Princton University Press, 1965.

Raeper, W. and Hoftum, M. *Spring Awakening: An Account of the 1990 Revolution in Nepal.* New Delhi: Viking, 1992.

Rajbhandari, Achyut and B. Srivastav, S. Pokhrel, P. Indra. *Nepalma Prajatantra Ko Ek Dasak* (A Decade in Nepal's Democracy). Lalitpur: Centre for Democracy and Good Governance and FES, 2057.

Rana, Pashupati S.J.B. and Kamal Prakash Malla (eds.). *Nepal in Perspective.* Kathmandu: CEDA, 1973.

Reilly, Benjamin, *Democracy in Divided Societies:* Electoral *Engineering for Conflict Management*, Cambridge: Cambridge University Press,2001.

Robertson, David. *Dictionary of Politics.* London: Penguin Books, 1993.

Rose, Leo E. and J.T. Scholz. *Nepal: Profile of a Himalayan Kingdom.* New Delhi: Select Book Syndicate, 1980.

Rosenbaum, Walter. *Political Culture.* New York: Praeger, 1975.

Russel, Bertrand. H*uman Society in Ethics and Politics,* London: George Allen and Unwin LTD.1954.

Sanwal, B.D. *Social and Political History of Nepal.* New Delhi: Monohar Publication, 1993.

SEARCH. *Strengthening Democratic Processes in Nepal; Voter Education Program, 1991.* Kathmandu: SEARCH, 1991.

— *Strengthening Democratic Process in Nepal: General Elections Monitoring Program 1991.* Kathmandu: SEARCH, 1991.

— *Political Opinion Survey in Nepal.* Kathmandu: SEARCH, 1994.

Shaha, Rishikesh. *Nepali Politics: Retrospect and Prospect.* Delhi: Oxford University Press, 1975.

— *Essays in the Practice of Government in Nepal.* Delhi: Manohar Publications, 1982.

— *Modern Nepal: A Political History 1769-1955,* Vol. 1: 1769-1885. New Delhi: Manohar Publication, 1990.

— *Modern Nepal: A Political History 1969-1955.* Vol. II: 1885-1955, New Delhi: Manohar Publication, 1990.

— *Politics in Nepal, 1980-1990: Refrendum, Stalemate and Triumph of People's Power.* New Delhi: Manohar Publication, 1990.

— *Ancient and Medieval Nepal.* Kathmandu: Ratna Pustak Bhandar, 1992.

Sharma, Prayag Raj. "Nepali Culture and Society. Reflection on some Historical Currents." K.P. Malla (ed.), *Nepal; Perspective on Continuity and Change,* CNAS, 1989.

Shrestha, Tirtha B. *Education, Development, Population and Literacy, in Population Monograph of Nepal.* Kathmandu: Central Bureau of Statistics (CBS), 1995.

Shrestha, Tulsi Narayan, *Nepalese Administration: A Historical Perspective,* Kathmandu: Rhino Publication, 1989.

Thapa, Ganga B. *Promoting Participatory Democracy in Nepal: An Assessment of Local Self–Government.* POLSAN, Kathmandu: Modern Printing Press, 1998.

Uprety, Prem R. *Political Awakening in Nepal: The Search for a New Identity.* New Delhi: Common Wealth Publishers, 1992.

Vaidya, T.R. *Nepal: A Study of Socio-Economic and Political Changes.* New Delhi; Anmol Publications, 1992.

Vaidya, Tulsi Ram, Manandhar, Tri Ratna and Joshi, Shankar Lal. *Social History of Nepal.* New Delhi: Anmol Publication 1993.

Verba, Sidney. "Conclusion: Comparative Political Culture." Pye and Verba (eds.), *Political Culture and Political Development.* New Jersey: Princton University Press, 1965.

Yadav, Lal Babu. "Republican State: Continuity and Change." *Political Parties and Parliamentary Process in Nepal: A Study of Transitional Phase.* Kathmandu: Jeewan Printing Press, 1992.

# Index